What Readers Are Saying About
Arduino: A Quick-Start Guide

The most comprehensive book on the Arduino platform I have read. Loaded with excellent examples and references, *Arduino: A Quick-Start Guide* gets beginners up and running in no time and provides experienced developers with a wealth of inspiration for their own projects.

▶ **Haroon Baig**
Creator of the Twitwee Clock, http://www.haroonbaig.com

Excellently paced for those who have never experimented with electronics or microcontrollers before and packed with valuable tidbits even for advanced Arduino tinkerers.

▶ **Georg Kaindl**
Creator, Arduino DHCP, DNS, and Bonjour libs

The Arduino platform is a great way for anyone to get into embedded systems, and this book is the road map. From first baby steps to complex sensors and even game controllers, there is no better way to get going on the Arduino.

▶ **Tony Williamitis**
Senior embedded systems engineer

I recommend this engaging and informative book to software developers who want to learn the basics of electronics, as well as to anyone looking to interface their computers with the physical world.

▶ **René Bohne**
Software developer and creator of LumiNet

Arduino
A Quick-Start Guide

Arduino
A Quick-Start Guide

Maik Schmidt

The Pragmatic Bookshelf
Raleigh, North Carolina   Dallas, Texas

Pragmatic Bookshelf

Our Pragmatic courses, workshops, and other products can help you and your team create better software and have more fun. For more information, as well as the latest Pragmatic titles, please visit us at http://www.pragprog.com.

The team that produced this book includes:

Editor:	Susannah Pfalzer
Indexing:	Potomac Indexing, LLC
Copy edit:	Kim Wimpsett
Layout:	Samuel Langhorne
Production:	Janet Furlow
Customer support:	Ellie Callahan
International:	Juliet Benda

ISBN-10: 1-934356-66-2

ISBN-13: 978-1-934356-66-1

Printed on acid-free paper.

P3.0 printing, August, 2011

Version: 2011-7-28

For Yvonne.

The greatest little sister on earth.

Contents

Acknowledgments

Writing books doesn't get easier the more often I do it—I think there will never be a time when I can do it on my own. I will always depend on the help of others, and a lot of wonderful people contributed to this book.

I have to start by thanking my unbelievably talented editor, Susannah Davidson Pfalzer. Only because of her insightful advice, her patience, and her encouragement have I finished this book. I owe her so much!

Also, the Pragmatic Bookshelf team again has been amazingly professional, and my publishers have been very sympathetic when I went through some hard times. I am so thankful for that!

This book would not have been possible without the stunning work of the whole Arduino team! Thank you so much for creating the Arduino!

A big "thank-you!" goes to all the people who contributed material to this book: Christian Rattat took all the book's photos, Kaan Karaca created the Blaminatr's display, and Tod E. Kurt kindly allowed me to use his excellent C code for accessing an Arduino via serial port.

I have created all circuit diagrams with Fritzing,[1] and I'd like to thank the Fritzing team for making such a great tool available for free!

For an author, there's nothing more motivating than feedback. I'd like to thank my reviewers: René Bohne, Stefan Christoph, Georg Kaindl, Kaan Karaca, Christian Rattat, Stefan Rödder, Christoph Schwaeppe, Federico Tomassetti, and Tony Williamitis. This book is so much better because of your insightful comments and suggestions! I am also grateful to all readers who have sent in errata during the beta book period.

When I had written the first half of this book, my mother passed away in February 2010. It has been one of the hardest times in my life, and

---

1. http://fritzing.org/

without the support of my family and my friends, I would have never finished this book. We miss you so much, Mom!

Finally, I'd like to thank Tanja for giving me confidence and for bringing fun back into my life when I needed it most!

Preface

Welcome to the Arduino, and welcome to the exciting world of physical computing! Arduino[2] is an open source project consisting of both hardware and software. It was originally created to give designers and artists a prototyping platform for interaction design courses. Today hobbyists and experts all over the world use it to create physical computing projects, and you can too.

The Arduino lets us get hands-on again with computers in a way we haven't been able to since the 1980s, when you could build your own computer. And Arduino makes it easier than ever to develop handcrafted electronics projects ranging from prototypes to sophisticated gadgets. Gone are the days when you had to learn lots of theory about electronics and arcane programming languages before you could even get an LED blinking. You can create your first Arduino project in a few minutes without needing advanced electrical engineering course work.

In fact, you don't need to know anything about electronics projects to read this book, and you'll get your hands dirty right from the beginning. You'll not only learn how to use some of the most important electronic parts in the first pages, you'll also learn how to write the software needed to bring your projects to life.

This book dispenses with theory and stays hands-on throughout. I'll explain all the basics you need to build the book's projects, and every chapter has a troubleshooting section to help when things go wrong. This book is a quick-start guide that gets you up to speed quickly and enables you to immediately create your own projects.

---

2. http://arduino.cc

Who Should Read This Book

If you are interested in electronics—and especially in building your own toys, games, and gadgets—then this book is for you. Although the Arduino is a nice tool for designers and artists, only software developers are able to unleash its full power. So, if you've already developed some software—preferably with C/C++ or Java—then you'll get a lot out of this book.

But there's one more thing: you have to build, try, and modify the projects in this book. Have fun. Don't worry about making mistakes. The troubleshooting sections—and the hands-on experience you'll gain as you become more confident project by project—will make it all worthwhile. Reading about electronics without doing the projects yourself isn't even half the battle (you know the old saying: we remember 5 percent of what we hear, 10 percent of what we write, and 95 percent of what we personally suffer). And don't be afraid: you really don't need any previous electronics project experience!

If you've never written a piece of software before, start with a programming course or read a beginner's book about programming first (*Learn to Program* [Pin06] is a nice starting point). Then, learn to program in C with *The C Programming Language* [KR98] or in C++ with *The C++ Programming Language* [Str00].

What's in This Book

This book consists of three parts ("Getting Started with Arduino," "Eight Arduino Projects," and the appendixes). In the first part, you'll learn all the basics you need to build the projects in the second part, so read the chapters in order and do all the exercises. The chapters in the second part also build on each other, reusing techniques and code from earlier chapters.

Here's a short walk-through:

- The book starts with the basics of Arduino development. You'll learn how to use the IDE and how to compile and upload programs. You'll quickly build your first project—electronic dice—that shows you how to work with basic parts such as LEDs, buttons, and resistors. By implementing a Morse code generator, you'll see how easy it is to create your own Arduino libraries.

- Then you'll learn how to work with analog and digital sensors. You'll use a temperature sensor and an ultrasonic sensor to build a very accurate digital metering ruler. Then you'll use a three-axis accelerometer to build your own motion-sensing game controller, together with a cool breakout game clone.

- In electronics, you don't necessarily have to build gadgets yourself. You can also tinker with existing hardware, and you'll see how easy it is to take full control of Nintendo's Wii Nunchuk so you can use it in your own applications.

- Using a Nunchuk to control applications or devices is nice, but often it's more convenient to have a wireless remote control. So, you'll learn how to build your own universal remote control that you can even control using a web browser.

- Speaking of web browsers: connecting the Arduino to the Internet is easy, so you'll build a burglar alarm that sends you an email whenever someone is moving in your living room during your absence.

- Finally, you'll work with motors by creating a fun device for your next software project. It connects to your continuous integration system, and whenever the build fails, it moves an arrow to point to the name of the developer who is responsible.

- In the appendixes, you'll learn about the basics of electricity and soldering. You'll also find advanced information about programming a serial port and programming the Arduino in general.

Every chapter starts with a detailed list of all parts and tools you need to build the chapter's projects. Every chapter contains lots of photos and diagrams showing how everything fits together. You'll get inspired with descriptions of real-world Arduino projects in sidebars throughout the book.

Things won't always work out as expected, and debugging circuits can be a difficult and challenging task. So in every chapter you'll find a "What If It Doesn't Work?" section that explains the most common problems and their solutions.

Before you read the solutions in the "What If It Doesn't Work?" sections, though, try to solve the problems yourself, because that's the most effective way of learning. In the unlikely case that you *don't* run into any problems, you'll find a list of exercises to build your skills at the end of every chapter.

All the projects in this book have been tested on the Arduino Uno, the Arduino Duemilanove, and with the Arduino IDE versions 18 to 21. If possible, you should always use the latest version.

Arduino Uno and the Arduino Platform

After releasing several Arduino boards and Arduino IDE versions, the Arduino team decided to specify a version 1.0 of the platform. It will be the reference for all future developments, and they announced it on the first day of 2010.[3] Since then, they have released the Arduino Uno, and they have also improved the IDE and its supporting libraries step-by-step.

At the moment of this writing, it is still not completely clear what Arduino 1.0 will look like. The Arduino team tries to keep this release as backward compatible as possible. This book is up-to-date for the new Arduino Uno boards. All the projects will also work with older Arduino boards such as the Duemilanove or Diecimila. This book is current for version 21 of the Arduino platform. You can follow the progress of the Arduino platform online.[4]

Code Examples and Conventions

Although this is a book about open source hardware and electronics, you will find a lot of code examples. We need them to bring the hardware to life and make it do what we want it to do.

We use C/C++ for all programs that will eventually run on the Arduino. For applications running on our PC, we use Processing,[5] but in Section C.2, *Serial Communication Using Various Programming Languages*, on page 241, you'll also learn how to use several other programming languages to communicate with an Arduino.

 Whenever you find a slippery road icon beside a paragraph, slow down and read carefully. They announce difficult or dangerous techniques.

---

3. http://arduino.cc/blog/2010/01/01/uno-punto-zero/
4. http://code.google.com/p/arduino/issues/list?q=milestone=1.0
5. http://processing.org

Online Resources

This book has its own web page at http://pragprog.com/titles/msard where you can download the code for all examples (if you have the ebook version of this book, clicking the little gray box above each code example downloads that source file directly). You can also participate in a discussion forum and meet other readers and me. If you find bugs, typos, or other annoyances, please let me and the world know about them on the book's errata page.[6]

On the web page you will also find a link to a Flickr[7] photo set. It contains all the book's photos in high resolution. There you can also see photos of reader projects, and we'd really like to see photos of your projects, too!

Let's get started!

---

6. http://www.pragprog.com/titles/msard/errata
7. http://flickr.com

The Parts You Need

Here's a list of the parts you need to work through all the projects in this book. In addition, each chapter lists the parts you'll need for that chapter's projects, so you can try projects chapter-by-chapter without buying all the components at once. Although there look to be a lot of components here, they're all fairly inexpensive, and you can buy all the parts you need for all the projects in this book for about $200.

Starter Packs

Many online shops sell Arduino components and electronic parts. Some of the best are Makershed[8] and Adafruit.[9] They have awesome starter packs, and I strongly recommend buying one of these.

The best and cheapest solution is to buy the Arduino Projects Pack from Makershed (product code MSAPK). It contains nearly all the parts you need to build the book's examples, as well as many more useful parts that you can use for your own side projects. If you buy the Arduino Projects Pack, you'll need to buy these additional parts separately:

- Parallax PING))) sensor
- TMP36 temperature sensor from Analog Devices
- ADXL335 accelerometer breakout board
- 6 pin 0.1" standard header
- Nintendo Nunchuk controller
- A Passive Infrared Sensor
- An infrared LED
- An infrared receiver
- An Ethernet shield

---

8. http://makershed.com
9. http://adafruit.com

Alternatively, Adafruit also sells an Arduino Starter Pack (product ID 170). It's cheaper, but it doesn't contain as many parts. For example, it doesn't have a Protoshield or a tilt sensor.

All shops constantly improve their starter packs, so it's a good idea to scan their online catalogs carefully.

Complete Parts List

If you prefer to buy parts piece by piece (or chapter by chapter) rather than a starter pack, here is a list of all the parts used in the book. Each chapter also has a parts list and photo with all parts needed for that chapter. Suggested websites where you can buy the parts are listed here for your convenience, but many of these parts are available elsewhere also, so feel free to shop around.

Good shops for buying individual components parts are RadioShack,[10] Digi-Key,[11] sparkfun,[12] and Mouser.[13]

- An Arduino board such as the Uno, Duemilanove, or Diecimila available from Adafruit (product ID 50) or Makershed (product code MKSP4).

- A standard A-B USB cable for USB 1.1 or 2.0. You might already have a few. If not, you can order it at RadioShack (catalog number 55011289).

- A half-size breadboard from Makershed (product code MKKN2) or from Adafruit (product ID 64).

- Three LEDs (four additional ones are needed for an optional exercise). Buying LEDs one at a time isn't too useful; a better idea is to buy a pack of 20 at RadioShack (catalog number 276-1622).

- One 100Ω resistor, two $10k\Omega$ resistors, and three $1k\Omega$ resistors. It's also not too useful to buy single resistors; buy a value pack such as catalog number 271-308 from RadioShack.

- Two pushbuttons. Don't buy a single button switch; buy at least four instead, available at Digi-Key (part number 450-1650-ND) or Mouser (101-TS6111T1602-EV).

---

10. http://radioshack.com
11. http://digikey.com
12. http://sparkfun.com
13. http://mouser.com

- Some wires, preferably breadboard jumper wires. You can buy them at Makershed (product code MKSEEED3) or Adafruit (product ID 153).

- A Parallax PING))) sensor (product code MKPX5) from Makershed.

- A Passive Infrared Sensor (number 2906724) from RadioShack.

- A TMP36 temperature sensor from Analog Devices.[14] You can get it from Adafruit (product ID165).

- An ADXL335 accelerometer breakout board. You can buy it at Adafruit (product ID 163).

- A 6 pin 0.1" standard header (included, if you order the ADXL335 from Adafruit). Alternatively, you can order from sparkfun (search for *breakaway headers*). Usually, you can only buy stripes that have more pins. In this case, you have to cut it accordingly.

- A Nintendo Nunchuk controller. You can buy it at nearly every toy store or at http://www.amazon.com/, for example.

- An Arduino Ethernet shield (product code MKSP7) from Makershed.

- An infrared sensor such as the PNA4602. You can buy it a Adafruit (product ID 157) or Digi-Key (search for *PNA4602*).

- An infrared LED. You can get it from RadioShack (catalog number 276-143) or from sparkfun (search for *infrared LED*).

- A 5V servo motor such as the Hitec HS-322HD or the Vigor Hextronic. You can get one from Adafruit (product id 155) or sparkfun. Search for standard servos with an operating voltage of 4.8V–6V.

For some of the exercises, you'll need some optional parts:

- An Arduino Proto Shield from Adafruit (product ID 51) or Makershed (product code MKAD6). You'll also need a tiny breadboard (product code MKKN1 at Makershed). I highly recommend this shield!

- A piezo speaker or buzzer. Search for *piezo buzzer* at RadioShack or get it from Adafruit (product ID 160).

---

14. http://www.analog.com/en/sensors/digital-temperature-sensors/tmp36/products/product.html

- A tilt sensor. Get it from Adafruit (product ID 173), or buy it at Mouser (part number 107-2006-EV).

For the soldering tutorial, you need the following things:

- A 25W–30W soldering iron with a tip (preferably 1/16") and a soldering stand.

- Standard 60/40 solder (rosin-core) spool for electronics work. It should have a 0.031" diameter.

- A sponge.

You can find these things in every electronics store, and many have soldering kits for beginners that contain some useful additional tools. Take a look at Adafruit (product ID 136) or Makershed (product code MKEE2).

Part I

Getting Started with Arduino

Chapter 1

Welcome to the Arduino

The Arduino was originally built for designers and artists—people with little technical expertise. Even without programming experience, the Arduino enabled them to create sophisticated design prototypes and some amazing interactive artworks. So, it should come as no surprise that the first steps with the Arduino are very easy, even more so for people with a strong technical background.

But it's still important to get the basics right. You'll get the most out of working with the Arduino if you're familiar with the Arduino board itself, with its development environment, and with techniques such as serial communication.

One thing to understand before getting started is *physical computing*. If you have worked with computers before, you might wonder what this means. After all, computers are physical objects, and they accept input from physical keyboards and mice. They output sound and video to physical speakers and displays. So, isn't all computing physical computing in the end?

In principle, regular computing is a subset of physical computing: keyboard and mouse are *sensors* for real-world inputs, and displays or printers are *actuators*. But controlling special sensors and actuators, using a regular computer is very difficult. Using an Arduino, it's a piece of cake to control sophisticated and sometimes even weird devices. In the rest of this book, you'll learn how, and in this chapter you'll get started with physical computing by learning how to control the Arduino, what tools you need, and how to install and configure them. Then we'll quickly get to the fun part: you'll develop your first program for the Arduino.

1.1 What You Need

- An Arduino board such as the Uno, Duemilanove, or Diecimila.

- A USB cable to connect the Arduino to your computer.

- An LED.

- The Arduino IDE (see Section 1.4, *Installing the Arduino IDE*, on page 11). You will need it in every chapter, so after this chapter, I'll no longer mention it explicitly.

1.2 What Exactly Is an Arduino?

Beginners often get confused when they discover the Arduino project. When looking for the Arduino, they hear and read strange names such as Uno, Duemilanove, Diecimila, LilyPad, or Seeduino. The problem is that there is no such thing as "the Arduino."

A couple of years ago the Arduino team designed a microcontroller board and released it under an open source license. You could buy fully assembled boards in a few electronics shops, but people interested in electronics could also download its schematic[1] and build it themselves.

Over the years the Arduino team improved the board's design and released several new versions. They usually had Italian names such as Uno, Duemilanove, or Diecimila, and you can find a list of all boards that were ever created by the Arduino team online.[2]

Figure 1.1, on the facing page shows a small selection of Arduinos. They may differ in their appearance, but they have a lot in common, and you can program them all with the same tools and libraries.

The Arduino team did not only constantly improve the hardware design. They also invented new designs for special purposes. For example, they created the Arduino LilyPad[3] to embed a microcontroller board into textiles. You can use it to build interactive T-shirts, for example.

In addition to the official boards, you can find countless Arduino clones on the Web. Everybody is allowed to use and change the original board design, and many people created their very own version of an Arduino-compatible board. Among many others, you can find the Freeduino,

---

1. http://arduino.cc/en/uploads/Main/arduino-uno-schematic.pdf
2. http://arduino.cc/en/Main/Boards
3. http://arduino.cc/en/Main/ArduinoBoardLilyPad

Figure 1.1: YOU CAN CHOOSE FOM MANY DIFFERENT ARDUINOS.

Seeduino, Boarduino, and the amazing Paperduino,[4] an Arduino clone without a printed circuit board. All its parts are attached to an ordinary piece of paper.

Arduino is a registered trademark—only the official boards are named "Arduino."—so clones usually have names ending with "duino." You can use every clone that is fully compatible with the original Arduino to build all the book's projects.

1.3 Exploring the Arduino Board

In Figure 1.2, on the next page, you can see a photo of an Arduino Uno board and its most important parts. I'll explain them one by one. Let's start with the USB connector. To connect an Arduino to your computer,

---

4. http://lab.guilhermemartins.net/2009/05/06/paperduino-prints/

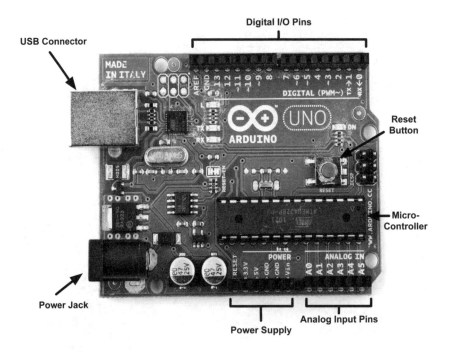

Figure 1.2: THE ARDUINO'S MOST IMPORTANT COMPONENTS

you just need an USB cable. Then you can use the USB connection for various purposes:

- Upload new software to the board (you'll see how to do this in Section 1.6, *Compiling and Uploading Programs*, on page 18).

- Communicate with the Arduino board and your computer (you'll learn that in Section 2.4, *Using Serial Ports*, on page 30).

- Supply the Arduino board with power.

As an electronic device, the Arduino needs power. One way to power it is to connect it to a computer's USB port, but that isn't a good solution in some cases. Some projects don't necessarily need a computer, and it would be overkill to use a whole computer just to power the Arduino. Also, the USB port only delivers 5 volts, and sometimes you need more.

Figure 1.3: YOU CAN POWER AN ARDUINO WITH AN AC ADAPTER.

In these situations, the best solution usually is an AC adapter (see Figure 1.3) supplying 9 volts (the recommended range is 7V to 12V).[5] You need an adapter with a 2.1 mm barrel tip and a positive center (you don't need to understand what that means right now; just ask for it in your local electronics store). Plug it into the Arduino's power jack, and it will start immediately, even if it isn't connected to a computer. By the way, even if you connect the Arduino to an USB port, it will use the external power supply if available.

Please note that older versions of the Arduino board (Arduino-NG and Diecimila) don't switch automatically between an external power supply and a USB supply. They come with a power selection jumper labeled *PWR_SEL*, and you manually have to set it to EXT or USB, respectively (see Figure 1.4, on the next page).

Now you know two ways to supply the Arduino with power. But the Arduino isn't greedy and happily shares its power with other devices. At the bottom of Figure 1.2, on the facing page, you can see several sockets (sometimes I'll also call them *pins*, because internally they are connected to pins in the microcontroller) related to power supply:

- Using the pins labeled *3V3* and *5V*, you can power external devices connected to the Arduino with 3.3 volts or 5 volts.

---

5.   http://www.arduino.cc/playground/Learning/WhatAdapter

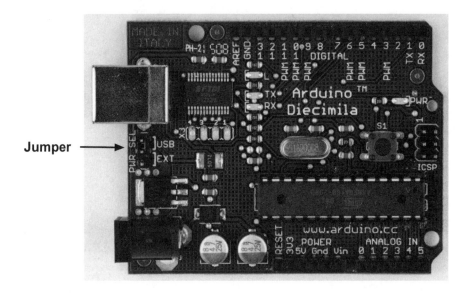

Jumper

Figure 1.4: OLDER ARDUINOS HAVE A POWER SOURCE SELECTION JUMPER.

- Two ground pins labeled *Gnd* allow your external devices to share a common ground with the Arduino.

- Some projects need to be portable, so they'll use a portable power supply such as batteries. You connect an external power source such as a battery pack to the *Vin* and *Gnd* sockets.

  If you connect an AC adapter to the Arduino's power jack, you can supply the adapter's voltage through this pin.

On the lower right of the board, you see six analog input pins named A0–A5. You can use them to connect analog sensors to the Arduino. They take sensor data and convert it into a number between 0 and 1023. In Chapter 5, *Sensing the World Around Us*, on page 87, we'll use them to connect a temperature sensor to the Arduino.

At the board's top are 14 digital IO pins named D0–D13. Depending on your needs, you can use these pins for both digital input and output, so you can read the state of a pushbutton or switch to turn on and off an LED (we'll do this in Section 3.5, *Working with Buttons*, on page 56). Six of them (D3, D5, D6, D9, D10, and D11) can also act as analog

Analog and Digital Signals

Nearly all physical processes are analog. Whenever you observe a natural phenomenon such as electricity or sound, you're actually receiving an analog signal. One of the most important properties of these analog signals is that they are continuous. For every given point in time, you can measure the strength of the signal, and in principle you could register even the tiniest variation of the signal.

But although we live in an analog world, we are also living in the digital age. When the first computers were built a few decades ago, people quickly realized that it's much easier to work with real-world information when it's represented as numbers and not as an analog signal such as voltage or volume. For example, it's much easier to manipulate sounds using a computer when the sound waves are stored as a sequence of numbers. Every number in this sequence could represent the signal's loudness at a certain point in time.

So instead of storing the complete analog signal (as is done on records), we measure the signal only at certain points in time (see Figure 1.5, on the following page). We call this process *sampling*, and the values we store are called *samples*. The frequency we use to determine new samples is called *sampling rate*. For an audio CD, the sampling rate is 44.1 kHz: we gather 44,100 samples per second.

We also have to limit the samples to a certain range. On an audio CD, every sample uses 16 bits. In Figure 1.5, on the next page, the range is denoted by two dashed lines, and we had to cut off a peak at the beginning of the signal.

Although you can connect both analog and digital devices to the Arduino, you usually don't have to think much about it. The Arduino automatically performs the conversion from analog to digital, and vice versa, for you.

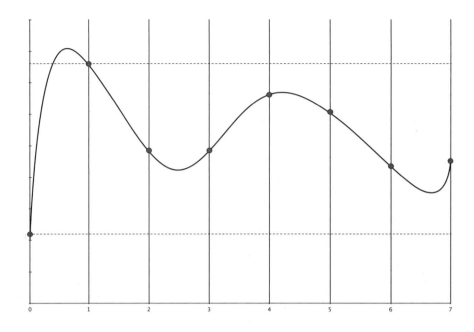

Figure 1.5: DIGITIZING AN ANALOG SIGNAL

output pins. In this mode, they convert values from 0 to 255 into an analog voltage.

All these pins are connected to a *microcontroller*. A microcontroller combines a CPU with some peripheral functions such as IO channels. Many different types of microcontrollers are available, but the Arduino usually comes with an ATmega328 or an ATmega168. Both are 8-bit microcontrollers produced by a company named Atmel.

Although modern computers load programs from a hard drive, microcontrollers usually have to be programmed. That means you have to load your software into the microcontroller via a cable, and once the program has been uploaded, it stays in the microcontroller until it gets overwritten with a new program. Whenever you supply power to the Arduino, the program currently stored in its microcontroller gets executed automatically. Sometimes you want the Arduino to start right from the beginning. With the reset button on the right side of the board, you can do that. If you press it, everything gets reinitialized, and the program stored in the microcontroller starts again (we use it in Section 3.4, *First Version of a Binary Die*, on page 51).

In this section, we had a closer look at the Arduino Uno, the newest Arduino board. But several other types are available, and although they're the same in principle, they differ in some details. The Arduino Mega2560[6] has many more IO pins than all other Arduinos and uses the powerful ATmega2560 microcontroller, while the Arduino Nano[7] was designed to be used on a breadboard, so it doesn't have any sockets. From my experience, beginners should start with one of the "standard" boards, that is, with an Uno or a Duemilanove.

1.4 Installing the Arduino IDE

To make it as easy as possible to get started with the Arduino, the Arduino developers have created a simple but useful integrated development environment (IDE). It runs on many different operating systems. Before you can create your first projects, you have to install it.

Installing the Arduino IDE on Windows

The Arduino IDE runs on all the latest versions of Microsoft Windows, such as Windows XP, Windows Vista, and Windows 7. Installing the software is easy, because it comes as a self-contained ZIP archive,[8] so you don't even need an installer. Download the archive, and extract it to a location of your choice.

Before you first start the IDE, you must install drivers for the Arduino's USB port. This process depends on the Arduino board you're using and on your flavor of Windows, but you always have to plug the Arduino into a USB port first to start the driver installation process.

On Windows Vista, driver installation usually happens automatically. Lean back and watch the hardware wizard's messages pass by until it says that you can use the newly installed USB hardware.

Windows XP and Windows 7 may not find the drivers on Microsoft's update sites automatically. Sooner or later the hardware wizard asks you for the path to the right drivers after you have told it to skip automatic driver installation from the Internet. Depending on your Arduino board, you have to point it to the right location in the Arduino installation directory. For the Arduino Uno and the Arduino Mega 2560, choose

---

6. http://arduino.cc/en/Main/ArduinoBoardMega2560
7. http://arduino.cc/en/Main/ArduinoBoardNano
8. http://arduino.cc/en/Main/Software

Arduino UNO.inf (respectively, Arduino MEGA 2560.inf) in the drivers directory. For older boards such as the Duemilanove, Diecimila, or Nano,
choose the drivers/FTDI USB Drivers directory

After the drivers have been installed, you can start the Arduino executable from the archive's main directory by double-clicking it. Follow
the instructions on the screen to install the IDE.

Please note that the USB drivers don't change as often as the Arduino
IDE. Whenever you install a new version of the IDE, check whether you
have to install new drivers, too. Usually, it isn't necessary.

Installing the Arduino IDE on Mac OS X

The Arduino IDE is available as a disk image for the most recent Mac
OS X.[9] Download it, double-click it, and then drag the Arduino icon to
your Applications folder.

If you're using an Arduino Uno or an Arduino Mega 2560, you are
done and can start the IDE. Before you can use the IDE with an older
Arduino such as the Duemilanove, Diecimila, or Nano, you have to
install drivers for the Arduino's serial port. A universal binary is in the
disk image—double-click the FTDIUSBSerialDriver_10_4_10_5_10_6.pkg file for
your platform, and follow the installation instructions on the screen.

When installing a new version of the Arduino IDE, you usually don't
have to install the FTDI drivers again (only when a more recent version
of the drivers is available).

Installing the Arduino IDE on Linux

Installation procedures on Linux distributions are still not very homo-
geneous. The Arduino IDE works fine on nearly all modern Linux versions, but the installation process heavily differs from distribution to
distribution. Also, you often have to install additional software (the Java
virtual machine, for example) that comes preinstalled with other operating systems.

It's best to check the official documentation[10] and look up the instructions for your preferred system.

Now that we have the drivers and the IDE installed, let's see what it has
to offer.

---

9. http://arduino.cc/en/Main/Software
10. http://www.arduino.cc/playground/Learning/Linux

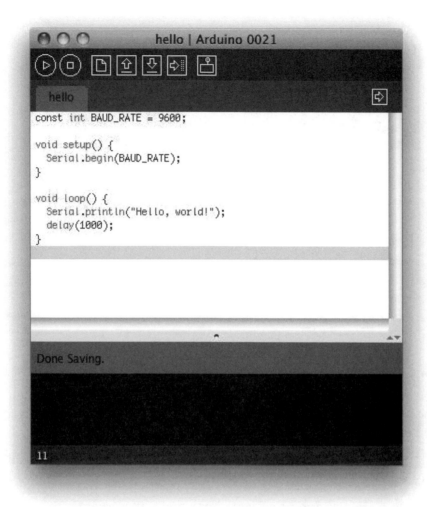

Figure 1.6: THE ARDUINO IDE IS WELL ARRANGED.

1.5 Meeting the Arduino IDE

If you have used an IDE such as Eclipse, Xcode, or Microsoft Visual Studio before, you'd better lower your expectations, because the Arduino IDE is really simple. It mainly consists of an editor, a compiler, a loader, and a serial monitor (see Figure 1.6 or, even better, start the IDE on your computer).

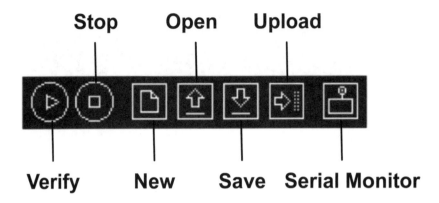

Figure 1.7: The IDE's toolbar gives you quick access to important functions.

It has no advanced features such as a debugger or code completion. You can change only a few preferences, and as a Java application it does not fully integrate into the Mac desktop. It's still usable, though, and even has decent support for project management.

In Figure 1.7, you can see the IDE's toolbar that gives you instant access to the functions you'll need most:

- With the Verify button, you can compile the program that's currently in the editor. So, in some respects, "Verify" is a bit of a misnomer, because clicking the button does not only verify the program syntactically. It also turns it into a representation suitable for the Arduino board.

- The New button creates a new program by emptying the content of the current editor window. Before that happens, the IDE gives you the opportunity to store all unsaved changes.

- With Open, you can open an existing program from the file system.

- Save saves the current program.

- When you click the Upload button, the IDE compiles the current program and uploads it to the Arduino board you have chosen in

Figure 1.8: THE ARDUINO BOARD COMES WITH SEVERAL LEDS.

the IDE's Tools > Serial Port menu (you'll learn more about this in Section 1.6, *Compiling and Uploading Programs*, on page 18).

- The Arduino can communicate with a computer via a serial connection. Clicking the Serial Monitor button opens a serial monitor window that allows you to watch the data sent by an Arduino and also to send data back.

- The Stop button stops the serial monitor.

Although using the IDE is easy, you might run into problems or want to look up something special. In such cases, take a look at the Help menu. It points to many useful resources at the Arduino's website that provide quick solutions not only to all typical problems but also to reference material and tutorials.

To get familiar with the IDE's most important features, we'll create a simple program that makes an light-emitting diode (LED) blink. An LED is a cheap and efficient light source, and the Arduino already comes with several LEDs. One LED shows whether the Arduino is currently powered, and two other LEDs blink when data is transmitted or received via a serial connection (see them in Figure 1.8).

In our first little project, we'll make the Arduino's status LED blink. The status LED is connected to digital IO pin 13. Digital pins act as a kind of switch and can be in one of two states: HIGH or LOW. If set to HIGH, the output pin is set to 5 volts, causing a current to flow through the LED, so it lights up. If it's set back to LOW, the current flow stops, and the LED turns off. You do not need to know exactly how electricity works at the moment, but if you're curious, take a look at Section A.1, *Current, Voltage, and Resistance*, on page 225.

Open the IDE, and enter the following code in the editor:

`welcome/HelloWorld/HelloWorld.pde`

```
Line 1  const unsigned int LED_PIN = 13;
   -    const unsigned int PAUSE = 500;
   -
   -    void setup() {
   5      pinMode(LED_PIN, OUTPUT);
   -    }
   -
   -    void loop() {
   -      digitalWrite(LED_PIN, HIGH);
  10      delay(PAUSE);
   -      digitalWrite(LED_PIN, LOW);
   -      delay(PAUSE);
   -    }
```

Let's see how this works and dissect the program's source code piece by piece. In the first two lines we define two **int** constants using the **const** keyword. LED_PIN refers to the number of the digital IO pin we're using, and PAUSE defines the length of the blink period in milliseconds.

Every Arduino program needs a function named setup(), and ours starts in line 4. A function definition always adheres to the following scheme:

<return value type> <function name> '(' <list of parameters> ')'

In our case the function's name is setup(), and its return value type is **void**: it returns nothing. setup() doesn't expect any arguments, so we left the parameter list empty. Before we continue with the dissection of our program, you should learn a bit more about the Arduino's data types.

Arduino Data Types

Every piece of data you store in an Arduino program needs a type. Depending on your needs, you can choose from the following:

- **boolean** values take up one byte of memory and can be **true** or **false**.

- **char** variables take up one byte of memory and store numbers from -128 to 127. These numbers usually represent characters encoded in ASCII; that is, in the following example, c1 and c2 have the same value:

  ```
  char c1 = 'A';
  char c2 = 65;
  ```

  Note that you have to use single quotes for **char** literals.

- **byte** variables use one byte and store values from 0 to 255.

- An **int** variable needs two bytes of memory; you can use it to store numbers from -32,768 to 32,767. Its unsigned pendant **unsigned int** also consumes two bytes of memory but stores numbers from 0 to 65,535.

- For bigger numbers, use **long**. It consumes four bytes of memory and stores values from -2,147,483,648 to 2,147,483,647. The unsigned variant **unsigned long** also needs four bytes but ranges from 0 to 4,294,967,295.

- **float** and **double** are the same at the moment, and you can use these types for storing floating-point numbers. Both use four bytes of memory and are able to store values from -3.4028235E+38 to 3.4028235E+38.

- You need **void** only for function declarations. It denotes that a function doesn't return a value.

- Arrays store collections of values having the same type:

```
int values[2];        // A two-element array
int values[0] = 42;   // Set the first element
int values[1] = -42;  // Set the second element
int more_values[] = { 42, -42 };
int first = more_values[0]; // first == 42
```

In the preceding example, the arrays values and more_values contain the same elements. We have used only two different ways of initializing an array. Note that the array index starts at 0, and keep in mind that uninitialized array elements contain random values.

- A string is an array of **char** values. The Arduino environment supports the creation of strings with some syntactic sugar—all these declarations create strings with the same contents.

```
char string1[8] = { 'A', 'r', 'd', 'u', 'i', 'n', 'o', '\0' };
char string2[]  = "Arduino";
char string3[8] = "Arduino";
char string4[]  = { 65, 114, 100, 117, 105, 110, 111, 0 };
```

Strings should always be terminated by a zero byte. When you use double quotes to create a string, the zero byte will be added automatically. That's why you have to add one byte to the size of the corresponding array.

In Section 8.7, *Emailing Directly from an Arduino*, on page 173, you'll learn how to use the Arduino's new String class.

Arduino calls setup() once when it boots, and we use it for initializing the Arduino board and all the hardware we have connected to it. We use the pinMode() method to turn pin 13 into an output pin. This makes sure the pin is able to provide enough current to light up an LED. The default state of a pin is INPUT, and both INPUT and OUTPUT are predefined constants.[11]

Another mandatory function named loop() begins in line 8. It contains the main logic of a program, and the Arduino calls it in an infinite loop. Our program's main logic has to turn on the LED connected to pin 13 first. To do this, we use digitalWrite() and pass it the number of our pin and the constant HIGH. This means the pin will output 5 volts until further notice, and the LED connected to the pin lights up.

The program then calls delay() and waits for 500 milliseconds doing nothing. During this pause, pin 13 remains in HIGH state, and the LED continues to burn. The LED is eventually turned off when we set the pin's state back to LOW using digitalWrite() again. We wait another 500 milliseconds, and then the loop() function ends. The Arduino starts it again, and the LED blinks.

In the next section, you'll learn how to bring the program to life and transfer it to the Arduino.

1.6 Compiling and Uploading Programs

Before you compile and upload a program to the Arduino, you have to configure two things in the IDE: the type of Arduino you're using and the serial port your Arduino is connected to.

Identifying the Arduino type is easy, because it is printed on the board. Popular types are Uno, Duemilanove, Diecimila, Nano, Mega, Mini, NG, BT, LilyPad, Pro, or Pro Mini. In some cases, you also have to check what microcontroller your Arduino uses—most have an ATmega168 or an ATmega328. You can find the microcontroller type printed on the microcontroller itself. When you have identified the exact type of your Arduino, choose it from the Tools > Board menu.

Now you have to choose the serial port your Arduino is connected to from the Tools > Serial Port menu. On Mac OS X, the name of the serial port starts with /dev/cu.usbserial or /dev/cu.usbmodem (on my

---

11. See http://arduino.cc/en/Tutorial/DigitalPins for the official documentation.

MacBook Pro, it's /dev/cu.usbmodemfa141). On Linux systems, it should be /dev/ttyUSB0, /dev/ttyUSB1, or something similar depending on the number of USB ports your computer has.

On Windows systems, it's a bit more complicated to find out the right serial port, but it's still not difficult. Go to the Device Manager, and look for USB Serial Port below the Ports (COM & LPT) menu entry (see Figure 1.9, on the following page). Usually the port is named COM1, COM2, or something similar.

After you have chosen the right serial port, click the Verify button, and you should see the following output in the IDE's message area (the Arduino IDE calls programs *sketches*):

```
Binary sketch size: 1010 bytes (of a 32256 byte maximum)
```

This means the IDE has successfully compiled the source code into 1,010 bytes of machine code that we can upload to the Arduino. If you see an error message instead, check whether you have typed in the program correctly (when in doubt, download the code from the book's website).[12] Depending on the Arduino board you're using, the byte maximum may differ. On an Arduino Duemilanove, it's usually 14336, for example.

Now click the Upload button, and after a few seconds, you should see the following output in the message area:

```
Binary sketch size: 1010 bytes (of a 32256 byte maximum)
```

This is exactly the same message we got after compiling the program, and it tells us that the 1,010 bytes of machine code were transferred successfully to the Arduino. In case of any errors, check whether you have selected the correct Arduino type and the correct serial port in the Tools menu.

During the upload process, the TX and RX LEDs will flicker for a few seconds. This is normal, and it happens whenever the Arduino and your computer communicate via the serial port. When the Arduino sends information, it turns on the TX LED. When it gets some bits, it turns on the RX LED. Because the communication is pretty fast, the LEDs start to flicker, and you cannot identify the transmission of a single byte (if you can, you are probably an alien).

---

12. http://www.pragprog.com/titles/msard

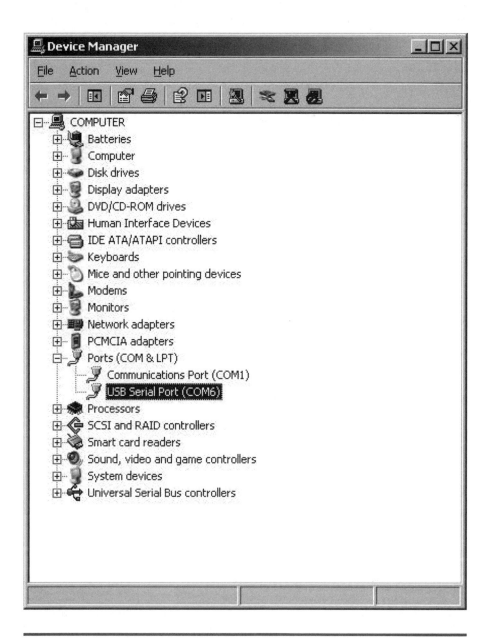

Figure 1.9: Look up the serial port an Arduino is connected to on Windows XP.

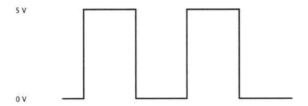

Figure 1.10: WHAT'S HAPPENING ON PIN 13 WHILE THE LED BLINKS.

As soon as the code has been transmitted completely, the Arduino executes it. In our case, this means the status LED starts to blink. It turns on for half a second, then it turns off for half a second, and so on.

In Figure 1.10, you can see a diagram showing the activity on the pin while the program is running. The pin starts in LOW state and does not output any current. We set it to HIGH in the software using digitalWrite() and let it output 5 volts for 500 milliseconds. Finally, we set it back to LOW for 500 milliseconds and repeat the whole process.

Admittedly, the status LED does not look very spectacular. So, in the next section, we'll attach a "real" LED to the Arduino.

1.7 Working with LEDs

The LEDs that come with the Arduino are nice for testing purposes, but you should not use them in your own electronics projects. They all have a specific meaning, and it's bad style to use them in a different context. Also, they are very small and not very bright, so it's a good idea to get some additional LEDs and learn how to connect them to the Arduino. It's really easy.

We will not use the same type of LEDs that are mounted on the Arduino board. They are surface-mounted devices (SMD) that are difficult to handle. You will rarely work with SMD parts, because for most of them you need special equipment and a lot of experience. They save costs as soon as you start mass production of an electronic device, but pure hobbyists won't need them often.

The LEDs that we need are through-hole parts; you can see some in Figure 1.11, on the following page. They are named through-hole parts because they are mounted to a circuit board through holes. That's

Figure 1.11: A COLLECTION OF THROUGH-HOLE LEDS

why they usually have one or more long wires. First you put the wires through holes in a printed circuit board. Then you usually bend, solder, and cut them to attach the part to the board. Where available, you can also plug them into sockets as we have them on the Arduino or on breadboards (you'll learn more about breadboards in Section 3.2, *Working with Breadboards*, on page 46).

In Figure 1.12, on the facing page, you can see how to attach an LED to an Arduino. Put the short connector of the LED to the ground pin (GND) and the longer one to pin 13. You can do that while the blink sketch is still running. Both the status LED and the external LED will start to blink.

Make absolutely sure that you're using pin 13! If you connect the LED to any other pin, it will probably be destroyed. The reason is that pin 13 has an internal resistor that the other pins don't have (you'll learn more about this in Chapter 3, *Building Binary Dice*, on page 45).

That's it! You've just added your first external electronics part to your Arduino, and you have created your first physical computing project. You've written some code, and it makes the world a bit brighter. Your very own digital version of "fiat lux."[13]

You will need the theory and skills you have learned in this chapter for nearly every Arduino project. In the next chapter, you'll see how to gain more control over LEDs, and you'll learn how to benefit from more advanced features of the Arduino IDE.

---

13. http://en.wikipedia.org/wiki/Fiat_lux

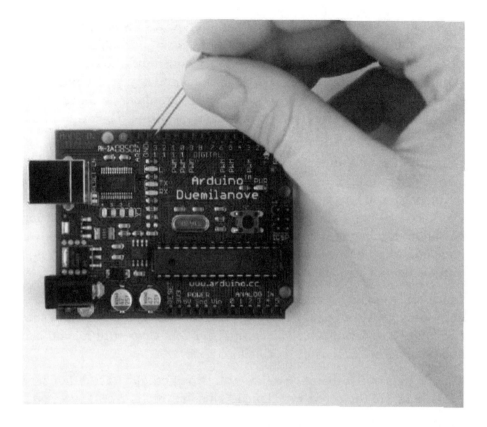

Figure 1.12: CONNECT AN LED TO THE ARDUINO.

1.8 What If It Doesn't Work?

Don't panic! If it doesn't work, you've probably attached the LED in the wrong way. When assembling an electronics project, parts fall into two categories: those you can mount any way you like and those that need a special direction. An LED has two connectors: an anode (positive) and a cathode (negative). It's easy to mix them up, and my science teacher taught me the following mnemonic: the *c*athode is ne*c*ative. It's also easy to remember what the negative connector of an LED is: it is shorter, minus, less than. If you are a more positive person, then think of the anode as being bigger plus more. You can alternatively identify a LED's connectors using its case. On the negative side the case is flat, while it's round on the positive side.

Choosing the wrong serial port or Arduino type also is a common mistake. If you get an error message such as "Serial port already in use" when uploading a sketch, check whether you have chosen the right serial port from the Tools > Serial Port menu. If you get messages such as "Problem uploading to board" or "programmer is not responding," check whether you have chosen the right Arduino board from the Tools > Board menu.

Your Arduino programs, like all programs, will contain bugs. Typos and syntax errors will be detected by the compiler. In Figure 1.13, on the facing page, you can see a typical error message. Instead of pinMode(), we called pinMod(), and because the compiler did not find a function having that name, it stopped with an error message. The Arduino IDE highlights the line, showing the error with a yellow background, and prints a helpful error message.

Other bugs might be more subtle and sometimes you have to carefully study your code and use some plain old debugging techniques (in *Debug It! Find, Repair, and Prevent Bugs in Your Code* [But09] you can find plenty of useful advice on this topic).

It might happen—although it's rare—that you actually have a damaged LED. If none of the tricks mentioned helps, try another LED.

1.9 Exercises

- Try different blink patterns using more pauses and vary the pause length (they don't necessarily have to be all the same). Also, experiment with very short pauses that make the LED blink at a high frequency. Can you explain the effect you're observing?

- Let the LED output your name in Morse code.[14]

---

14. http://en.wikipedia.org/wiki/Morse_code

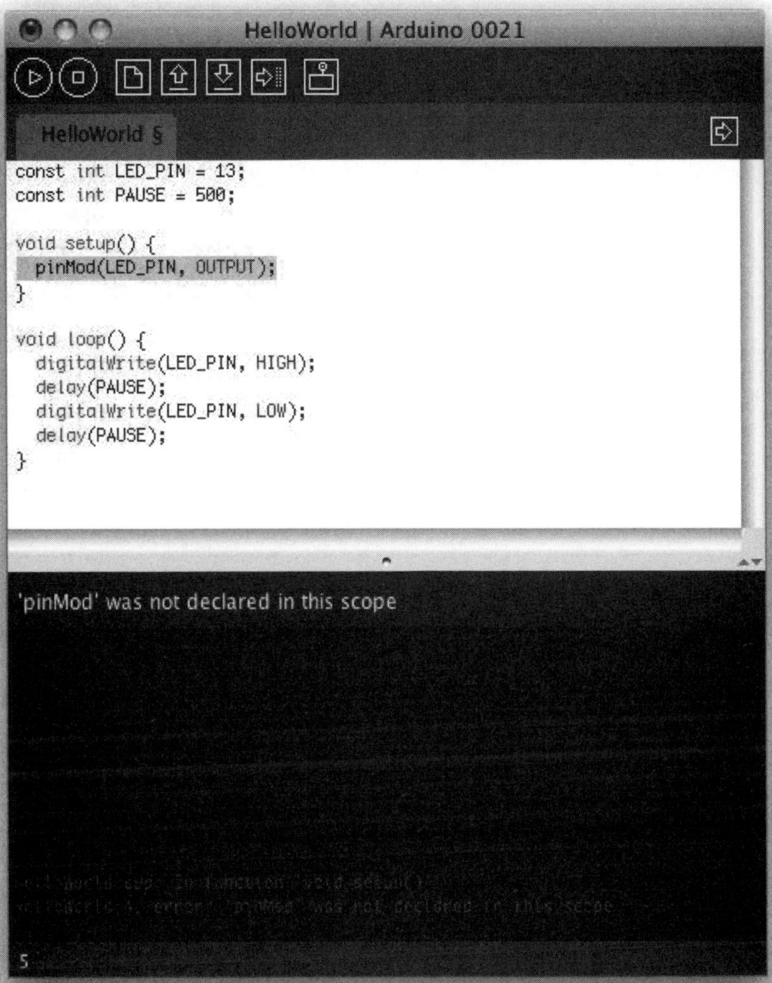
HelloWorld | Arduino 0021
HelloWorld §
const int LED_PIN = 13;
const int PAUSE = 500;
void setup() {
pinMod(LED_PIN, OUTPUT);
}
void loop() {
digitalWrite(LED_PIN, HIGH);
delay(PAUSE);
digitalWrite(LED_PIN, LOW);
delay(PAUSE);
}
'pinMod' was not declared in this scope
5

Figure 1.13: THE ARDUINO IDE EXPLAINS SYNTAX ERRORS NICELY.

Chapter 2

Inside the Arduino

For simple applications, all you have learned about the Arduino IDE in the preceding chapter is sufficient. But soon your projects will get more ambitious, and then it will come in handy to split them into separate files that you can manage as a whole. So in this chapter, you'll learn how to stay in control over bigger projects with the Arduino IDE.

Usually, bigger projects need not only more software but also more hardware—you will rarely use the Arduino board in isolation. For example, you will use many more sensors than you might imagine, and you'll have to transmit the data they measure back to your computer. To exchange data with the Arduino, you'll use its serial port. This chapter explains everything you need to know about serial communication. To make things more tangible, you'll learn how to turn your computer into a very expensive light switch that lets you control an LED using the keyboard.

2.1 What You Need

To try this chapter's examples, you need only a few things:

- An Arduino board such as the Uno, Duemilanove, or Diecimila

- A USB cable to connect the Arduino to your computer

- An LED (optional)

- A software serial terminal such as Putty (for Windows users) or screen for Linux and Mac OS X users (optional)

2.2 Managing Projects and Sketches

Modern software developers can choose from a variety of development tools that automate repetitive and boring tasks. That's also true for embedded systems like the Arduino. You can use integrated development environments (IDEs) to manage your programs, too. The most popular one has been created by the Arduino team.

The Arduino IDE manages all files belonging to your project. It also provides convenient access to all the tools you need to create the binaries that will run on your Arduino board. Conveniently, it does so unobtrusively. For example, you might have noticed that the Arduino IDE stores all code you enter automatically. This is to prevent beginners from losing data or code accidentally (not to mention that even the pros lose data from time to time, too).

Organizing all the files belonging to a project automatically is one of the most important features of an IDE. Under the hood, the Arduino IDE creates a directory for every new project, and it stores all the files belonging to the project in this directory. To add new files to a project, click the tabs button on the right to open the tabs pop-up menu, and then choose New Tab (see Figure 2.1). To add an existing file, use the Sketch > Add File menu item.

As you might have guessed already from the names of the menu items, the Arduino IDE calls projects *sketches*. If you do not choose a name, it gives them a name starting with sketch_. You can change the name whenever you like using the Save As command. If you do not save a sketch explicitly, the IDE stores it in a predefined folder you can look

Figure 2.1: THE TABS MENU IN ACTION

up in the preferences menu. You can change this behavior so that the IDE asks you for a name when you create a new sketch. Whenever you get lost, you can check what folder the current sketch is in using the Sketch > Show Sketch Folder menu item.

The IDE uses directories not only to organize projects. It also stores some interesting things in the following folders:

- The examples folder contains sample sketches that you can use as a basis for your own experiments. Get to them via the File > Open dialog box. Take some time to browse through them, even if you do not understand anything you see right now.

- The libraries directory contains libraries for various purposes and devices. Whenever you use a new sensor, for example, chances are good that you have to copy a supporting library to this folder.

The Arduino IDE makes your life easier by choosing reasonable defaults for a lot of settings. But it also allows you to change most of these settings, and you'll see how in the next section.

2.3 Changing Preferences

For your early projects, the IDE's defaults might be appropriate, but sooner or later you'll want to change some things. As you can see in Figure 2.2, on the following page, the IDE lets you change only a few preferences directly. But the dialog box refers to a file named preferences.txt containing more preferences. This file is a Java properties file consisting of key/value pairs. Here you see a few of them:

```
...
editor.external.bgcolor=#168299
preproc.web_colors=true
editor.font.macosx=Monaco,plain,10
sketchbook.auto_clean=true
update.check=true
build.verbose=true
upload.verbose=true
...
```

Most of these properties control the user interface; that is, they change fonts, colors, and so on. But they can also change the application's behavior. For example, you can enable more verbose output for operations such as compiling or uploading a sketch. Edit preferences.txt, and set both build.verbose and upload.verbose to true. Then load the blinking LED sketch from Chapter 1, *Welcome to the Arduino*, on page 3 and

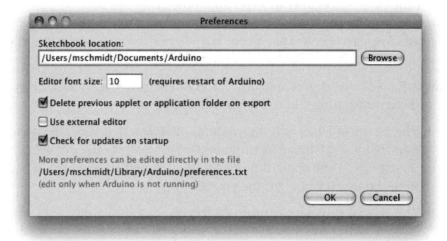

Figure 2.2: THE IDE LETS YOU CHANGE SOME PREFERENCES.

compile it again. The output in the message panel should look similar to Figure 2.3, on the facing page (in recent versions of the IDE, you can achieve the same effect by holding down the Shift key when you click the Verify/Compile or Upload button in the toolbar).

Note that the IDE updates some of the preferences' values when it shuts down. So before you change any preferences directly in the pref-erences.txt file, you have to stop the Arduino IDE first.

Now that you're familiar with the Arduino IDE, let's do some program-ming. We'll make the Arduino talk to the outside world.

2.4 Using Serial Ports

Arduino makes many stand-alone applications possible—projects that do not involve any additional computers. In such cases you need to con-nect the Arduino to a computer once to upload the software, and after that, it needs only a power supply. More often, people use the Arduino to enhance the capabilities of a computer using sensors or by giving access to additional hardware. Usually, you control external hardware via a serial port, so it is a good idea to learn how to communicate seri-ally with the Arduino.

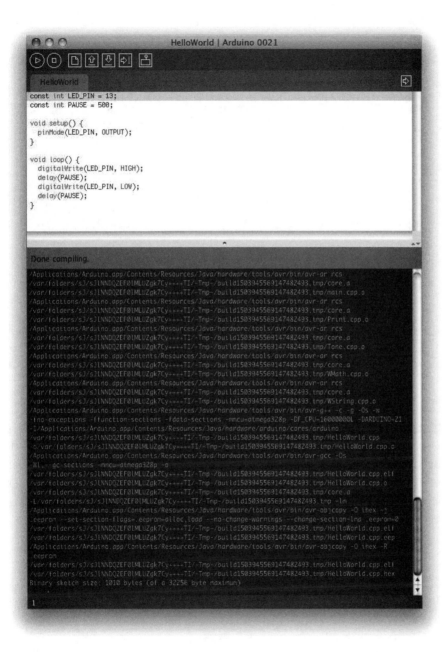

Figure 2.3: IDE IN VERBOSE MODE SHOWING OUTPUT OF COMMAND-LINE
TOOLS

The Arduino Programming Language

People sometimes seem to be a bit irritated when it comes to the language the Arduino gets programmed in. That's mainly because the typical sample sketches look as if they were written in a language that has been exclusively designed for programming the Arduino. But that's not the case—it is plain old C++ (which implies that it supports C, too).

Every Arduino uses an AVR microcontroller designed by a company named Atmel. (Atmel says that the name AVR does not stand for anything.) These microcontrollers are very popular, and many hardware projects use them. One of the reasons for their popularity is the excellent tool chain that comes with them. It is based on the GNU C++ compiler tools and has been optimized for generating code for AVR microcontrollers.

That means you feed C++ code to the compiler that is not translated into machine code for *your* computer but for an AVR microcontroller. This technique is called *cross-compiling* and is the usual way to program embedded devices.

Although the standards for serial communication have changed over the past few years (for example, we are using USB today, and our computers no longer have RS232 connectors), the basic working principles remain the same. In the simplest case, we can connect two devices using only three wires: a common ground, a line for transmitting data (TX), and one for receiving data (RX).

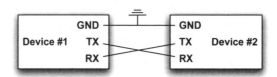

Serial communication might sound a bit old-school, but it's still the preferred way for hardware devices to communicate. For example, the S in USB stands for "serial"—and when was the last time you saw a parallel port? (Perhaps this is a good time to clean up the garage and throw out that old PC that you wanted to turn into a media center someday....)

For uploading software, the Arduino has a serial port, and we can use it to connect the Arduino to other devices, too (in Section 1.6, *Compiling and Uploading Programs*, on page 18, you learn how to look up the serial port your Arduino is connected to). In this section, we will use it to control Arduino's status LED using our computer's keyboard. The LED should be turned on when you press 1, and it should be turned off when you press 2. Here's all the code we need:

```
welcome/LedSwitch/LedSwitch.pde
```

```
Line 1  const unsigned int LED_PIN = 13;
   -    const unsigned int BAUD_RATE = 9600;

   -    void setup() {
   5      pinMode(LED_PIN, OUTPUT);
   -      Serial.begin(BAUD_RATE);
   -    }

   -    void loop() {
  10      if (Serial.available() > 0) {
   -        int command = Serial.read();
   -        if (command == '1') {
   -          digitalWrite(LED_PIN, HIGH);
   -          Serial.println("LED on");
  15        } else if (command == '2') {
   -          digitalWrite(LED_PIN, LOW);
   -          Serial.println("LED off");
   -        } else {
   -          Serial.print("Unknown command: ");
  20          Serial.println(command);
   -        }
   -      }
   -    }
```

As in our previous examples, we define a constant for the pin the LED is connected to and set it to OUTPUT mode in the setup() function. In line 6, we initialize the serial port using the begin() function of the Serial class, passing a baud rate of 9600 (you can learn what a baud rate is in Section C.1, *Learning More About Serial Communication*, on page 239). That's all we need to send and receive data via the serial port in our program.

So, let's read and interpret the data. The loop() function starts by calling Serial's available() method in line 10. available() returns the number of bytes waiting on the serial port. If any data is available, we read it using Serial.read(). read() returns the first byte of incoming data if data is available and -1 otherwise.

Fashionable LEDs

Both pervasive and wearable computing got very popular over the past years, so T-shirts with an equalizer are still cool but not that exciting any longer.* But by using a few LEDs, you can create some astonishing accessories for the ladies. For example, Japanese engineers have created LED eyelashes.[†]

This particular product does not use an Arduino, but with the Lilypad,[‡] you can easily create similar things yourself. You have to be extremely careful with LEDs, because most of them are very bright and can cause serious damage to your eyes!

---

*. http://www.thinkgeek.com/tshirts-apparel/interactive/8a5b/
†. http://blog.makezine.com/archive/2009/10/led_eyelashes.html
‡. http://www.arduino.cc/en/Main/ArduinoBoardLilyPad

If the byte we have read represents the character 1, we switch on the LED and send back the message "LED on" over the serial port. We use Serial.println(), which adds a carriage return character (ASCII code 13) followed by a newline (ASCII code 10) to the text.

If we received the character 2, we switch off the LED. If we received an unsupported command, we send back a corresponding message and the command we did not understand. Serial.print() works exactly like Serial.println(), but it does not add carriage return and newline characters to the message.

Let's see how the program works in practice. Compile it, upload it to your Arduino, and then switch to the serial monitor (optionally you can attach an LED to pin 13; otherwise, you can only control the Arduino's status LED). At first glance, nothing has happened. That's because we have not sent a command to the Arduino yet. Enter a 1 in the text box, and then click the Send button. Two things should happen now: the LED is switched on, and the message "LED on" appears in the serial monitor window (see Figure 2.4, on the next page). We are controlling a LED using our computer's keyboard!

Play around a bit with the commands 1 and 2, and also observe what happens when you send an unknown command. If you type in an uppercase *A*, for example, the Arduino will send back the message "Unknown command: 65." The number 65 is the ASCII code of the letter *A*, and the Arduino outputs the data it got in its most basic form.

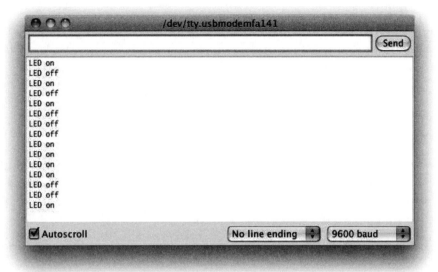

Figure 2.4: The Arduino IDE's serial monitor

That's the default behavior of Serial's print() method, and you can change it by passing a format specifier to your function calls. To see the effect, replace line 20 with the following statements:

```
Serial.println(command, DEC);
Serial.println(command, HEX);
Serial.println(command, OCT);
Serial.println(command, BIN);
Serial.println(command, BYTE);
```

The output looks as follows when you send the character *A* again:

```
Unknown command: 65
41
101
1000001
A
```

Depending on the format specifier, Serial.println() automatically converts a byte into another representation. DEC outputs a byte as a decimal number, HEX as a hexadecimal number, and so on. Note that such an operation usually changes the length of the data that gets transmitted. The binary representation of the single byte 65, for example, needs 7 bytes, because it contains seven characters.

Numbering Systems

It's an evolutionary accident that 10 is the basis for our numbering system. If we had only four fingers on each hand, it'd be probably eight, and we'd probably have invented computers a few centuries earlier.

For thousands of years, people have used denominational number systems, and we represent a number like 4711 as follows:

$4{\times}10^3 + 7{\times}10^2 + 1{\times}10^1 + 1{\times}10^0$

This makes arithmetic operations very convenient. But when working with computers that only interpret binary numbers, it's often advantageous to use numbering systems based on the numbers 2 (binary), 8 (octal), or 16 (hexadecimal).

For example, the decimal number 4711 can be represented in octal and hexadecimal as follows:

- $1{\times}8^4 + 1{\times}8^3 + 1{\times}8^2 + 4{\times}8^1 + 7{\times}8^0 = 011147$
- $1{\times}16^3 + 2{\times}16^2 + 6{\times}16^1 + 7{\times}16^0 = 0x1267$

In Arduino programs, you can define literals for all these numbering systems:

```
int decimal = 4711;
int binary = B1001001100111;
int octal = 011147;
int hexadecimal = 0x1267;
```

Binary numbers start with a B character, octal numbers with a 0, and hexadecimal numbers start with 0x.

Using Different Serial Terminals

For trivial applications, the IDE's serial monitor is sufficient, but you cannot easily combine it with other applications, and it lacks some features (for example, it could not send newline characters in older IDE versions). That means you should have an alternative serial terminal to send data, and you can find plenty of them for every operating system.

Serial Terminals for Windows

Putty[1] is an excellent choice for Windows users. It is free, and it comes as an executable that does not even have to be installed. Figure 2.5, on the facing page shows how to configure it for communication on a serial port.

---

1. http://www.chiark.greenend.org.uk/~sgtatham/putty/

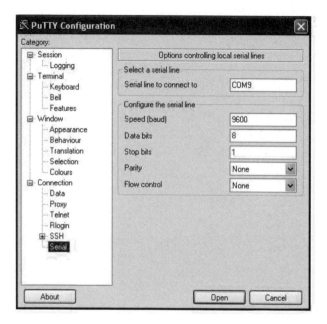

Figure 2.5: CONFIGURING PUTTY TO MAKE IT WORK WITH ARDUINO

After you have configured Putty, you can open a serial connection to the Arduino. In Figure 2.6, on the next page, you can see the corresponding dialog box. Click Open, and you'll see an empty terminal window.

Now press 1 and 2 a few times to switch on and off the LED. In Figure 2.7, on the following page, you can see a typical session.

Serial Terminals for Linux and Mac OS X

Linux and Mac users can use the screen command to communicate with the Arduino on a serial port. Check which serial port the Arduino is connected to (for example, in the IDE's Tools > Board menu), and then run a command like this (with an older board the name of the serial port might be something like /dev/cu.usbserial-A9007LUY, and on Linux systems it might be /dev/ttyUSB1 or something similar):

```
$ screen /dev/cu.usbmodemfa141 9600
```

screen expects the name of the serial port and the baud rate to be used. In Figure 2.8, on page 39, you can see a typical session. To quit the screen command, press Ctrl-a followed by Ctrl-k.

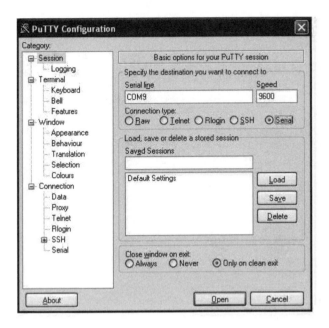

Figure 2.6: OPENING A SERIAL SESSION TO ARDUINO WITH PUTTY

Figure 2.7: PUTTY COMMUNICATES WITH ARDUINO.

Figure 2.8: The screen command communicates with Arduino.

We can now communicate with the Arduino, and this has great implications: whatever is controlled by the Arduino can also be controlled by your computer, and vice versa. Switching LEDs on and off is not too spectacular, but try to imagine what's possible now. You could move robots, automate your home, or create interactive games.

Here are some more important facts about serial communication:

- The Arduino's serial receive buffer can hold up to 128 bytes. When sending large amounts of data at high speed, you have to synchronize sender and receiver to prevent data loss. Usually, the receiver sends an acknowledgment to the sender whenever it is ready to consume a new chunk of data.

Exciting LED Projects

From what you have seen in this and the preceding sections, you might think that LEDs are useful but not very exciting. You can use them for showing a device's status or even to build a complete TV set, but that's something you are used to.

But LEDs are the basis for some really spectacular projects. One of the most amazing ones is the *BEDAZZLER*.* The BEDAZZLER is a nonlethal weapon that uses blinking LEDs to cause nausea, dizziness, headache, flash blindness, eye pain, and vomiting. Originally it has been developed for the military, but now it is available as an open source project.†

All scientific curiosity aside, you should keep in mind that the BEDAZZLER is a weapon. Do not use it as a toy, and do not target it at humans or animals.

*.   http://www.instructables.com/id/Bedazzler-DIY-non-lethal-weaponry/
†.   http://www.ladyada.net/make/bedazzler/

- You can control many devices using serial communication, but the regular Arduino has only one serial port. If you need more, take a look at the Arduino Mega 2560, which has four serial ports.[2]

- A Universal Asynchronous Receiver/Transmitter (UART)[3] device supports serial communication on the Arduino. This device handles serial communication while the CPU can take care of other tasks. This greatly improves the system's overall performance. The UART uses digital pins 0 (RX) and 1 (TX), which means you cannot use them for other purposes when communicating on the serial port. If you need them, you can disable serial communication using Serial.end().

- With the SoftwareSerial[4] library, you can use any digital pin for serial communication. It has some serious limitations regarding speed and reliability, and it does not support all functions that are available when using a regular serial port.

---

2. http://arduino.cc/en/Main/ArduinoBoardMega2560
3. http://en.wikipedia.org/wiki/UART
4. http://www.arduino.cc/en/Reference/SoftwareSerial

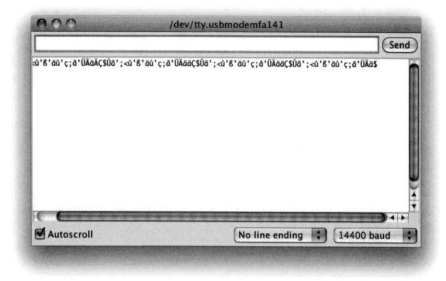

Figure 2.9: A WRONG BAUD RATE CREATES A LOT OF GARBAGE.

In this chapter, you saw how to communicate with the Arduino using the serial port, which opens the door to a whole new world of physical computing projects (see Section C.1, *Learning More About Serial Communication*, on page 239 for more details about serial communication). In the next chapters, you'll learn how to gather interesting facts about the real world using sensors, and you'll learn how to change the real world by moving objects. Serial communication is the basis for letting you control all these actions using the Arduino and your PC.

2.5 What If It Doesn't Work?

If anything goes wrong with the examples in this chapter, you should take a look at Section 1.8, *What If It Doesn't Work?*, on page 23 first. If you still run into problems, it may be because of some issues with serial communication. For example, you might have set the wrong baud rate; in Figure 2.9, you can see what's happening in such a case.

Make sure that the baud rate you have set in your call to Serial.begin() matches the baud rate in the serial monitor.

2.6 Exercises

- Add new commands to the sample program. For example, the command 3 could make the LED blink for a while.

- Try to make the commands more readable; that is, instead of 1, use the command on, and instead of 2, use off.

If you have problems solving this exercise, read Chapter 4, *Building a Morse Code Generator Library*, on page 71 first.

Part II

Eight Arduino Projects

Chapter 3

Building Binary Dice

Things will really start to get interesting now that you've learned the basics of Arduino development. You now have the skills to create your first complex, stand-alone projects. After you have worked through this chapter, you'll know how to work with LEDs, buttons, breadboards, and resistors. Combining these parts with an Arduino gives you nearly endless opportunities for new and cool projects.

Our first project will be creating an electronic die. While regular dice display their results using one to six dots, ours will use LEDs instead. For our first experiments, a single LED has been sufficient, but for the dice we need more than one. You need to connect several external LEDs to the Arduino. Because you cannot attach them all directly to the Arduino, you'll learn how to work with breadboards. Also, you need a button that rolls the dice, so you'll learn how to work with pushbuttons, too. To connect pushbuttons and LEDs to the Arduino, you need another important electronic part: the resistor. So, at the end of the chapter, you'll have many new tools in your toolbox.

3.1 What You Need

1. A half-size breadboard
2. Three LEDs (for the exercises you'll need additional LEDs)
3. Two 10kΩ resistors (see Section A.1, *Current, Voltage, and Resistance*, on page 225 to learn more about resistors)
4. Three 1kΩ resistors
5. Two pushbuttons
6. Some wires

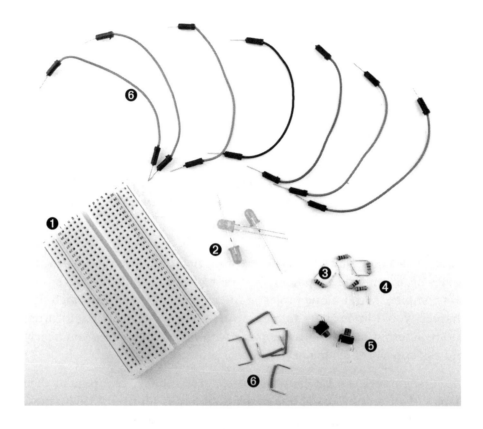

Figure 3.1: ALL THE PARTS YOU NEED FOR THIS CHAPTER

7. An Arduino board such as the Uno, Duemilanove, or Diecimila
8. A USB cable to connect the Arduino to your computer
9. A tilt sensor (optional)

Figure 3.1 shows the parts needed to build the projects in this chapter. You'll find such photos in most of the following chapters. The numbers in the photo correspond to the numbers in the parts list. The photos do not show standard parts such as the Arduino board or an USB cable.

3.2 Working with Breadboards

Connecting parts such as LEDs directly to the Arduino is only an option in the most trivial cases. Usually, you will prototype your projects on a breadboard that you connect to the Arduino. A breadboard "emulates"

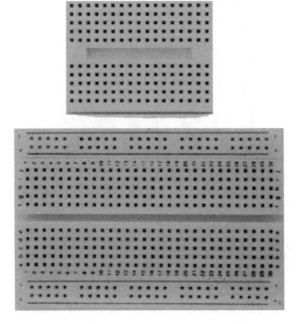

Figure 3.2: A COLLECTION OF BREADBOARDS

a circuit board. You don't have to solder parts to the board; instead, you can simply plug them into it.

Breadboards come in various types and sizes (in Figure 3.2, you can see two of them), but they all work the same way. They have a lot of sockets that you can use for plugging in through-hole parts or wires. That alone wouldn't be a big deal, but the sockets are connected in a special way. In Figure 3.3, on the next page, you can see how.

As you can see, most sockets are connected in columns. If one socket of a column is connected to a power supply, then automatically all the other sockets in this column are powered, too. On the bigger board in the photo, you can also see four rows of connected sockets. This is convenient for bigger circuits. Usually, you connect one row to your power supply and one to the ground. This way, you can distribute power and ground to any point on the board. Now let's see how to put parts on a breadboard.

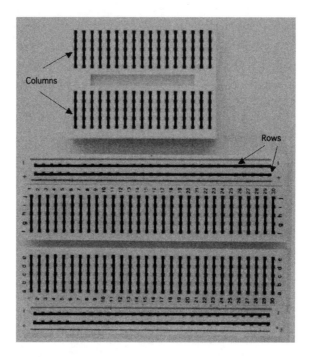

Figure 3.3: HOW SOCKETS ON A BREADBOARD ARE CONNECTED

3.3 Using an LED on a Breadboard

Up to now, we used the LEDs that are installed on the Arduino board, and we connected one LED directly to the Arduino. In this section, we'll plug an LED into a breadboard and then connect the breadboard to the Arduino.

In Figure 3.4, on the facing page, you can see a photo of our final circuit. It consists of an Arduino, a breadboard, an LED, three wires, and a 1kΩ resistor (more on that part in a few minutes). Connect the Arduino to the breadboard using two wires. Connect pin 12 with the ninth column of the breadboard, and connect the ground pin with the tenth column. This automatically connects all sockets in column 9 to pin 12 and all sockets in column 10 to the ground. This choice of columns was arbitrary, and you could have used other columns instead.

Plug the LED's negative connector (the shorter one) into column 10 and its positive connector into column 9. When you plug in parts or wires into a breadboard, you have to press them firmly until they slip in. You

Figure 3.4: CONNECTING AN LED ON A BREADBOARD TO THE ARDUINO

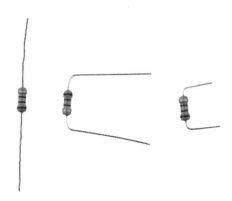

Figure 3.5: A RESISTOR IN VARIOUS PROCESSING STAGES

might need more than one try, especially on new boards, and it often comes in handy to shorten the connectors before plugging them into the breadboard. Make sure that you can still identify the negative and the positive connector after you have shortened them. Shorten the negative one a bit more, for example. Also wear safety glasses to protect your eyes when cutting the connectors!

The things we have done until now have been straightforward. That is, in principle we have only extended the Arduino's ground pin and its IO pin number 12. Why do we have to add a resistor, and what is a resistor? A resistor limits the amount of current that flows through an electric connection. In our case, it protects the LED from consuming too much power, because this would destroy the LED. You always have to use a resistor when powering an LED! In Section A.1, *Current, Voltage, and Resistance*, on page 225, you can learn more about resistors and their color bands. In Figure 3.5, you can see a resistor in various stages: regular, bent, and cut.

You might ask yourself why we didn't have to use a resistor when we connected the LED directly to the Arduino. The answer is simple: pin 13 comes with an internal resistor of 1kΩ. Now that we use pin 12, we have to add our own resistor.

We don't want to fiddle around too much with the connectors, so we build the circuit as shown in Figure 3.6, on the next page. That is, we use both sides of the breadboard by connecting them with a short wire. Note that the resistor bridges the sides, too.

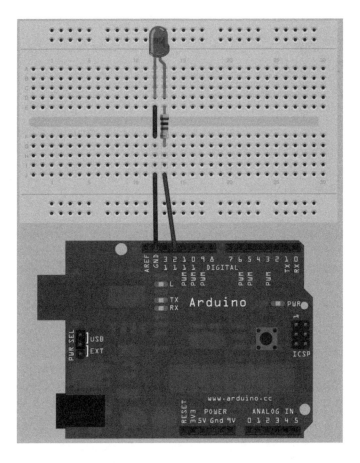

Figure 3.6: YOU CAN USE BOTH SIDES OF A BREADBOARD.

3.4 First Version of a Binary Die

You're certainly familiar with regular dice displaying results in a range from one to six. To emulate such dice exactly with an electronic device, you'd need seven LEDs and some fairly complicated business logic. We'll take a shortcut and display the result of a die roll in binary.

For a binary die, we need only three LEDs that represent the current result. We turn the result into a binary number, and for every bit that is set, we will light up a corresponding LED. The following diagram shows how the die results are mapped to LEDs (a black triangle stands for a shining LED).

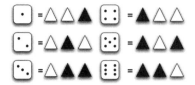

We already know how to control a single LED on a breadboard. Controlling three LEDs is similar and requires only more wires, LEDs, 1kΩ resistors, and pins. In Figure 3.7, on the facing page, you can see the first working version of a binary die.

The most important difference is the common ground. When you need ground for a single LED, you can connect it to the LED directly. But we need ground for three LEDs now, so we'll use the breadboard's rows for the first time. Connect the row marked with a hyphen (-) to the Arduino's ground pin, and all sockets in this row will work as ground pins, too. Then you can connect this row's sockets to the LEDs using short wires.

Everything else in this circuit should look familiar, because we only had to clone the basic LED circuit from the previous section three times. Note that we have connected the three circuits to pins 10, 11, and 12. The only thing missing is some software:

```
BinaryDice/BinaryDice.pde
const unsigned int LED_BIT0 = 12;
const unsigned int LED_BIT1 = 11;
const unsigned int LED_BIT2 = 10;

void setup() {
  pinMode(LED_BIT0, OUTPUT);
  pinMode(LED_BIT1, OUTPUT);
  pinMode(LED_BIT2, OUTPUT);

  randomSeed(analogRead(A0));
  long result = random(1, 7);
  output_result(result);
}

void loop() {
}

void output_result(const long result) {
  digitalWrite(LED_BIT0, result & B001);
  digitalWrite(LED_BIT1, result & B010);
  digitalWrite(LED_BIT2, result & B100);
}
```

Figure 3.7: A FIRST WORKING VERSION OF OUR BINARY DIE

More LEDs, Dice, and Cubes

Building binary dice is fun, and it's an easy project even for beginners. But what about the opposite—reading real dice? Steve Hoefer[*] has built a dice reader using an Arduino, and it's really impressive. He uses five pairs of infrared emitters and receivers to "scan" a die's surface. It's a fairly advanced project, and you can learn a lot from it.

Another interesting project is an LED cube: building a cube consisting of LEDs.[†] It's surprisingly difficult to control more than a few LEDs, but you can produce astonishing results.

[*]. http://grathio.com/2009/08/dice-reader-version-2.html
[†]. http://arduinofun.com/blog/2009/12/02/led-cube-and-arduino-lib-build-it/

This is all the code we need to implement the first version of binary dice. As usual, we define some constants for the output pins the LEDs are connected to. In the setup() function, we set all the pins into OUTPUT mode. For the dice, we need random numbers in the range between one and six. The random() function returns random numbers in a specified range using a pseudorandom number generator. In line 10, we initialize the generator with some noise we read from analog input pin A0 (see the sidebar on the next page to learn why we have to do that). You might wonder where the constant A0 is from. Since version 19, the Arduino IDE defines constants for all analog pins named A0, A1, and so on. Then we actually generate a new random number between one and six and output it using the output_result() function. (the seven in the call to random() is correct, because it expects the upper limit plus one).

The function output_result() takes a number and outputs its lower three bits by switching on or off our three LEDs accordingly. Here we use the & operator and binary literals. The & operator takes two numbers and combines them bitwise. When two corresponding bits are 1, the result of the & operator is 1, too. Otherwise, it is 0. The B prefix allows you to put binary numbers directly into your source code. For example, B11 is the same as 3.

You might have noticed that the loop() function was left empty, and you might wonder how such dice work. It's pretty simple: whenever you restart the Arduino, it outputs a new number, and to roll the dice again, you have to press the reset button.

Generating Random Numbers

Some computing problems are surprisingly difficult, and creating good random numbers is one of them. After all, one of the most important properties of a computer is deterministic behavior. Still, we often need—at least seemingly—random behavior for a variety of purposes, ranging from games to cryptographic algorithms.

The most popular approach (used in Arduino's random() function, for example) is to create pseudorandom numbers.* They seem to be random, but they actually are the result of a formula. Different kinds of algorithms exist, but usually each new pseudorandom number is calculated from its predecessors. This implies that you need an initialization value to create the first random number of the sequence. This initialization value is called a *random seed*, and to create different sequences of pseudorandom numbers, you have to use different random seeds.

Creating pseudorandom numbers is cheap, but if you know the algorithm and the random seed, you can easily predict them. So, you shouldn't use them for cryptographic purposes.

In the real world, you can find countless random processes, and with the Arduino, it's easy to measure them to create real random numbers. Often it's sufficient to read some random noise from analog pin 0 and pass it as the random seed to the randomSeed() function. You can also use this noise to create real random numbers; there is even a library for that purpose.†

If you need strong random numbers, the Arduino is a perfect device for creating them. You can find many projects that observe natural processes solely to create random numbers. One of them watches an hourglass using the Arduino, for example.‡

---

*. http://en.wikipedia.org/wiki/Pseudo-random_numbers
†. http://code.google.com/p/tinkerit/wiki/TrueRandom
‡. http://www.circuitlake.com/usb-hourglass-sand-timer.html

Compile the code, upload it to the Arduino, and play a bit with your binary dice. You have mastered your first advanced electronics project! Enjoy it for a moment!

So, whenever you want to see a new result, you have to reset the Arduino. That's probably the most pragmatic user interface you can build, and for a first prototype, this is OK. But often you need more than one button, and it's also more elegant to add your own button anyway. So, that's what we'll do in the next section.

3.5 Working with Buttons

In this section, we'll add our own pushbutton to our binary dice, so we no longer have to abuse the Arduino's reset button to roll the dice. We'll start small and build a circuit that uses a pushbutton to control a single LED.

So, what exactly is a pushbutton? Here are three views of a typical pushbutton that can be used as the Arduino's reset button.

It has four connectors that fit perfectly on a breadboard (at least after you have straightened them with a pair of pliers). Two opposite pins connect when the button is pushed; otherwise, they are disconnected.

In Figure 3.8, on the facing page, you can see a simple circuit using a pushbutton. Connect pin 7 (chosen completely arbitrarily) to the pushbutton, and connect the pushbutton via a 10kΩ resistor to ground. Then connect the 5 volts power supply to the other pin of the button. Make sure the pushbutton's orientation is right. Its connected pins have to bridge the gap of the breadboard.

All in all, this approach seems straightforward, but why do we need a resistor again? The problem is that we expect the pushbutton to return a default value (LOW) in case it isn't pressed. But when the button isn't pressed, it would be directly connected to ground and would flicker because of static and interference. Only a little bit of current flows through the resistor, and this helps prevent random noise from changing the voltage that the input pin sees.

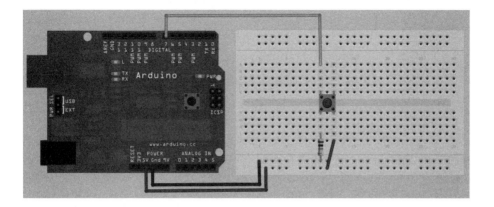

Figure 3.8: A SIMPLE PUSHBUTTON CIRCUIT

When the button is pressed, there will still be 5 volts at the Arduino's digital pin, but when the button isn't pressed, it will cleanly read the connection to ground. We call this a *pull-down resistor*; a *pull-up resistor* works exactly the other way around. That is, you have to connect the Arduino's signal pin to power through the pushbutton and connect the other pin of the pushbutton to ground using a resistor.

Now that we've eliminated all this ugly unstable real-world behavior, we can return to the stable and comforting world of software development. The following program checks whether a pushbutton is pressed and lights an LED accordingly:

`BinaryDice/SimpleButton/SimpleButton.pde`

```
const unsigned int BUTTON_PIN = 7;
const unsigned int LED_PIN    = 13;

void setup() {
  pinMode(LED_PIN, OUTPUT);
  pinMode(BUTTON_PIN, INPUT);
}

void loop() {
  const int BUTTON_STATE = digitalRead(BUTTON_PIN);

  if (BUTTON_STATE == HIGH)
    digitalWrite(LED_PIN, HIGH);
  else
    digitalWrite(LED_PIN, LOW);
}
```

We connect the button to pin 7 and the LED to pin 13 and initialize the pins accordingly in the setup() function. In loop(), we read the current state of the pin connected to the button. If it is HIGH, we turn the LED on. Otherwise, we turn it off.

Upload the program to the Arduino, and you'll see that the LED is on as long as you press the button. As soon as you release the button, the LED turns off. This is pretty cool, because now we nearly have everything we need to control our dice using our own button. But before we proceed, we'll slightly enhance our example and turn the button into a real light switch.

To build a light switch, we start with the simplest possible solution. Do not change the current circuit, and upload the following program to your Arduino:

BinaryDice/UnreliableSwitch/UnreliableSwitch.pde

```
Line 1  const unsigned int BUTTON_PIN = 7;
        const unsigned int LED_PIN    = 13;

        void setup() {
5         pinMode(LED_PIN, OUTPUT);
          pinMode(BUTTON_PIN, INPUT);
        }

        int led_state = LOW;
10
        void loop() {
          const int CURRENT_BUTTON_STATE = digitalRead(BUTTON_PIN);

          if (CURRENT_BUTTON_STATE == HIGH) {
15          led_state = (led_state == LOW) ? HIGH : LOW;
            digitalWrite(LED_PIN, led_state);
          }
        }
```

We begin with the usual pin constants, and in setup() we set the modes of the pins we use. In line 9, we define a global variable named led_state to store the current state of our LED. It will be LOW when the LED is on and HIGH otherwise. In loop(), we check the button's current state. When we press the button, its state switches to HIGH, and we toggle the content of led_state. That is, if led_state was HIGH, we set it to LOW, and vice versa. At the end, we set the physical LED's state to our current software state accordingly.

Our solution is really simple, but unfortunately, it does not work. Play around with it a bit, and you'll quickly notice some annoying behavior.

If you press the button, for example, the LED sometimes will turn on and then off immediately. Also, if you release it, the LED will often remain in a more or less arbitrary state; that is, sometimes it will be on and sometimes off.

The problem is that the Arduino executes the loop() method over and over again. Although the Arduino's CPU is comparatively slow, this would happen very often—no matter if we currently press the button or not. But if you press it and keep it pressed, its state will constantly be HIGH, and you'd constantly toggle the LED's state (because this happens so fast it seems like the LED's constantly on). When you release the button, the LED is in a more or less arbitrary state.

To improve the situation, we have to store not only the LED's current state but also the pushbutton's previous state:

BinaryDice/MoreReliableSwitch/MoreReliableSwitch.pde

```
const unsigned int BUTTON_PIN = 7;
const unsigned int LED_PIN    = 13;

void setup() {
  pinMode(LED_PIN, OUTPUT);
  pinMode(BUTTON_PIN, INPUT);
}

int old_button_state = LOW;
int led_state = LOW;

void loop() {
  const int CURRENT_BUTTON_STATE = digitalRead(BUTTON_PIN);
  if (CURRENT_BUTTON_STATE != old_button_state &&
      CURRENT_BUTTON_STATE == HIGH)
  {
    led_state = (led_state == LOW) ? HIGH : LOW;
    digitalWrite(LED_PIN, led_state);
  }
  old_button_state = CURRENT_BUTTON_STATE;
}
```

After initializing the button and LED pins, we declare two variables now: old_button_state stores the previous state of our pushbutton, and led_state stores the LED's current state. Both can be either HIGH or LOW.

In the loop() function, we still have to read the current button state, but now we not only check whether it is HIGH. We also check whether it has changed since the last time we read it. Only when both conditions are met do we toggle the LED's state. So, we no longer turn the LED

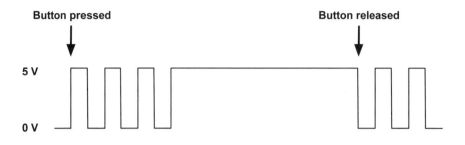

Figure 3.9: MECHANICAL SWITCHES HAVE TO BE DEBOUNCED.

on and off over and over again as long as the button is pressed. At
the end of our program, we have to store the button's current state in
old_button_state.

Upload our new version, and you'll see that this solution works much
better than our old one. But you will still find some edge cases when
the button does not fully behave as expected. Problems mainly occur in
the moment you release the button.

The cause of these problems is that mechanical buttons bounce for a
few milliseconds when you press them. In Figure 3.9, you can see a
typical signal produced by a mechanical button. Right after you have
pressed the button, it doesn't emit a clear signal. To overcome this
effect, you have to *debounce* the button. It's usually sufficient to wait
a short period of time until the button's signal stabilizes. Debouncing
makes sure that we react only once to a push of the button. In addition
to debouncing, we still have to store the current state of the LED in a
variable. Here's how to do that:

`BinaryDice/DebounceButton/DebounceButton.pde`

```
Line 1   const unsigned int BUTTON_PIN = 7;
     -   const unsigned int LED_PIN    = 13;
     -
     -   void setup() {
     5     pinMode(LED_PIN, OUTPUT);
     -     pinMode(BUTTON_PIN, INPUT);
     -   }
     -
     -   int old_button_state = LOW;
    10   int led_state = LOW;
     -
```

```
   void loop() {
     const int CURRENT_BUTTON_STATE = digitalRead(BUTTON_PIN);
     if (CURRENT_BUTTON_STATE != old_button_state &&
15       CURRENT_BUTTON_STATE == HIGH)
     {
       led_state = (led_state == LOW) ? HIGH : LOW;
       digitalWrite(LED_PIN, led_state);
       delay(50);
20     }
     old_button_state = CURRENT_BUTTON_STATE;
   }
```

This final version of our LED switch differs from the previous one in only a single line: to debounce the button, we wait for 50 milliseconds in line 19 before we enter the main loop again.

This is everything you need to know about pushbuttons for now. In the next section, we'll use two buttons to turn our binary dice into a real game.

3.6 Adding Our Own Button

Up to now, we had to abuse the Arduino's reset button to control the dice. This solution is far from optimal, so we'll add our own buttons. In Figure 3.10, on page 63, you can see that we need to change our current circuit only slightly. Actually, we don't have to change the existing parts at all; we only need to add some things. First we plug a button into the breadboard and connect it to pin 7. Then we connect the button to the ground via a 10kΩ resistor and use a small piece of wire to connect it to the 5 volts pin. That's all the hardware we need. Here's the corresponding software:

BinaryDice/DiceWithButton/DiceWithButton.pde

```
const unsigned int LED_BIT0 = 12;
const unsigned int LED_BIT1 = 11;
const unsigned int LED_BIT2 = 10;
const unsigned int BUTTON_PIN = 7;

void setup() {
  pinMode(LED_BIT0, OUTPUT);
  pinMode(LED_BIT1, OUTPUT);
  pinMode(LED_BIT2, OUTPUT);
  pinMode(BUTTON_PIN, INPUT);
  randomSeed(analogRead(A0));
}

int current_value = 0;
```

```
int old_value = 0;

void loop() {
  current_value = digitalRead(BUTTON_PIN);
  if (current_value != old_value && current_value == HIGH) {
    output_result(random(1, 7));
    delay(50);
  }
  old_value = current_value;
}

void output_result(const long result) {
  digitalWrite(LED_BIT0, result & B001);
  digitalWrite(LED_BIT1, result & B010);
  digitalWrite(LED_BIT2, result & B100);
}
```

That's a perfect merge of the original code and the code needed to control a debounced button. As usual, we initialize all pins we use: three output pins for the LEDs and one input pin for the button. We also initialize the random seed, and in the loop() function we wait for new button presses. Whenever the button gets pressed, we roll the dice and output the result using the LEDs. We've replaced the reset button with our own!

Now that we know how easy it is to add a pushbutton, we'll add another one in the next section to turn our simple dice into a game.

3.7 Building a Dice Game

Turning our rudimentary dice into a full-blown game requires adding another pushbutton. With the first one we can still roll the dice, and with the second one we can program a guess. When we roll the dice again and the current result equals our guess, the three LEDs on the die will blink. Otherwise, they will remain dark.

To enter a guess, press the guess button the right number of times. If you think the next result will be a 3, for example, press the guess button three times and then press the start button.

To add another button to the circuit, do exactly the same thing as for the first one. In Figure 3.11, on page 64, you can see that we have added yet another button circuit to the breadboard. This time we've connected it to pin 5.

Figure 3.10: OUR BINARY DICE WITH ITS OWN START BUTTON

Now we need some code to control the new button, and you might be tempted to copy it from our last program. After all, we copied the hardware design also, right? In the real world, some redundancy is totally acceptable, because we actually need two physical buttons, even if they are in principle the same. In the world of software, redundancy is a no-go, so we won't copy our debounce logic but use a library[1] that was written for this purpose. Download the library, and unpack its content into ~/Documents/Arduino/libraries (on a Mac) or My Documents\Arduino\libraries (on a Windows box). Usually that's all you have to do, but it never

---

1.   http://www.arduino.cc/playground/Code/Bounce

Figure 3.11: OUR BINARY DIE NOW HAS A "GUESS" BUTTON.

hurts to read the installation instructions and documentation on the web page.

Here's the final version of our binary dice code:

BinaryDice/DiceGame/DiceGame.pde

```
Line 1   #include <Bounce.h>
    -
    -    const unsigned int LED_BIT0 = 12;
    -    const unsigned int LED_BIT1 = 11;
    5    const unsigned int LED_BIT2 = 10;
    -    const unsigned int START_BUTTON_PIN = 5;
    -    const unsigned int GUESS_BUTTON_PIN = 7;
    -    const unsigned int BAUD_RATE = 9600;
    -
    10   void setup() {
    -      pinMode(LED_BIT0, OUTPUT);
    -      pinMode(LED_BIT1, OUTPUT);
    -      pinMode(LED_BIT2, OUTPUT);
    -      pinMode(START_BUTTON_PIN, INPUT);
    15     pinMode(GUESS_BUTTON_PIN, INPUT);
    -      randomSeed(analogRead(A0));
    -      Serial.begin(BAUD_RATE);
    -    }
    -
    20   const unsigned int DEBOUNCE_DELAY = 20;
    -    Bounce start_button(START_BUTTON_PIN, DEBOUNCE_DELAY);
    -    Bounce guess_button(GUESS_BUTTON_PIN, DEBOUNCE_DELAY);
    -    int guess = 0;
    -
    25   void loop() {
    -      handle_guess_button();
    -      handle_start_button();
    -    }
    -
    30   void handle_guess_button() {
    -      if (guess_button.update()) {
    -        if (guess_button.read() == HIGH) {
    -          guess = (guess % 6) + 1;
    -          output_result(guess);
    35           Serial.print("Guess: ");
    -          Serial.println(guess);
    -        }
    -      }
    -    }
    40
    -    void handle_start_button() {
    -      if (start_button.update()) {
    -        if (start_button.read() == HIGH) {
    -          const int result = random(1, 7);
    45           output_result(result);
```

```
          Serial.print("Result: ");
          Serial.println(result);
          if (guess > 0) {
            if (result == guess) {
50            Serial.println("You win!");
              hooray();
            } else {
              Serial.println("You lose!");
            }
55        }
          delay(2000);
          guess = 0;
        }
      }
60  }

    void output_result(const long result) {
      digitalWrite(LED_BIT0, result & B001);
      digitalWrite(LED_BIT1, result & B010);
65    digitalWrite(LED_BIT2, result & B100);
    }

    void hooray() {
      for (int i = 0; i < 3; i++) {
70      output_result(7);
        delay(500);
        output_result(0);
        delay(500);
      }
75  }
```

Admittedly that is a lot of code, but we know most of it already, and the new parts are fairly easy. In the first line, we include the Bounce library we'll use later to debounce our two buttons. Then we define constants for all the pins we use, and in the setup() method, we initialize all our pins and set the random seed. We also initialize the serial port, because we'll output some debug messages.

The Bounce library declares a class named Bounce, and you have to create a Bounce object for every button you want to debounce. That's what happens in lines 21 and 22. The constructor of the Bounce class expects the number of the pin the button is connected to and the debounce delay in milliseconds. Finally, we declare and initialize a variable named guess that stores our current guess.

Our loop() function has been reduced to two function calls. One is responsible for dealing with guess button pushes, and the other one handles pushes of the start button. In handle_guess_button(), we use the

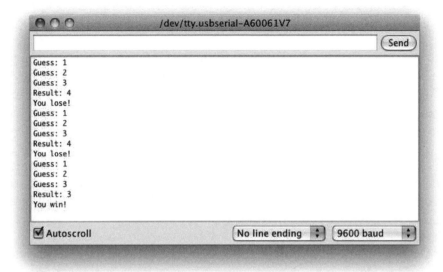

Figure 3.12: WE HAVE A WINNER!

Bounce class for the first time. To determine the current state of our guess_button object, we have to call its update() method. Afterward, we read its current status using the read() method.

If the button was pressed, its state is set to HIGH, and we increment the guess variable. To make sure that the guess is always in the range between 1 and 6, we use the modulus operator (%) in line 33. This operator divides two values and returns the remainder. For 6, it returns values between 0 and 5, because when you divide a number by 6, the remainder is always between 0 and 5. Add 1 to the result, and you get values between 1 and 6. Finally, we output the current guess using the three LEDs, and we also print it to the serial port.

The handling of the start button in handle_start_button() works exactly the same as the handling of the guess button. When the start button was pressed, we calculate a new result and output it on the serial port. Then we check whether the user has entered a guess (guess is greater than zero in this case) and whether the user has guessed the right result. In either case, we print a message to the serial port, and if the user guessed right, we also call the hooray() method. hooray() lets all three LEDs blink several times.

At the end of the method, we wait for two seconds until the game starts again, and we set back the current guess to zero.

After you've uploaded the software to the Arduino, start the IDE's serial monitor. It will print the current value of the guess variable whenever you press the guess button. Press the start button, and the new result appears. In Figure 3.12, on the preceding page, you can see a typical output of our binary dice.

In this chapter, you completed your first really complex Arduino project. You needed a breadboard, LEDs, buttons, resistors, and wires, and you wrote a nontrivial piece of software to make all the hardware come to life.

In the next chapter, we'll write an even more sophisticated program for generating Morse code. You'll also learn how to create your own Arduino libraries that you can easily share with the rest of the world.

3.8 What If It Doesn't Work?

A lot of things will probably go wrong when you work with breadboards for the first time. The biggest problem usually is that you didn't connect parts correctly. It takes some time to find the right technique for plugging LEDs, wires, resistors, and buttons into the breadboard. You have to press firmly but not too hard—otherwise you'll bend the connectors, and they won't fit. It's usually easier to plug parts in after you've shortened the connectors. When cutting the connectors, wear safety glasses to protect your eyes!

While fiddling around with the parts, don't forget that some of them—LEDs, for example—need a certain direction. Pushbuttons are candidates for potential problems, too. Take a close look at the pushbuttons on page 56 and make sure that you've mounted them in the right direction.

Even simple things such as ordinary wires can lead to problems, especially if they aren't the right length. If a wire is too short and might potentially slip out of its socket, replace it immediately. Wires are too cheap to waste your valuable time with unnecessary and annoying debugging sessions.

3.9 Exercises

- Binary dice are all very well when you're playing Monopoly with your geeky friends, but most people prefer more familiar dice. Try turning binary dice into decimal dice with seven LEDs. Arrange the LEDs like the eyes on regular dice.

- The 1kΩ resistors we have used to protect our LEDs in this chapter are rather big. Read Section A.1, *Resistors*, on page 227, and replace them with smaller ones. Can you see the difference in brightness?

- LEDs can be used for more than displaying binary dice results. Provided you have enough LEDs, you can easily build other things, such as a binary clock.[2]

  You already know enough about electronics and Arduino programming to build your own binary clock. Try it or think about other things you could display using a few LEDs.

- Using a button to roll the dice seems a bit awkward, doesn't it? Usually, you take dice into both hands and shake them. You can easily simulate that with a tilt sensor.

  Tilt sensors detect the tilting of an object and are perfect devices for simulating the roll of a dice. In principle, they work like a push-button, but you don't press them—you shake them. Try to add one to the binary dice by working your way through the tutorial on the Arduino website.[3]

---

2. http://www.instructables.com/id/LED-Binary-Clock/
3. http://www.arduino.cc/en/Tutorial/TiltSensor

Chapter 4

Building a Morse Code Generator Library

You now know enough about the Arduino development environment and about blinking LEDs to start a bigger project. In this chapter, we'll develop a Morse code generator that reads text from the serial port and outputs it as light signals using an LED.

By building this project, you'll deepen your understanding of serial communication between the Arduino and your computer. You'll also learn a lot about the typical Arduino development process: how to use existing libraries and how to structure bigger projects into your own libraries. At the end, you'll be able to create a library that is ready for publishing on the Internet.

4.1 What You Need

- An Arduino board such as the Uno, Duemilanove, or Diecimila
- A USB cable to connect the Arduino to your computer
- An LED
- A speaker or a buzzer (they are optional)

4.2 Learning the Basics of Morse Code

Morse code was invented to turn text into sounds.[1] In principle, it works like a character set encoding such as ASCII. But while ASCII

---

1. http://en.wikipedia.org/wiki/Morse_Code

encodes characters as numbers, in Morse code they're sequences of dots and dashes (also called *dits* and *dahs*). Dits are shorter in length than dahs. An *A* is encoded as · – and – – · · is *Z*.

Morse code also specifies a timing scheme that defines the length of the dits and dahs. It also specifies how long the pauses between symbols and words have to be. The base unit of Morse code is the length of a dit, and a dah is as long as three dits. You insert a pause of one dit between two symbols, and you separate two letters by three dits. Insert a pause of seven dits between two words.

To transmit a message encoded in Morse code, you need a way to emit signals of different lengths. The classic approach is to use sounds, but we will use an LED that is turned on and off for varying periods of time. Sailors still transmit Morse code using blinking lights.

Let's implement a Morse code generator!

4.3 Building a Morse Code Generator

The main part of our library will be a C++ class named Telegraph. In this section, we'll define its interface, but we will start with a new sketch that looks as follows:

Telegraph/Telegraph.pde

```
void setup() {
}

void loop() {
}
```

This is the most minimalistic Arduino program possible. It does not do anything except define all mandatory functions, even if they are empty. We do this so we can compile our work in progress from time to time and check whether there are any syntactical errors. Save the sketch as Telegraph, and the IDE will create a folder named Telegraph and a file named Telegraph.pde in it. All the files and directories we need for our library will be stored in the Telegraph folder.

Now open a new tab, and when asked for a filename, enter telegraph.h. Yes, we will create a good old C header file (to be precise, it will even be a C++ header file). The listing in on the next page.

Telegraph/telegraph.h

```
#ifndef __TELEGRAPH_H__
#define __TELEGRAPH_H__

class Telegraph {
public:
  Telegraph(const int output_pin, const int dit_length);
  void send_message(const char* message);

private:
  void dit();
  void dah();
  void output_code(const char* code);
  void output_symbol(const int length);

  int _output_pin;
  int _dit_length;
  int _dah_length;
};

#endif
```

Ah, obviously object-oriented programming is not only for the big CPUs anymore! This is an interface description of a Telegraph class that you could use in your next enterprise project (provided that you need to transmit some information as Morse code, that is).

We start with the classic double-include prevention mechanism; that is, the body of header file defines a preprocessor macro with the name __TELEGRAPH_H__. We wrap the body (that contains this definition) in an #ifndef, so that the body is only complied if the macro has not been defined. That way, you can include the header as many times as you want, and the body will only be compiled once.

The interface of the Telegraph class consists of a public part that users of the class have access to and a private part only members of the class can use. In the public part, you find two things: a constructor that creates new Telegraph objects and a method named send_message() that sends a message by emitting it as Morse code. In your applications, you can use the class as follows:

```
Telegraph telegraph(13, 200);
telegraph.send_message("Hello, world!");
```

In the first line, we create a new Telegraph object that communicates on pin 13 and emits dits that are 200 milliseconds long. Then we emit the message "Hello, world!" as Morse code. This way, we are able to send whatever message we want, and we can change the pin and the length of a dit easily.

Now that we have defined the interface, we will implement it in the next section.

4.4 Fleshing Out the Generator's Interface

Declaring interfaces is important, but it's as important to implement them. Create a new tab, enter the filename telegraph.cpp, and then enter the following code:[2]

Telegraph/telegraph.cpp

```
#include <ctype.h>
#include <WProgram.h>
#include "telegraph.h"

char* LETTERS[] = {
    ".-",    "-...", "-.-.", "-..",   ".",     // A-E
    "..-.", "--.",   "....", "..",    ".---", // F-J
    "-.-",  ".-..", "--",   "-.",    "---", // K-O
    ".--.", "--.-", ".-.",   "...",   "-", // P-T
    "..-",  "...-", ".--",   "-..-", "-.--", // U-Y
    "--.."                                    // Z
};

char* DIGITS[] = {
    "-----", ".----", "..---", "...--", // 0-3
    "....-", ".....", "-....", "--...", // 4-7
    "---..", "----."                    // 8-9
};
```

Like most C++ programs, ours imports some libraries first. Because we need functions such as toupper() later, we include ctype.h. and we have to include telegraph.h to make our class declaration and its corresponding function declarations available. But what is WProgram.h good for?

Until now we haven't thought about where constants such as HIGH, LOW, or OUTPUT came from. They are defined in several header files that come with the Arduino IDE, and you can find them in the hardware/cores/arduino directory of the IDE. Have a look at WProgram.h, and

---

2. Older versions of the Arduino IDE have an annoying bug that will prevent you from creating a new file this way. The IDE claims that a file having the same name already exists. See http://www.arduino.cc/cgi-bin/yabb2/YaBB.pl?num=1251245246 for a workaround.

notice that it includes a file named wiring.h that contains all the constants we have used so far and many more. It also declares many useful macros and the Arduino's most basic functions.

When you edit regular sketches, you do not have to worry about including any standard header files, because the IDE does it automatically behind the scenes. As soon as you start to create more complex projects that contain "real" C++ code, you have to manage everything yourself. You have to explicitly import all the libraries you need, even for basic stuff such as the Arduino constants.

After importing all necessary header files, we define two string arrays named LETTERS and DIGITS. They contain the Morse code for all letters and digits, and we'll use them later to translate regular text into Morse code. Before we do that, we define the constructor that is responsible for creating and intializing new Telegraph objects:

Telegraph/telegraph.cpp

```
Telegraph::Telegraph(const int output_pin, const int dit_length) {
  _output_pin = output_pin;
  _dit_length = dit_length;
  _dah_length = dit_length * 3;
  pinMode(_output_pin, OUTPUT);
}
```

The constructor expects two arguments: the number of the pin the Morse code should be sent to and the length of a dit measured in milliseconds. Then it stores these values in corresponding instance variables, calculates the correct length of a dah, and turns the communication pin into an output pin.

You've probably noticed that all private instance variables start with an underscore. That is a convention that I like personally. It is not enforced by C++ or the Arduino IDE.

4.5 Outputting Morse Code Symbols

After everything has been initialized, we can start to output Morse code symbols. We use several small helper methods to make our code as readable as possible:

Telegraph/telegraph.cpp

```
void Telegraph::output_code(const char* code) {
  const unsigned int code_length = strlen(code);
  for (int i = 0; i < code_length; i++) {
```

```
      if (code[i] == '.')
        dit();
      else
        dah();
      if (i != code_length - 1)
        delay(_dit_length);
    }
  }

  void Telegraph::dit() {
    Serial.print(".");
    output_symbol(_dit_length);
  }

  void Telegraph::dah() {
    Serial.print("-");
    output_symbol(_dah_length);
  }

  void Telegraph::output_symbol(const int length) {
    digitalWrite(_output_pin, HIGH);
    delay(length);
    digitalWrite(_output_pin, LOW);
  }
```

The function output_code() takes a Morse code sequence consisting of
dots and dashes and turns it into calls to dit() and dah(). The dit() and
dah() methods then print a dot or a dash to the serial port and delegate
the rest of the work to output_symbol(), passing it the length of the Morse
code symbol to be emitted. output_symbol() sets the output pin to HIGH
for the length of the symbol, and then it sets it back to LOW. Everything
works exactly as described in the Morse code timing scheme, and only
the implementation of send_message() is missing:

Telegraph/telegraph.cpp

```
Line 1   void Telegraph::send_message(const char* message) {
  -        for (int i = 0; i < strlen(message); i++) {
  -          const char current_char = toupper(message[i]);
  -          if (isalpha(current_char)) {
  5            output_code(LETTERS[current_char - 'A']);
  -            delay(_dah_length);
  -          } else if (isdigit(current_char)) {
  -            output_code(DIGITS[current_char - '0']);
  -            delay(_dah_length);
 10          } else if (current_char == ' ') {
  -            Serial.print(" ");
  -            delay(_dit_length * 7);
  -          }
  -        }
```

```
15    Serial.println();
  -   }
```

send_message() outputs a message character by character in a loop. In line 3, we turn the current character into uppercase, because lowercase characters are not defined in Morse code (that's the reason why you can't implement a chat client using Morse code). Then we check whether the current character is a letter using C's isalpha() function. If it is, we use it to determine its Morse code representation that is stored in the LETTERS array. To do that, we use an old trick: in the ASCII table all letters (and digits) appear in the right order, that is, A=65, B=66, and so on. To transform the current character into an index for the LETTERS array, we have to subtract 65 (or 'A') from its ASCII code. When we have determined the correct Morse code, we pass it to output_symbol() and delay the program for the length of a dah afterward.

The algorithm works exactly the same for outputting digits; we only have to index the DIGITS array instead of the LETTERS array, and we have to subtract the ASCII value of the character 0.

In line 10, we check whether we received a blank character. If yes, we print a blank character to the serial port and wait for seven dits. All other characters are ignored: we only process letters, digits, and blanks. At the end of the method, we send a newline character to the serial port to mark the end of the message.

4.6 Installing and Using the Telegraph Class

Our Telegraph class is complete, and we should now create some example sketches that actually use it. This is important for two reasons: we can test our library code, and for users of our class it's good documentation for how to use it.

The Arduino IDE looks for libraries in two places: in its global libraries folder relative to its installation directory and in the user's local sketchbook directory. During development it's best to use the local sketchbook directory. You can find its location in the IDE's preferences (see Figure 4.1, on the next page). Create a new directory named libraries in the sketchbook directory.

To make our Telegraph class available, create a Telegraph subfolder in the libraries folder. Then copy telegraph.h and telegraph.cpp to that folder (do not copy Telegraph.pde). Restart the IDE.

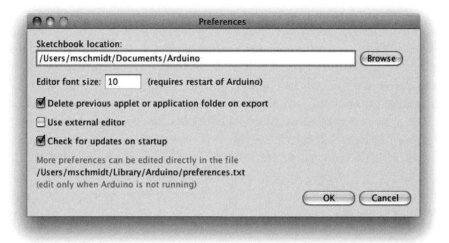

Figure 4.1: FIND THE SKETCHBOOK LOCATION IN THE PREFERENCES.

Let's start with the mother of all programs: "Hello, world!" Create a new sketch named HelloWorld, and enter the following code:

Telegraph/examples/HelloWorld/HelloWorld.pde

```
#include "telegraph.h"

const unsigned int BAUD_RATE  = 9600;
const unsigned int OUTPUT_PIN = 13;
const unsigned int DIT_LENGTH = 200;

Telegraph telegraph(OUTPUT_PIN, DIT_LENGTH);

void setup() {
  Serial.begin(BAUD_RATE);
}

void loop() {
  telegraph.send_message("Hello, world!");
  delay(5000);
}
```

This sketch emits the string "Hello, world!" as Morse code every five seconds. To achieve this, we include the definition of our Telegraph class, and we define constants for the pin our LED is connected to and for the length of our dits. Then we create a global Telegraph object and an empty setup() function. In loop(), then we invoke send_message() on our Telegraph instance every five seconds.

When you compile this sketch, the Arduino IDE automatically compiles the telegraph library, too. So if you made any syntactical errors in the library, you'll be notified now. If you have to correct some errors, make sure you change your original source code files. After you've fixed the errors, copy the files to the libraries folder again, and don't forget to restart the IDE.

Turning a static string into Morse code is nice, but wouldn't it be great if our program could work for arbitrary strings? So, let's add a more sophisticated example. This time, we'll write code that reads messages from the serial port and feeds them into a Telegraph instance. Create a new sketch named MorseCodeGenerator, and enter the following code:

Telegraph/examples/MorseCodeGenerator/MorseCodeGenerator.pde

```
#include "telegraph.h"

const unsigned int OUTPUT_PIN = 13;
const unsigned int DIT_LENGTH = 200;
const unsigned int MAX_MESSAGE_LEN = 128;
const unsigned int BAUD_RATE = 9600;
const int LINE_FEED = 13;

char message_text[MAX_MESSAGE_LEN];
int index = 0;

Telegraph telegraph(OUTPUT_PIN, DIT_LENGTH);

void setup() {
  Serial.begin(BAUD_RATE);
}

void loop() {
  if (Serial.available() > 0) {
    int current_char = Serial.read();
    if (current_char == LINE_FEED || index == MAX_MESSAGE_LEN - 1) {
      message_text[index] = 0;
      index = 0;
      telegraph.send_message(message_text);
    } else {
      message_text[index++] = current_char;
    }
  }
}
```

Again, we include the header file of the Telegraph class, and as usual we define some constants: OUTPUT_PIN defines the pin our LED is connected to, and DIT_LENGTH contains the length of a dit measured in milliseconds. LINE_FEED is set to the ASCII code of the linefeed character. We need it to determine the end of the message to be emitted as Morse code. Finally, we set MAX_MESSAGE_LEN to the maximum length of the messages we are able to send.

Next we define three global variables: message_text is a character buffer that gets filled with the data we receive on the serial port. index keeps track of our current position in the buffer, and telegraph is the Telegraph object we'll use to convert a message into "blinkenlights."[3]

setup() initializes the serial port, and in loop() we check whether new data has arrived, calling Serial.available(). We read the next byte if new data is available, and we check whether it is a linefeed character or whether it is the last byte that fits into our character buffer. In both cases, we set the last byte of message_text to 0, because strings in C/C++ are null-terminated. We also reset index so we can read the next message, and finally we send the message using our telegraph. In all other cases, we add the latest byte to the current message text and move on.

You should compile and upload the program now. Open the serial monitor, and choose "Carriage return" from the line endings drop-down menu at the bottom of the window. With this option set, the serial monitor will automatically append a newline character to every line it sends to the Arduino. Enter a message such as your name, click the Send button, and see how the Arduino turns it into light.

Because we've encapsulated the whole Morse code logic in the Telegraph class, our main program is short and concise. Creating software for embedded devices doesn't mean we can't benefit from the advantages of object-oriented programming.

Still, we have some minor things to do to turn our project into a first-class library. Read more about it in the next section.

4.7 Final Touches

One of the nice features of the Arduino IDE is its syntax coloring. Class names, function names, variables, and so on, all have different colors in the editor. This makes it much easier to read source code, and it's

---

3. http://en.wikipedia.org/wiki/Blinkenlights

possible to add syntax coloring for libraries. You only have to add a file named keywords.txt to your project:

Telegraph/keywords.txt

```
# Syntax-coloring for the telegraph library

Telegraph       KEYWORD1
send_message    KEYWORD2
```

Lines starting with a # character contain comments and will be ignored. The remaining lines contain the name of one of the library's members and the member's type. Separate them with a tab character. Classes have the type KEYWORD1, while functions have the type KEYWORD2. For constants, use LITERAL1.

To enable syntax coloring for the telegraph library, copy keywords.txt to the libraries folder, and restart the IDE. Now the name of the Telegraph class will be orange, and send_message() will be colored brown.

Before you finally publish your library, you should add a few more things:

- Store all example sketches in a folder named examples, and copy it to the libraries folder. Every example sketch should get its own subdirectory within that folder.

- Choose a license for your project, and copy its terms into a file named LICENSE.[4] You might think this is a bit over the top for many libraries, but it will give your potential audience confidence.

- Add installation instructions and documentation. Usually, users expect to find documentation in a file named README, and they will look for installation instructions in a file named INSTALL. You should try to install your library on as many operating systems as possible and provide installation instructions for all of them.

After you've done all this, your library folder should look like Figure 4.2, on the following page.

Finally, create a ZIP archive containing all the files in your project. On most operating systems, it's sufficient to right-click the directory in the Explorer, Finder, or whatever you are using and turn the directory into

---

4. At http://www.opensource.org/, you can find a lot of background information and many standard licenses.

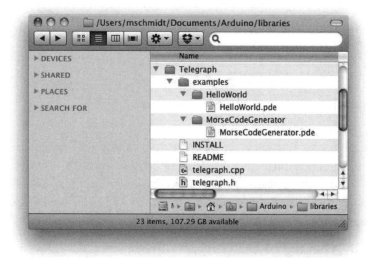

Figure 4.2: This is what a typical Arduino library needs.

a ZIP archive. On Linux systems and on a Mac, you can also use one of the following command-line statements to create an archive:

```
maik> zip -r Telegraph Telegraph
maik> tar cfvz Telegraph.tar.gz Telegraph
```

The first command creates a file named Telegraph.zip, and the second one creates Telegraph.tar.gz. Both formats are widespread, and it's best to offer them both for download.

Although you have to perform a lot of manual file operations, it's still easy to create an Arduino library. So, there's no excuse: whenever you think you've built something cool, make it publicly available.

Until now our projects have communicated with the outside world using LEDs (output) and pushbuttons (input). In the next chapter, you'll learn how to work with more sophisticated input devices, such as ultrasonic sensors. You'll also learn how to visualize data that an Arduino sends to programs running on your computer.

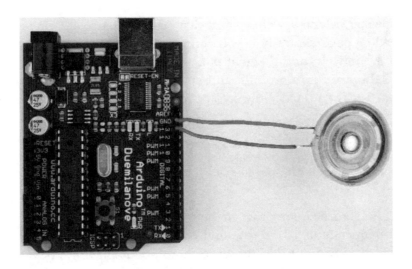

Figure 4.3: IT'S EASY TO CONNECT A SPEAKER TO AN ARDUINO.

4.8 What If It Doesn't Work?

The Arduino IDE has a strong opinion on naming files and directories, and it was built for creating sketches, not libraries. So, you need to perform a few manual file operations to get everything into the right place. In Figure 4.2, on the preceding page, you can see the final directory layout. If you have more than one version of the Arduino IDE installed, make sure that you're using the right libraries folder.

Remember that you have to restart the IDE often. Whenever you change one of the files belonging to your library, restart the IDE.

If syntax coloring doesn't work, make sure your keywords file is actually named keywords.txt. Double-check if you have separated all objects and type specifiers by a tab character! Restart your IDE!

4.9 Exercises

- Morse code supports not only letters and digits. It also defines symbols such as commas. Improve the Telegraph class so it understands all characters of the Morse code.

- Blinking LEDs are great, but when we think of Morse code, we usually think of beeping sounds, so replace the LED with a piezo speaker, which are cheap and easy to use. Figure 4.3, on the preceding page shows how you connect it to an Arduino. They have a ground pin and a signal pin, so connect the speaker's ground to the Arduino's ground, and connect the signal pin to Arduino pin 13. Then replace the output_symbol() method with the following code:

```
void Telegraph::output_symbol(const int length) {
  const int frequency = 131;
  tone(_output_pin, frequency, length);
}
```

This sends a square wave to the speaker, and it plays a tone having a frequency of 131 Hertz (find the "Melody" example that comes with the Arduino IDE to learn more about playing notes with a piezo speaker).

• Improve the library's design to make it easier to support different output devices. For example, you could pass some kind of Output-Device object to the Telegraph constructor. Then derive a LedDevice and a SpeakerDevice from OutputDevice. It could look as follows:

```
class OutputDevice {
  public:
  virtual void output_symbol(const int length);
};

class Led : public OutputDevice {
  public:
  void output_symbol(const int length) {
    // ...
  }
};

class Speaker : public OutputDevice {
  public:
  void output_symbol(const int length) {
    // ...
  }
};
```

You can then use these classes as follows:

```
Led led;
Speaker speaker;
OutputDevice* led_device = &led;
OutputDevice* speaker_device = &speaker;

led_device->output_symbol(200);
speaker_device->output_symbol(200);
```

The rest is up to you.

- Try to learn Morse code. Let someone else type some messages into the serial terminal and try to recognize what he or she sent. That's not necessary for learning Arduino development, but it's a lot of fun!

Chapter 5

Sensing the World Around Us

Instead of communicating via mouse or keyboard as with regular computers, you need to connect special sensors to the Arduino so that it can sense changes around it. You can attach sensors that measure the current temperature, the acceleration, or the distance to the nearest object.

Sensors make up an important part of physical computing, and the Arduino makes using various sensor types a breeze. In this chapter, we will use both digital and analog sensors to capture some real-world state, and all we need is a couple of wires and some small programs.

We will take a close look at two sensor types: an ultrasonic sensor that measures distances and a temperature sensor that measures, well, temperatures. With the ultrasonic sensor, we will build a digital metering rule that helps us measure distances remotely. Although ultrasonic sensors deliver quite accurate results, we can still improve their precision with some easy tricks. Interestingly, the temperature sensor will help us with this, and at the end of the chapter, we will have created a fairly accurate digital metering rule. We will also build a nice graphical application that visualizes the data we get from the sensors.

But the Arduino doesn't only make using sensors easy. It also encourages good design for both your circuits and your software. For example, although we end up using two sensors, they are completely independent. All the programs we'll develop in this chapter will run without changes on the final circuit.

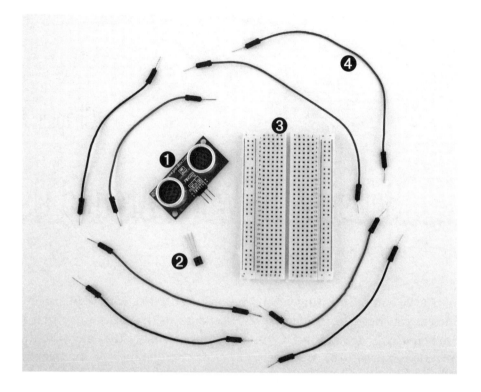

Figure 5.1: ALL THE PARTS YOU NEED IN THIS CHAPTER

5.1 What You Need

1. A Parallax PING))) sensor

2. A TMP36 temperature sensor from Analog Devices

3. A breadboard

4. Some wires

5. An Arduino board such as the Uno, Duemilanove, or Diecimila

6. A USB cable to connect the Arduino to your computer

7. An installation of the Processing programming language[1]

---

1. http://processing.org

5.2 Measuring Distances with an Ultrasonic Sensor

Measuring distances automatically and continuously comes in handy in many situations. Think of a robot that autonomously tries to find its way or of an automatic burglar alarm that rings a bell or calls the police whenever someone is too near to your house or to the *Mona Lisa*. All this is possible with Arduino. But before you can create that burglar alarm or robot, you need to understand some key concepts.

Many different types of sensors for measuring distances are available, and the Arduino plays well with most of them. Some sensors use ultrasound, while others use infrared light or even laser. But in principle all sensors work the same way: they emit a signal, wait for the echo to return, and measure the time the whole process took. Because we know how fast sound and light travel through the air, we can then convert the measured time into a distance.

In our first project, we will build a device that measures the distance to the nearest object and outputs it on the serial port. For this project, we use the Parallax PING))) ultrasonic sensor,[2] because it's easy to use, comes with excellent documentation, and has a nice feature set. It can detect objects in a range between 2 centimeters and 3 meters, and we use it directly with a breadboard, so we do not have to solder. It's also a perfect example of a sensor that provides information via variable-width pulses (more on that in a few paragraphs). With the PING))) sensor, we can easily build a sonar or a robot that automatically finds its way through a maze without touching a wall.

As mentioned earlier, ultrasonic sensors usually do not return the distance to the nearest object. Instead, they return the time the sound needed to travel to the object and back to the sensor. The PING))) is no exception (see Figure 5.2, on the next page), and its innards are fairly complex. Fortunately, they are hidden behind three simple pins: power, ground, and signal.

This makes it easy to connect the sensor to the Arduino. First, connect Arduino's ground and 5V power supply to the corresponding PING))) pins. Then connect the PING)))'s sensor pin to one of the Arduino's digital IO pins (we're using pin 7 for no particular reason). For a diagram

---

2. http://www.parallax.com/StoreSearchResults/tabid/768/txtSearch/28015/List/0/SortField/4/ProductID/92/Default.aspx

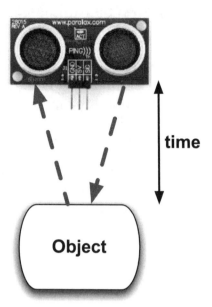

Figure 5.2: Basic working principle of the PING))) sensor

of our circuit, see Figure 5.3, on the facing page, and for a photo see Figure 5.5, on page 93.

To bring the circuit to life, we need some code that communicates with the PING))) sensor:

`ultrasonic/simple/simple.pde`

```
const unsigned int PING_SENSOR_IO_PIN = 7;
const unsigned int BAUD_RATE = 9600;

void setup() {
  Serial.begin(BAUD_RATE);
}

void loop() {
  pinMode(PING_SENSOR_IO_PIN, OUTPUT);
  digitalWrite(PING_SENSOR_IO_PIN, LOW);
  delayMicroseconds(2);

  digitalWrite(PING_SENSOR_IO_PIN, HIGH);
  delayMicroseconds(5);
  digitalWrite(PING_SENSOR_IO_PIN, LOW);
```

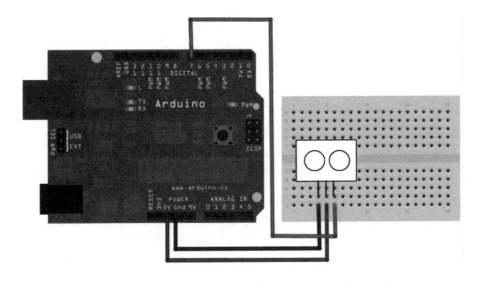

Figure 5.3: PING))) BASIC CIRCUIT

```
     pinMode(PING_SENSOR_IO_PIN, INPUT);
     const unsigned long duration = pulseIn(PING_SENSOR_IO_PIN, HIGH);
     if (duration == 0) {
20     Serial.println("Warning: We did not get a pulse from sensor.");
     } else {
       Serial.print("Distance to nearest object: ");
       Serial.print(microseconds_to_cm(duration));
       Serial.println(" cm");
25   }

     delay(100);
   }

30 unsigned long microseconds_to_cm(const unsigned long microseconds) {
     return microseconds / 29 / 2;
   }
```

First we define a constant for the IO pin the PING))) sensor is connected
to. If you want to connect your sensor to another digital IO pin, you
have to change the program's first line. In the setup() method, we set
the serial port's baud rate to 9600, because we'd like to see some sensor
data on the serial monitor.

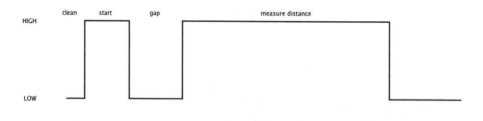

Figure 5.4: PING))) PULSE DIAGRAM

The real action happens in loop() where we actually implement the PING))) protocol. According to the data sheet,[3] we can control the sensor using pulses, and it returns results as variable-width pulses, too.

In lines 9 to 11, we set the sensor's signal pin to LOW for 2 microseconds to bring it to a proper state. This will ensure clean HIGH pulses that are needed in the next steps (in the world of electronics, you should always be prepared for jitters in the power supply).

Finally, it's time to tell the sensor to do some work. In lines 13 to 15, we set the sensor's signal pin to HIGH for 5 microseconds to start a new measurement. Afterward, we set the pin to LOW again, because the sensor will respond with a HIGH pulse of variable length on the same pin.

With a digital pin, you have only a few options to transmit information. You can set the pin to HIGH or LOW, and you can control how long it remains in a particular state. For many purposes, this is absolutely sufficient, and in our case it is, too. When the PING))) sensor sends out its 40 kHz chirp, it sets the signal pin to HIGH and then sets it back to LOW when it receives the echo. That is, the signal pin remains in a HIGH state for exactly the time it takes the sound to travel to an object and back to the sensor. Loosely speaking, we are using a digital pin for measuring an analog signal. In Figure 5.4, you can see a diagram showing typical activity on a digital pin connected to a PING))) sensor.

We could measure the duration the pin remains in HIGH state manually, but the pulseIn() method already does all the dirty work for us. So, we use it in line 18 after we have set the signal pin into input mode again. pulseIn() accepts three parameters:

---

3. http://www.parallax.com/dl/docs/prod/acc/28015-PING-v1.5.pdf

Figure 5.5: PHOTO OF PING))) BASIC CIRCUIT

- *pin*: Number of the pin to read the pulse from.

- *type*: Type of the pulse that should be read. It can be HIGH or LOW.

- *timeout*: Timeout measured in microseconds. If no pulse could be detected within the timeout period, pulseIn() returns 0. This parameter is optional and defaults to one second.

Note that in the whole process only one pin is used to communicate with the PING))). Sooner or later, you will realize that IO pins are a scarce resource on the Arduino, so it's really a nice feature that the PING))) uses only one digital pin. When you can choose between different parts performing the same task, try to use as few pins as possible.

We have only one thing left to do: convert the duration we have measured into a length. Sound travels at 343 meters per second, which means it needs 29.155 microseconds per centimeter. So, we have to divide the duration by 29 and then by 2, because the sound has to travel the distance twice. It travels to the object and then back to the PING))) sensor. The microseconds_to_cm() method performs the calculation.

According to the specification of the PING))) sensor, you have to wait at least 200 microseconds between two measurements. For high-speed measurements, we could calculate the length of a pause more accurately by actually measuring the time the code takes. But in our case, this is pointless, because all the statements that are executed during two measurements in the loop() method take far more than 200 microseconds. And outputting data to the serial connection is fairly expensive. Despite this, we have added a small delay of 100 microseconds to slow down the output a bit.

You might wonder why we use the const keyword so often. The Arduino language is based on C/C++, and in these languages it's considered a good practice to declare constant values as const (see *Effective C++: 50 Specific Ways to Improve Your Programs and Designs* [Mey97]). Not only will using const make your program more concise and prevent logical errors early, it will also help the compiler to decrease your program's size.

Although most Arduino programs are comparatively small, software development for the Arduino is still software development and should be done according to all the best practices we know. So, whenever you define a constant value in your program, declare it as such (using const, not using #define). This is true for other programming languages, too, so we will use final in our Processing and Java programs a lot (you'll learn more about Processing in Section 5.5, *Transferring Data Back to Your Computer Using Processing*, on page 104).

Now it's time to play around with the sensor and get familiar with its strengths and weaknesses. Compile the program, upload it to your

Arduino board, and open the serial monitor (don't forget to set the baud rate to 9600). You should see something like this:

```
Distance to nearest object: 42 cm
Distance to nearest object: 33 cm
Distance to nearest object: 27 cm
Distance to nearest object: 27 cm
Distance to nearest object: 29 cm
Distance to nearest object: 36 cm
```

In addition to the output in the terminal, you will see that the LED on the PING))) sensor is turned on whenever the sensor starts a new measurement.

Test the sensor's capabilities by trying to detect big things or very small things. Try to detect objects from different angles, and try to detect objects that are below or above the sensor. You should also do some experiments with objects that do not have a flat surface. Try to detect stuffed animals, for example, and you will see that they are not detected as well as solid objects (that's probably the reason why bats don't hunt bears: they cannot see them).

With only three wires and a few lines of code, we have built a first version of a digital metering rule. At the moment, it only outputs centimeter distances in whole numbers, but we will increase its accuracy tremendously in the next section by changing our software and adding more hardware.

5.3 Increasing Precision Using Floating-Point Numbers

According to the specification, the PING))) sensor is accurate for objects that are between 2 centimeters and 3 meters away. (By the way, the reason for this is the length of the pulse that is generated. Its minimum length is 115 microseconds, and the maximum length is 18.5 milliseconds.) With our current approach, we do not fully benefit from its precision because all calculations are performed using integer values. We can only measure distances with an accuracy of a centimeter. To enter the millimeter range, we have to use floating-point numbers.

Normally it is a good idea to use integer operations, because compared to regular computers the Arduino's memory and CPU capacities are severely limited and calculations containing floating-point numbers are often expensive. But sometimes it's useful to enjoy the luxury of highly accurate floating-point numbers, and the Arduino supports them well. We will use them to improve our project now:

ultrasonic/float/float.pde

```
Line 1   const unsigned int PING_SENSOR_IO_PIN = 7;
    -    const unsigned int BAUD_RATE = 9600;
    -    const float MICROSECONDS_PER_CM = 29.155;
    -    const float MOUNTING_GAP = 0.2;
    5    const float SENSOR_OFFSET = MOUNTING_GAP * MICROSECONDS_PER_CM * 2;
    -
    -    void setup() {
    -      Serial.begin(BAUD_RATE);
    -    }
    10
    -    void loop() {
    -      const unsigned long duration = measure_distance();
    -      if (duration == 0)
    -        Serial.println("Warning: We did not get a pulse from sensor.");
    15      else
    -        output_distance(duration);
    -    }
    -
    -    const float microseconds_to_cm(const unsigned long microseconds) {
    20      const float net_distance = max(0, microseconds - SENSOR_OFFSET);
    -      return net_distance / MICROSECONDS_PER_CM / 2;
    -    }
    -
    -    const unsigned long measure_distance() {
    25      pinMode(PING_SENSOR_IO_PIN, OUTPUT);
    -      digitalWrite(PING_SENSOR_IO_PIN, LOW);
    -      delayMicroseconds(2);
    -
    -      digitalWrite(PING_SENSOR_IO_PIN, HIGH);
    30      delayMicroseconds(5);
    -      digitalWrite(PING_SENSOR_IO_PIN, LOW);
    -
    -      pinMode(PING_SENSOR_IO_PIN, INPUT);
    -      return pulseIn(PING_SENSOR_IO_PIN, HIGH);
    35    }
    -
    -    void output_distance(const unsigned long duration) {
    -      Serial.print("Distance to nearest object: ");
    -      Serial.print(microseconds_to_cm(duration));
    40      Serial.println(" cm");
    -    }
```

This program does not differ much from our first version. First, we use the more accurate value 29.155 for the number of microseconds it takes sound to travel 1 centimeter. In addition, the distance calculation now takes a potential gap between the sensor and the case into account.

If you plug the sensor into a breadboard, for example, usually a small gap between the sensor and the breadboard's edge exists. This gap is defined in line 5, and it will be used in the distance calculation later on. The gap is measured in centimeters, and it gets multiplied by two, because the sound travels out and back.

The loop() method looks much cleaner now, because the program's main functionality has been moved to separate functions. The whole sensor control logic lives in the measure_distance() method and output_distance() takes care of outputting values to the serial port. The big changes happened in the microseconds_to_cm() function. It returns a float value now, and it subtracts the sensor gap from the measured duration. To make sure we do not get negative values, we use the max() function.

Compile and upload the program, and you should see something like the following in your serial monitor window:

```
Distance to nearest object: 17.26 cm
Distance to nearest object: 17.93 cm
Distance to nearest object: 17.79 cm
Distance to nearest object: 18.17 cm
Distance to nearest object: 18.65 cm
Distance to nearest object: 18.85 cm
Distance to nearest object: 18.78 cm
```

This not only looks more accurate than our previous version, it actually is. If you have worked with floating-point numbers in any programming language before, you might ask yourself why the Arduino rounds them automatically to two decimal digits. The secret lies in the print() method of the Serial class. In recent versions of the Arduino platform it works for all possible data types, and when it receives a float variable, it rounds it to two decimal digits before it gets output. You can specify the number of decimal digits. For example, Serial.println(3.141592, 4); prints 3.1416.

Only the output is affected by this; internally it is still a float variable (by the way, on the Arduino float and double values are the same at the moment).

So, what does it actually cost to use float variables? Their memory consumption is 4 bytes—that is, they consume as much memory as long variables. On the other hand, floating-point calculations are fairly expensive and should be avoided in time-critical parts of your software. The biggest costs are the additional library functions that have to be linked to your program for float support. Serial.print(3.14) might look harmless, but it increases your program's size tremendously. Comment line 39 out, and recompile the program to see the effect. It will no longer work properly, but we can see how this statement affects the program size. With my current setup, it needs 3,192 bytes without float support for Serial.print() and 4,734 bytes otherwise. That's a difference of 1,542 bytes!

In some cases, you can still get the best of both worlds: float support without paying the memory tax. You can save a lot of space by converting the float values to integers before sending them over a serial connection. To transfer values with a precision of two digits, multiply them by 100, and do not forget to divide them by 100 on the receiving side. We will use this trick (including rounding) later.

5.4 Increasing Precision Using a Temperature Sensor

Support for floating-point numbers is certainly an improvement, but it mainly increases the precision of our program's output. We could have achieved a similar effect using some integer math tricks. But now we will add an even better improvement that cannot be imitated using software: a temperature sensor.

When I told you that sound travels through air at 343m/s, I wasn't totally accurate, because the speed of sound is not constant—among other things it depends on the air's temperature. If you do not take temperature into account, the error can grow up to a quite significant 12 percent. We calculate the actual speed of sound C with a simple formula:

$$C = 331.5 + (0.6 * t)$$

To use it, we only have to determine the current temperature t in Celsius. We will use the TMP36 voltage output temperature sensor from Analog Devices.[4] It's cheap, and it's easy to use.

To connect the TMP36 to the Arduino, connect the Arduino's ground and power to the corresponding pins of the TMP36. Then connect the sensor's signal pin to the pin A0, that is, the analog pin number 0 (see Figure 5.6, on the facing page).

As you might have guessed from its vendor's name, the TMP36 is an analog device: it changes the voltage on its signal pin corresponding to

---

4. http://tinyurl.com/msard-analog

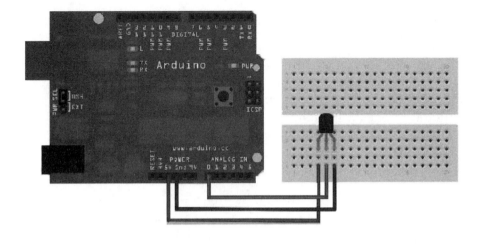

Figure 5.6: CONNECTING THE TEMPERATURE SENSOR TO THE ARDUINO

the current temperature. The higher the temperature, the higher the voltage. For us it is an excellent opportunity to learn how to use the Arduino's analog IO pins. So, let's see some code that uses the sensor:

`temperature/sensortest/sensortest.pde`

```
const unsigned int TEMP_SENSOR_PIN = 0;
const float SUPPLY_VOLTAGE = 5.0;
const unsigned int BAUD_RATE = 9600;

void setup() {
  Serial.begin(BAUD_RATE);
}

void loop() {
  Serial.print(get_temperature());
  Serial.println(" C");
  delay(1000);
}

const float get_temperature() {
  const int sensor_voltage = analogRead(TEMP_SENSOR_PIN);
  const float voltage = sensor_voltage * SUPPLY_VOLTAGE / 1024;
  return (voltage * 1000 - 500) / 10;
}
```

In the first two lines, we define constants for the analog pin the sensor is connected to and for the Arduino's supply voltage. Then we have a pretty normal setup() method followed by a loop() method that outputs the current temperature every second. The whole sensor logic has been encapsulated in the get_temperature() method.

For the PING))) sensor, we only needed a digital pin that could be HIGH or LOW. Analog pins are different and represent a voltage ranging from 0V to the current power supply (usually 5V). We can read Arduino's analog pins using the analogRead() method that returns a value between 0 and 1023, because analog pins have a resolution of ten bits ($1024 = 2^{10}$). We use it in line 16 to read the current voltage supplied by the TMP36.

There's one problem left, though: we have to turn the value returned by analogRead() into an actual voltage value, so we must know the Arduino's current power supply. It usually is 5V, but there are Arduino models (the Arduino Pro, for example) that use only 3.3V. You have to adjust the constant SUPPLY_VOLTAGE accordingly.

Knowing the supply voltage, we can turn the analog pin's output into a voltage value by dividing it by 1024 and by multiplying it with the supply voltage afterward. That's exactly what we do in line 17.

We now have to convert the voltage the sensor delivers into degree Celsius. In the sensor's data sheet, we find the following formula:

T = ((sensor output in mV) - 500) / 10

500 millivolts have to be subtracted, because the sensor always outputs a positive voltage. This way, we can represent negative temperatures, too. The sensor's resolution is 10 millivolts, so we have to divide by 10. A voltage value of 750 millivolts corresponds to a temperature of (750 - 500) / 10 = 25°C, for example. See it implemented in line 18.

Compile the program, upload it to the Arduino, and you'll see something like the following in your serial monitor:

```
10.06 C
26.64 C
28.62 C
28.50 C
28.50 C
29.00 C
29.00 C
28.50 C
29.00 C
```

As you can see, the sensor needs some time to calibrate, but its results get stable fairly quickly. By the way, you'll always need to insert a short

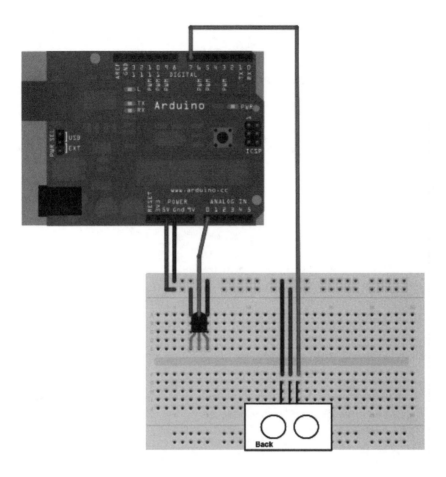

Figure 5.7: THE TMP36 AND THE PING))) SENSORS WORKING TOGETHER

delay between two calls to analogRead( ), because the Arduino's internal analog system needs some time (0.0001 seconds) between two readings. We have used a delay of a whole second to make the output easier to read and because we do not expect the temperature to change rapidly. Otherwise, a delay of a single millisecond would be enough.

Now we have two separate circuits: one for measuring distances and one for measuring temperatures. See them combined to a single circuit in Figure 5.7, as well as in Figure 5.8, on page 105. Use the following program to bring the circuit to life:

ultrasonic/PreciseSensor/PreciseSensor.pde

```
Line 1    const unsigned int TEMP_SENSOR_PIN = 0;
   -      const float SUPPLY_VOLTAGE = 5.0;
   -      const unsigned int PING_SENSOR_IO_PIN = 7;
   -      const float SENSOR_GAP = 0.2;
   5      const unsigned int BAUD_RATE = 9600;
   -
   -      float current_temperature = 0.0;
   -      unsigned long last_measurement = millis();
   -
  10      void setup() {
   -        Serial.begin(BAUD_RATE);
   -      }
   -
   -      void loop() {
  15        unsigned long current_millis = millis();
   -        if (abs(current_millis - last_measurement) >= 1000) {
   -          current_temperature = get_temperature();
   -          last_measurement = current_millis;
   -        }
  20        Serial.print(scaled_value(current_temperature));
   -        Serial.print(",");
   -        const unsigned long duration = measure_distance();
   -        Serial.println(scaled_value(microseconds_to_cm(duration)));
   -      }
  25
   -      long scaled_value(const float value) {
   -        float round_offset = value < 0 ? -0.5 : 0.5;
   -        return (long)(value * 100 + round_offset);
   -      }
  30
   -      const float get_temperature() {
   -        const int sensor_voltage = analogRead(TEMP_SENSOR_PIN);
   -        const float voltage = sensor_voltage * SUPPLY_VOLTAGE / 1024;
   -        return (voltage * 1000 - 500) / 10;
  35      }
   -
   -      const float microseconds_per_cm() {
   -        return 1 / ((331.5 + (0.6 * current_temperature)) / 10000);
   -      }
  40
   -      const float sensor_offset() {
   -        return SENSOR_GAP * microseconds_per_cm() * 2;
   -      }
   -
  45      const float microseconds_to_cm(const unsigned long microseconds) {
   -        const float net_distance = max(0, microseconds - sensor_offset());
   -        return net_distance / microseconds_per_cm() / 2;
   -      }
   -
```

```
50  const unsigned long measure_distance() {
      pinMode(PING_SENSOR_IO_PIN, OUTPUT);
      digitalWrite(PING_SENSOR_IO_PIN, LOW);
      delayMicroseconds(2);

55    digitalWrite(PING_SENSOR_IO_PIN, HIGH);
      delayMicroseconds(5);
      digitalWrite(PING_SENSOR_IO_PIN, LOW);

      pinMode(PING_SENSOR_IO_PIN, INPUT);
60    return pulseIn(PING_SENSOR_IO_PIN, HIGH);
    }
```

The code is nearly a perfect merge of the programs we used to get the PING))) and the TMP36 sensors working. Only a few things were changed:

- The constant MICROSECONDS_PER_CM has been replaced by the microseconds_per_cm() function that determines the microseconds sound needs to travel 1 centimeter dynamically depending on the current temperature.

- Because the current temperature will usually not change often or rapidly, we no longer measure it permanently but only once a second. We use millis() in line 8 to determine the number of milliseconds that have passed since the Arduino started. From lines 15 to 19, we check whether more than a second has passed since the last measurement. If yes, we measure the current temperature again.

- We no longer transfer the sensor data as floating-point numbers on the serial port but use scaled integer values instead. This is done by the scaled_value() function that rounds a float value to two decimal digits and converts it into a long value by multiplying it by 100. On the receiving side, you have to divide it by 100 again.

If you upload the program to your Arduino and play around with your hand in front of the sensor, you'll see an output similar to the following:

```
1940,2818
2914,3032
3045,34156
3005,2843
3045,2476
3085,2414
```

The output is a comma-separated list of values where the first value represents the current temperature in degree Celsius, and the second

---

How to Encode Sensor Data

Encoding sensor data is a problem that has to be solved often in Arduino projects, because all the nice data we collect usually has to be interpreted by applications running on regular computers.

When defining a data format, you have to take several things into account. For example, the format should not waste the Arduino's precious memory. In our case, we could have used XML for encoding the sensor data, for example:

```
<sensor-data>
  <temperature>30.05</temperature>
  <distance>51.19</distance>
</sensor-data>
```

Obviously this is not a good choice, because now we are wasting a multiple of the actual data's memory for creating the file format's structure. In addition, the receiving application has to use an XML parser to interpret the data.

But you shouldn't go to the other extreme either. That is, you should use binary formats only if it's absolutely necessary or if the receiving application expects binary data anyway.

All in all, the simplest data formats such as character-separated values (CSV) are often the best choice.

---

is the distance to the nearest object measured in centimeters. Both values have to be divided by 100 to get the actual sensor data.

Our little project now has two sensors. One is connected to a digital pin, while the other uses an analog one. In the next section, you'll learn how to transfer sensor data back to a PC and use it to create applications based on the current state of the real world.

5.5 Transferring Data Back to Your Computer Using Processing

All the programs in this chapter transfer sensor data back to your computer using a serial port. But until now we've only watched the data passing by in the IDE's serial monitor and haven't used it in our own applications.

Figure 5.8: Photo of final circuit

Save the Climate Using Sonar Sensors

Researchers from Northwestern and University of Michigan have created a sonar system that only uses a computer's microphone and speakers to detect whether the computer is currently used or not.* If it's not being used, the computer automatically powers off its screen, saving the environment.

Instead of using a microphone and speakers, you can also use a PING))) sensor. With the lessons you've learned in this chapter, you can build such a system yourself with ease. Try it!

* http://blog.makezine.com/archive/2009/10/using_sonar_to_save_power.html

In this section, we will build an application that graphically visualizes the sensor data. The program will implement a kind of inverted sonar: it draws a small dot on the screen showing the distance to the nearest object, while the position of the dot will move in a circle itself (see the picture on page 115).

To implement the application, we'll use the Processing programming language, and in Figure 5.9, on the next page you can see how we'll organize the project. The Processing code runs on our computer while all the PING))) sensor code still runs on the Arduino. Communication between the Processing code and the Arduino happens via serial port.

Processing is an extension of the Java programming language, and its focus is on computational art. With Processing, it's very easy to create multimedia applications: applications that produce sound and animated 2D or 3D graphics. It also has excellent support for user interactions and is well documented (for example, see *Processing: Creative Coding and Computational Art* [Gre07]).

It was originally built for design students who do not have a lot of programming experience but who still wanted to use computers and electronic devices to create interactive artwork. That's the reason why Processing is easy to learn and very beginner-friendly. But many people also use it for serious and advanced tasks, especially for presenting data in visually appealing ways.

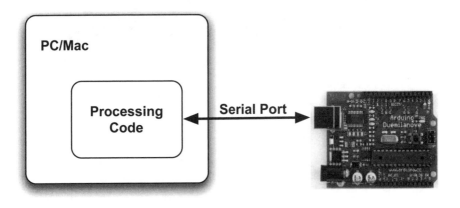

Figure 5.9: System architecture of our inverted Sonar project

You can download Processing for free,[5] and it comes with a one-click installer for all popular operating systems. Start it or take a look at Figure 5.10, on the following page. Looks familiar, doesn't it? That is not a coincidence, because the Arduino IDE was derived from the Processing IDE. Instead of writing a new programming environment from scratch, the Arduino team decided to modify the Processing IDE. That's the reason why both IDEs look so similar and why Arduino sketches have the file extension .pde (*Processing Development Environment*), for example.

Using Processing as the basis for the Arduino project provided a good and well-tested IDE for free. Processing and the Arduino are a good team for several other reasons:

- The Arduino simplifies embedded computing, and Processing simplifies the creation of multimedia applications. So, you can easily visualize sensor data in often spectacular ways.

- Processing is easy to learn, especially if you already know Java.

- Processing has excellent support for serial communication.

So, for many reasons, Processing is well worth a look, but it's especially useful when working with the Arduino. That's why we'll use it for several of the book's examples.

---

5. http://processing.org/download/

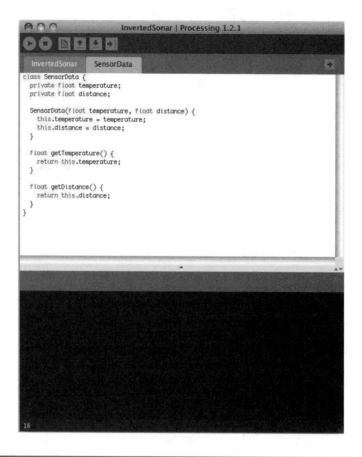

Figure 5.10: The Processing IDE is the basis for the Arduino IDE.

5.6 Representing Sensor Data

We start with a Processing class that represents the current sensor data we return from the Arduino via serial port. Open a new file in the Processing IDE, and enter the following code:

`ultrasonic/InvertedSonar/SensorData.pde`

```
class SensorData {
  private float temperature;
  private float distance;

  SensorData(float temperature, float distance) {
    this.temperature = temperature;
    this.distance = distance;
  }
```

```
float getTemperature() {
  return this.temperature;
}

float getDistance() {
  return this.distance;
}
}
```

If you are familiar with Java or C++, the SensorData class will be perfectly clear to you. It encapsulates a temperature value and a distance as floating-point numbers and provides access to the data via accessor methods (getTemperature() and getDistance()). You can create new SensorData objects using the constructor, passing it the current temperature and distance.

Processing is an object-oriented programming language and allows us to define new classes using the **class** keyword. Classes have a name and they contain data (often called *attributes* or *properties*) and functions (often called *methods*). Our SensorData class contains two attributes named temperature and distance. They are both of type **float**, and we have declared them both **private**. Now only members of the SensorData class are allowed to access them. This is considered good style, because it prevents unwanted side effects and makes future changes much easier. A class should never expose its innards.

To set and get the values of our attributes, we have to use public methods, and our class has three of them: SensorData(), getTemperature(), and getDistance(). (Java and C++ programmers should note that in Processing everything is public if not specified otherwise!) A method that has the same name as the class is called a *constructor*, and you can use it for creating and initializing new objects of that particular class. Constructors do not have return values, but they may specify parameters. Ours, for example, takes two arguments and uses them to initialize our two attributes.

There's a small problem, though: our method's parameters have the same names as our classes' attributes. What would happen if we simply assigned the method parameters to the attributes like this:

```
temperature = temperature;
distance = distance;
```

Right: we simply assigned every method parameter to itself, which is effectively a no-operation. That's why we use the **this** keyword. It refers

to the class itself, so we can distinguish between the method parameters and the classes' attributes. Alternatively, we could have used different names for the method parameters or the attributes, but I prefer to use **this**.

After the constructor, we define the methods getTemperature and getDistance. Their definitions are very similar; we declare the method's return type (**float**), the method's name, and a list of parameters in parentheses. In our case, the parameter list is empty. In the methods, we return the current value of the corresponding attributes using the **return** keyword. **return** stops the method and returns its argument to the method's caller.

Now we can create and initialize new SensorData objects:

```
SensorData sensorData = new SensorData(31.5, 11.76);
```

The previous statement creates a new SensorData object named sensorData. It sets temperature to 31.5 and distance to 11.76. To read those values, we use the corresponding "get" methods:

```
sensorData.getTemperature(); // -> 31.5
sensorData.getDistance();    // -> 11.76
```

Because getTemperature() and getDistance() are members of the SensorData class, you can only invoke them using an instance of the class. Our instance is named sensorData, and to call the "get" methods we have to use the instance name, followed by a dot, followed by the method name.

Now that we can store sensor data, we'll continue to build our inverted sonar application in the next section.

5.7   Building the Application's Foundation

In this section, we'll create all the boilerplate code we need for our application by importing some libraries and defining some global constants and variables:

`ultrasonic/InvertedSonar/InvertedSonar.pde`

```
import processing.serial.*;

final int WIDTH = 1000;
final int HEIGHT = 1000;
final int xCenter = WIDTH / 2;
final int yCenter = HEIGHT / 2;
final int LINE_FEED = 10;
```

```
Serial arduinoPort;
SensorData sensorData;
int degree = 0;
int radius = 0;
```

To communicate with the Arduino via a serial port, we import Processing's support for serial communication in the first line. The **import** statement imports all classes from the processing.serial package and makes them available in our program.

Our application will have a 1000x1000 pixel screen, so we define constants for its width, height, and its center. We set the LINE_FEED constant to the ASCII value of a linefeed character, because we need it later to interpret the data sent by the Arduino.

Then we define a few global variables (yes, you Java programmers out there: Processing allows you to define global variables!):

- *arduinoPort*: An instance of Processing's Serial class. It's from the processing.serial package we have imported and encapsulates the serial port communication with the Arduino.

- *sensorData*: The current sensor data that have been transferred from the Arduino to our application. We use the SensorData class we defined in Section 5.6, *Representing Sensor Data*, on page 108.

- *degree*: We will visualize the current distance to the nearest object on a circle. This variable stores on which degree of the circle we are right now. Values range from 0 to 359.

- *radius*: The current distance to the nearest object is interpreted as a radius value.

5.8 Implementing Serial Communication in Processing

The following functions read data from the serial port the Arduino is connected to, and they interpret the data the Arduino is sending:

ultrasonic/InvertedSonar/InvertedSonar.pde

```
Line 1   void setup() {
    -      size(WIDTH, HEIGHT);
    -      println(Serial.list());
    -      String arduinoPortName = Serial.list()[0];
    5      arduinoPort = new Serial(this, arduinoPortName, 9600);
    -      arduinoPort.bufferUntil(LINE_FEED);
    -    }
    -
```

```
     void serialEvent(Serial port) {
10     sensorData = getSensorData();
       if (sensorData != null) {
         println("Temperature: " + sensorData.getTemperature());
         println("Distance: " + sensorData.getDistance());
         radius = min(300, int(sensorData.getDistance() * 2));
15     }
     }

     SensorData getSensorData() {
       SensorData result = null;
20     if (arduinoPort.available() > 0) {
         final String arduinoOutput = arduinoPort.readStringUntil(LINE_FEED);
         result = parseArduinoOutput(arduinoOutput);
       }
       return result;
25   }

     SensorData parseArduinoOutput(final String arduinoOutput) {
       SensorData result = null;
       if (arduinoOutput != null) {
30       final int[] data = int(split(trim(arduinoOutput), ','));
         if (data.length == 2)
           result = new SensorData(data[0] / 100.0, data[1] / 100.0);
       }
       return result;
35   }
```

setup() is one of Processing's standard functions and has the same meaning as the Arduino's setup() method. The Processing runtime environment calls it only once at application startup time and initializes the application. With the size() method, we create a new screen having a certain width and height (by the way, you can find excellent reference material for all Processing classes online[6]).

After initializing the screen, we prepare the serial port communication. First we print a list of all serial devices that are currently connected to the computer using Serial.list(). Then we set the name of the serial port we are going to use to the first list entry. This might be the wrong port, so either you hard-code the name of your system's serial port into the code or you have a look at the list of serial ports and choose the right one!

In line 5, we create a new Serial object that is bound to our application (that's what this is for). We use the serial port name we have from the list of all serial ports and set the baud rate to 9600. If you'd like to

---

6. http://processing.org/reference/

communicate faster, you have to change both the baud rate here and in the Arduino sketch.

Finally, we tell the Serial object that we want to be notified of new serial data only when a linefeed has been detected. Whenever we find a linefeed, we know that a whole line of data was transmitted by the Arduino.

For our application, we chose an asynchronous programming model; that is, we do not poll for new data in a loop but get notified whenever there's new data on the serial port (to be concise, we want to be notified only if a new linefeed was found). This way, we can change our application's state in real time and can prevent disturbing delays between the arrival of data and graphics updates on the screen.

When new data arrives, serialEvent() gets called automatically and is passed the serial port the data was found on. We have only one port, so we can ignore this parameter. We try to read the current sensor data using getSensorData(), and if we find some, we print them to the console for debugging purposes and set the radius to the measured distance. To make the visualization more appealing, we multiply the distance by two, and we cut values bigger than 300 centimeters.

getSensorData()'s implementation is fairly simple. First it checks to see if data is available on the serial port in line 20. This might look redundant, because this method gets called only if data is available, but if we'd like to reuse it in a synchronous context, the check is necessary. Then we read all data until we find a linefeed character and pass the result to parseArduinoOutput().

Parsing the output is easy because of Processing's split() method. We use it in line 30 to split the line of text we get from the Arduino at the comma (trim() removes trailing and leading whitespace characters). It returns a two-element array containing the textual representation of two integer values. These strings are turned into integers afterward using int(). Please note that in our case int() takes an array containing two strings and returns an array containing two **int** values.

Because it's possible that we have an incomplete line of text from the Arduino (the serial communication might start at an arbitrary byte position), we'd better check whether we actually got two sensor values. If yes, we create a new SensorData object and initialize it with the temperature and distance (after we have divided them by 100).

That's all we need to read the sensor data asynchronously from the Arduino. From now on, sensor data will be read whenever it's available, and the global sensorData and radius variables will be kept up-to-date automatically.

5.9 Visualizing Sensor Data

Now that the serial communication between our computer and the Arduino works, let's visualize the distance to the nearest object:

ultrasonic/InvertedSonar/InvertedSonar.pde

```
Line 1   void init_screen() {
           background(255);
           stroke(0);
           strokeWeight(1);
      5    int[] radius_values = { 300, 250, 200, 150, 100, 50 };
           for (int r = 0; r < radius_values.length; r++) {
             final int current_radius = radius_values[r] * 2;
             ellipse(xCenter, yCenter, current_radius, current_radius);
           }
     10    strokeWeight(10);
         }

         void draw() {
           init_screen();
     15    int x = (int)(radius * Math.cos(degree * Math.PI / 180));
           int y = (int)(radius * Math.sin(degree * Math.PI / 180));
           point(xCenter + x, yCenter + y);
           if (++degree == 360)
             degree = 0;
     20    }
```

init_screen() clears the screen and sets its background color to white in line 2. It sets the drawing color to black using stroke(0) and sets the width of the stroke used for drawing shapes to 1 pixel. Then it draws six concentric circles around the screen's center. These circles will help us to see how far the nearest object is away from the PING))) sensor. Finally, it sets the stroke width to 10, so we can visualize the sensor with a single point that is 10 pixels wide.

Processing calls the draw() method automatically at a certain frame rate (default is 60 frames per second), and it is the equivalent of the Arduino's loop() method. In our case, we initialize the screen and calculate coordinates lying on a circle. The circle's radius depends on the distance we have from the Arduino, so we have a point that moves on

Some Fun with Sensors

With an ultrasonic sensor, you can easily detect whether someone is nearby. This automatically brings a lot of useful applications to mind. For example, you could open a door automatically as soon as someone is close enough.

Alternatively, you can use advanced technology for pure fun. What about some Halloween gimmicks like a pumpkin that shoots silly string whenever you cross an invisible line?[*] It could be a nice gag for your next party, and you can build it using the PING))) sensor.[†]

---

[*]. http://www.instructables.com/id/Arduino-controlled-Silly-String-shooter/
[†]. http://arduinofun.com/blog/2009/11/01/silly-string-shooting-spider-contest-entry/

a circle. Its distance to the circle's center depends on the data we measure with the PING))) sensor.

So, we've seen that there are two types of sensor: digital and analog. You have also learned how to connect both types of sensors to the Arduino and how to transfer their measurements to your computer. Working with these two different IO types is the basis for all physical computing, and nearly every project—no matter how complex—is a derivation of the things you have learned in this chapter.

5.10 What If It Doesn't Work?

See Section 3.8, *What If It Doesn't Work?*, on page 68, and make sure that you have connected all parts properly to the breadboard. Take special care with the PING))) and the TMP36 sensors, because you haven't worked with them before. Make sure you have connected the right pins to the right connectors of the sensors.

In case of any errors with the software—no matter if it's Processing or Arduino code—download the code from the book's website and see whether it works.

If you have problems with serial communication, double-check whether you have used the right serial port and the right Arduino type. It might be that you have connected your Arduino to another port. In this case, you have to change the index 0 in the statement arduinoPort = new Serial(this, Serial.list()[0], 9600); accordingly. Also check whether the baud rate in the Processing code and serial monitor matches the baud rate you have used in the Arduino code. Make sure that the serial port is not blocked by another application like a serial monitor window you forgot to close, for example.

5.11 Exercises

- Build an automatic burglar alarm that shows a stop sign whenever someone is too close to your computer.[7] Make the application as smart as possible. For example, it should have a small activation delay to prevent it from showing a stop sign immediately when it's started.

- The speed of sound not only depends on the temperature but also on humidity and atmospheric pressure. Do some research to find the right formula and the right sensors.[8] Use your research results to make our circuit for measuring distances even more precise.

- Use an alternative technology for measuring distances, for example, an infrared sensor. Try to find an appropriate sensor, read its data sheet, and build a basic circuit so you can print the distance to the nearest object to the serial port.

---

7. You can find a stop sign here: http://en.wikipedia.org/wiki/File:Stop_sign_MUTCD.svg.
8. Try http://parallax.com.

Chapter 6

Building a Motion-Sensing Game Controller

It's astonishing how quickly we get used to new technologies. A decade ago, not many people would have imagined that we'd use devices someday to unobtrusively follow our movements. Today it's absolutely normal for us to physically turn our smartphones when we want to change from portrait to landscape view. Even small children intuitively know how to use motion-sensing controllers for video game consoles such as Nintendo's Wii. You can build your own motion-sensing devices using an Arduino, and in this chapter you'll learn how.

We'll work with one of the most widespread motion-sensing devices: the *accelerometer*. Accelerometers detect movement in all directions—they notice if you move them up, down, forward, backward, to the left, or to the right. Many popular gadgets such as the iPhone and the Nintendo Wii controllers contain accelerometers. That's why accelerometers are cheap.

Both fun and serious projects can benefit from accelerometers. When working with your computer, you certainly think of projects such as game controllers or other input control devices. But you can also use them when exercising or to control a real-life marble maze. You can also use them to measure acceleration more or less indirectly, such as in a car.

You will learn how to interpret accelerometer data correctly and how to get the most accurate results. Then you'll use an accelerometer to build your own motion-sensing game controller, and you'll implement a game that uses it.

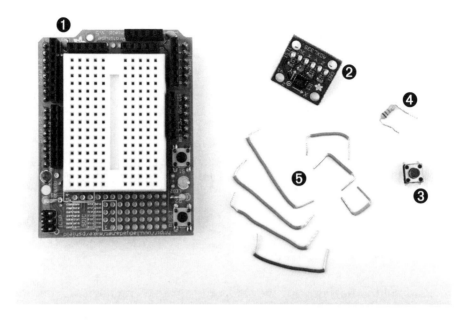

Figure 6.1: ALL THE PARTS YOU NEED IN THIS CHAPTER

6.1 What You Need

1. A half-size breadboard or—even better—an Arduino Prototyping shield with a tiny breadboard

2. An ADXL335 accelerometer

3. A pushbutton

4. A 10kΩ resistor

5. Some wires

6. An Arduino board such as the Uno, Duemilanove, or Diecimila

7. A USB cable to connect the Arduino to your computer

8. A 6 pin 0.1" standard header

Figure 6.2: AN ADXL335 SENSOR ON A BREAKOUT BOARD

6.2 Wiring Up the Accelerometer

There are many different accelerometers, differing mainly in the number of spacial axes they support (usually two or three). We use the ADXL335 from Analog Devices—it's easy to use and widely available.[1]

In this section, we'll connect the ADXL335 to the Arduino and create a small demo program showing the raw data the sensor delivers. At that point, we will have a quick look at the sensor's specification and interpret the data.

In Figure 6.2, you see a breakout board containing an ADXL335 sensor on the right. The sensor is the small black integrated circuit (IC), and the rest is just a carrier to allow connections. On the top, you see a 6 pin 0.1" standard header. The sensor has six connectors labeled GND, Z, Y, X, 3V, and TEST. To use the sensor on a breadboard, solder the standard header to the connectors. This not only makes it easier to attach the sensor to a breadboard but also stabilizes the sensor, so it

---

1. http://www.analog.com/en/sensors/inertial-sensors/adxl335/products/product.html

does not move accidentally. You can see the result on the left side of the photo (note that the breakout board on the left is not the same as on the right, but it's very similar). Don't worry if you've never soldered before. In Section A.2, *Learning How to Solder*, on page 229, you can learn how to do it.

You can ignore the connector labeled TEST, and the meaning of the remaining connectors should be obvious. To power the sensor, connect GND to the Arduino's ground pin and 3V to the Arduino's 3.3 volts power supply. X, Y, and Z will then deliver acceleration data for the x-, y-, and z-axes.

Like the TMP36 temperature sensor we used in Section 5.4, *Increasing Precision Using a Temperature Sensor*, on page 98, the ADXL335 is an analog device: it delivers results as voltages that have to be converted into acceleration values. So, the X, Y, and Z connectors have to be connected to three analog pins on the Arduino. We connect Z to analog pin 0, Y to analog pin 1, and X to analog pin 2 (see Figure 6.3, on the facing page, and double-check the pin labels on the breakout board you're using!).

Now that we've connected the ADXL335 to the Arduino, let's use it.

6.3 Bringing Your Accelerometer to Life

A pragmatic strategy to get familiar with a new device is to hook it up and see what data it delivers. The following program reads input values for all three axes and outputs them to the serial port:

MotionSensor/SensorTest/SensorTest.pde

```
const unsigned int X_AXIS_PIN = 2;
const unsigned int Y_AXIS_PIN = 1;
const unsigned int Z_AXIS_PIN = 0;
const unsigned int BAUD_RATE = 9600;

void setup() {
  Serial.begin(BAUD_RATE);
}

void loop() {
  Serial.print(analogRead(X_AXIS_PIN));
  Serial.print(" ");
  Serial.print(analogRead(Y_AXIS_PIN));
  Serial.print(" ");
  Serial.println(analogRead(Z_AXIS_PIN));
  delay(100);
}
```

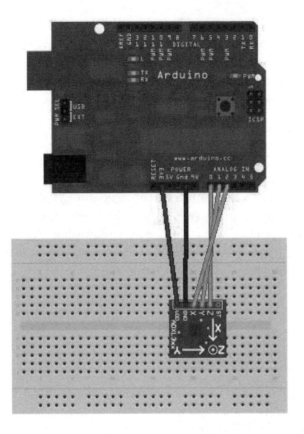

Figure 6.3: How to connect an ADXL335 sensor to an Arduino

Our test program is as simple as it can be. We define constants for the three analog pins and initialize the serial port in the setup() function. Note that we did not set the analog pins to INPUT explicitly, because that's the default anyway.

In the loop() function, we constantly output the values we read from the analog pins to the serial port. Open the serial monitor, and move the sensor around a bit—tilt it around the different axes. You should see an output similar to the following:

```
344 331 390
364 276 352
388 286 287
398 314 286
376 332 289
370 336 301
379 338 281
```

These values represent the data we get for the x-, y-, and z-axes. When you move the sensor only around the x-axis, for example, you can see that the first value changes accordingly. In the next section, we'll take a closer look at these values.

6.4 Finding and Polishing Edge Values

The physical world often is far from being perfect. That's especially true for the data many sensors emit, and accelerometers are no exception. They slightly vary in the minimum and maximum values they generate, and they often jitter a bit. They might change their output values even though you haven't moved them, or they might not change their output values correctly. In this section, we'll determine the sensor's minimum and maximum values, and we'll flatten the jitter.

Finding the edge values of the sensor is easy, but it cannot be easily automated. You have to constantly read the sensor's output while moving it. Here's a program that does the job:

MotionSensor/SensorValues/SensorValues.pde

```
const unsigned int X_AXIS_PIN = 2;
const unsigned int Y_AXIS_PIN = 1;
const unsigned int Z_AXIS_PIN = 0;
const unsigned int BAUD_RATE = 9600;

int min_x, min_y, min_z;
int max_x, max_y, max_z;

void setup() {
  Serial.begin(BAUD_RATE);
  min_x = min_y = min_z = 1000;
  max_x = max_y = max_z = -1000;
}

void loop() {
  const int x = analogRead(X_AXIS_PIN);
  const int y = analogRead(Y_AXIS_PIN);
  const int z = analogRead(Z_AXIS_PIN);

  min_x = min(x, min_x); max_x = max(x, max_x);
  min_y = min(y, min_y); max_y = max(y, max_y);
  min_z = min(z, min_z); max_z = max(z, max_z);

  Serial.print("x(");
  Serial.print(min_x);
  Serial.print("/");
  Serial.print(max_x);
```

```
Serial.print("), y(");
Serial.print(min_y);
Serial.print("/");
Serial.print(max_y);
Serial.print("), z(");
Serial.print(min_z);
Serial.print("/");
Serial.print(max_z);
Serial.println(")");
}
```

We declare variables for the minimum and maximum values of all three axes, and we initialize them with numbers that are definitely out of the sensor's range (-1000 and 1000). In the loop() function, we permanently measure the acceleration of all three axes and adjust the minimum and maximum values accordingly.

Compile and upload the sketch, then move the breadboard with the sensor in all directions, and then tilt it around all axes. Move it slowly, move it fast, tilt it slowly, and tilt it fast. Use long wires, and be careful when moving and rotating the breadboard so you do not accidentally loosen a connection.

After a short while the minimum and maximum values will stabilize, and you should get output like this:

```
x(247/649), y(253/647), z(278/658)
```

Write down these values, because we need them later, and you'll probably need them when you do your own sensor experiments.

Now let's see how to get rid of the jitter. In principle, it is simple. Instead of returning the acceleration data immediately, we collect the last readings and return their average. This way, small changes will be ironed out. The code looks as follows:

MotionSensor/Buffering/Buffering.pde

```
Line 1    const unsigned int X_AXIS_PIN = 2;
    -     const unsigned int Y_AXIS_PIN = 1;
    -     const unsigned int Z_AXIS_PIN = 0;
    -     const unsigned int NUM_AXES = 3;
    5     const unsigned int PINS[NUM_AXES] = {
    -       X_AXIS_PIN, Y_AXIS_PIN, Z_AXIS_PIN
    -     };
    -     const unsigned int BUFFER_SIZE = 16;
    -     const unsigned int BAUD_RATE = 9600;
    10
    -     int buffer[NUM_AXES][BUFFER_SIZE];
    -     int buffer_pos[NUM_AXES] = { 0 };
```

```
    void setup() {
15    Serial.begin(BAUD_RATE);
    }

    int get_axis(const int axis) {
      delay(1);
20    buffer[axis][buffer_pos[axis]] = analogRead(PINS[axis]);
      buffer_pos[axis] = (buffer_pos[axis] + 1) % BUFFER_SIZE;

      long sum = 0;
      for (int i = 0; i < BUFFER_SIZE; i++)
25      sum += buffer[axis][i];
      return round(sum / BUFFER_SIZE);
    }

    int get_x() { return get_axis(0); }
30  int get_y() { return get_axis(1); }
    int get_z() { return get_axis(2); }

    void loop() {
      Serial.print(get_x());
35    Serial.print(" ");
      Serial.print(get_y());
      Serial.print(" ");
      Serial.println(get_z());
    }
```

As usual, we define some constants for the pins we use first. This time, we also define a constant named NUM_AXES that contains the amount of axes we are measuring. We also have an array named PINS that contains a list of the pins we use. This helps us keep our code more generic later.

In line 11, we declare buffers for all axes. They will be filled with the sensor data we measure, so we can calculate average values when we need them. We have to store our current position in each buffer, so in line 12, we define an array of buffer positions.

setup() only initializes the serial port, and the real action takes place in the get_axis() function. It starts with a small delay to give the Arduino some time to switch between analog pins; otherwise, you might get bad data. Then it reads the acceleration for the axis we have passed and stores it at the current buffer position belonging to the axis. It increases the buffer position and sets it back to zero when the end of the buffer has been reached. Finally, we return the average value of the data we have gathered so far for the current axis.

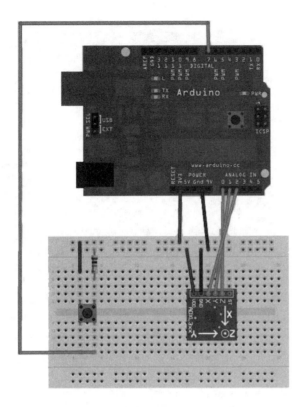

Figure 6.4: GAME CONTROLLER WITH ACCELEROMETER AND PUSHBUTTON

That's the whole trick. To see its effect, leave the sensor untouched on your desk, and run the program with different buffer sizes. If you do not touch the sensor, you would not expect the program's output to change. But if you set BUFFER_SIZE to 1, you will quickly see small changes. They will disappear as soon as the buffer is big enough.

The acceleration data we measure now is sufficiently accurate, and we can finally build a game controller that will not annoy users because of unexpected movements.

6.5 Building Your Own Game Controller

To build a full-blown game controller, we only need to add a button to our breadboard. In Figure 6.4, you can see how to do it (please, double-check the pin labels on your breakout board!).

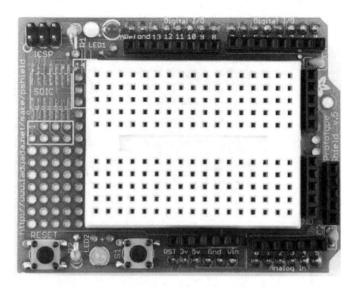

Figure 6.5: AN ARDUINO PROTOTYPING SHIELD

That's how it looks inside a typical modern game controller. We will not build a fancy housing for the controller, but we still should think about ergonomics for a moment. Our current breadboard solution is rather fragile, and you cannot really wave around the board when it's connected to the Arduino. Sooner or later you will disconnect some wires, and the controller will stop working.

To solve this problem, you could try to attach the breadboard to the Arduino using some rubber bands. That works, but it does not look very pretty, and it's still hard to handle.

A much better solution is to use an Arduino Prototyping shield (see Figure 6.5). It is a pluggable breadboard that lets you quickly build circuit prototypes. The breadboard is surrounded by the Arduino's pins, so you no longer need long wires. Shields are a great way to enhance an Arduino's capabilities, and you can get shields for many different purposes such as adding Ethernet, sound, displays, and so on.[2]

Using the Proto Shield our game controller looks as in Figure 6.6, on the next page. Neat, eh?

---

2. At http://shieldlist.org/, you find a comprehensive list of Arduino shields.

Figure 6.6: THE COMPLETE GAME CONTROLLER ON A PROTO SHIELD

Now that the hardware is complete, we need a final version of the game controller software. It supports the button we have added, and it performs the anti-jittering we have created in Section 6.4, *Finding and Polishing Edge Values*, on page 122:

MotionSensor/Controller/Controller.pde

```
#include <Bounce.h>

const unsigned int BUTTON_PIN = 7;
const unsigned int X_AXIS_PIN = 2;
const unsigned int Y_AXIS_PIN = 1;
const unsigned int Z_AXIS_PIN = 0;
const unsigned int NUM_AXES = 3;
const unsigned int PINS[NUM_AXES] = {
  X_AXIS_PIN, Y_AXIS_PIN, Z_AXIS_PIN
};
const unsigned int BUFFER_SIZE = 16;
const unsigned int BAUD_RATE = 19200;

int buffer[NUM_AXES][BUFFER_SIZE];
int buffer_pos[NUM_AXES] = { 0 };

Bounce button(BUTTON_PIN, 20);

void setup() {
  Serial.begin(BAUD_RATE);
  pinMode(BUTTON_PIN, INPUT);
}
```

```
int get_axis(const int axis) {
  delay(1);
  buffer[axis][buffer_pos[axis]] = analogRead(PINS[axis]);
  buffer_pos[axis] = (buffer_pos[axis] + 1) % BUFFER_SIZE;

  long sum = 0;
  for (int i = 0; i < BUFFER_SIZE; i++)
    sum += buffer[axis][i];
  return round(sum / BUFFER_SIZE);
}

int get_x() { return get_axis(0); }
int get_y() { return get_axis(1); }
int get_z() { return get_axis(2); }

void loop() {
  Serial.print(get_x());
  Serial.print(" ");
  Serial.print(get_y());
  Serial.print(" ");
  Serial.print(get_z());
  Serial.print(" ");
  if (button.update())
    Serial.println(button.read() == HIGH ? "1" : "0");
  else
    Serial.println("0");
}
```

As in Section 3.7, *Building a Dice Game*, on page 62, we use the Bounce class to debounce the button. The rest of the code is pretty much standard, and the only thing worth mentioning is that we use a 19200 baud rate to transfer the controller data sufficiently fast.

Compile and upload the code, open the serial terminal, and play around with the controller. Move it, press the button sometimes, and it should output something like the following:

```
324 365 396 0
325 364 397 0
325 364 397 1
325 364 397 0
325 365 397 0
325 365 397 1
326 364 397 0
```

A homemade game controller is nice, but wouldn't it be even nicer if we also had a game that supports it? That's what we will build in the next section.

6.6 Writing Your Own Game

To test our game controller, we will program a simple Breakout[3] clone in Processing. The game's goal is to destroy all bricks in the upper half of the screen with a ball. You can control the ball with the paddle at the bottom of the screen, and you can tilt the controller around the x-axis to move the paddle horizontally. It'll look something like this:

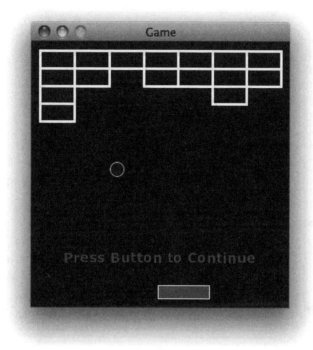

Although this is not a book about game programming, it will not hurt to take a look at the game's innards, especially because game programming with Processing is really pure fun! Download the code from the book's website[4] and play the game before you dive into the code.

Because we will connect our game controller to the serial port, we have to initialize it:

MotionSensor/Game/Game.pde

```
import processing.serial.*;
Serial arduinoPort;
```

---

3. http://en.wikipedia.org/wiki/Breakout_%28arcade_game%29
4. http://www.pragprog.com/titles/msard

Then we define some constants that will help us to customize the game easily:

MotionSensor/Game/Game.pde

```
final int COLUMNS = 7;
final int ROWS = 4;
final int BALL_RADIUS = 8;
final int BALL_DIAMETER = BALL_RADIUS * 2;
final int MAX_VELOCITY = 8;
final int PADDLE_WIDTH = 60;
final int PADDLE_HEIGHT = 15;
final int BRICK_WIDTH = 40;
final int BRICK_HEIGHT = 20;
final int MARGIN = 10;
final int WIDTH = COLUMNS * BRICK_WIDTH + 2 * MARGIN;
final int HEIGHT = 300;
final int X_AXIS_MIN = 252;
final int X_AXIS_MAX = 443;
final int LINE_FEED = 10;
final int BAUD_RATE = 19200;
```

Most of these values should be self-explanatory—they define the size of the objects that appear on the screen. For example, PADDLE_WIDTH is width of the paddle measured in pixels, and COLUMNS and ROWS set the layout of the bricks. You should replace X_AXIS_MIN and X_AXIS_MAX the minimum and maximum values you measured for your sensor in Section 6.4, *Finding and Polishing Edge Values*, on page 122.

Next we choose how to represent the game's objects:

MotionSensor/Game/Game.pde

```
int px, py;
int vx, vy;
int xpos = WIDTH / 2;
int[][] bricks = new int[COLUMNS][ROWS];
```

We store the balls' current x and y coordinates in px and py. For its current x and y velocity, we use vx and vy. We store the paddle's x position in xpos.

bricks is a two-dimensional array and contains the current state of the bricks on the screen. If an array element is set to 1, the corresponding brick is still on the screen. 0 means that it has been destroyed already.

Finally, we need to store the possible states of the game:

MotionSensor/Game/Game.pde

```
boolean buttonPressed = false;
boolean paused = true;
boolean done = true;
```

Unsurprisingly, we set buttonPressed to true when the button on the controller is pressed. Otherwise, it is false. paused tells you whether the game is currently paused, and done is true when the current level is done, that is, when all bricks have been destroyed.

Every Processing program needs a setup() function, and here is ours:

`MotionSensor/Game/Game.pde`

```
void setup() {
  size(WIDTH, HEIGHT);
  noCursor();
  textFont(loadFont("Verdana-Bold-36.vlw"));
  initGame();
  println(Serial.list());
  arduinoPort = new Serial(this, Serial.list()[0], BAUD_RATE);
  arduinoPort.bufferUntil(LINE_FEED);
}

void initGame() {
  initBricks();
  initBall();
}

void initBricks() {
  for (int x = 0; x < COLUMNS; x++)
    for (int y = 0; y < ROWS; y++ )
      bricks[x][y] = 1;
}

void initBall() {
  px = width / 2;
  py = height / 2;
  vx = int(random(-MAX_VELOCITY, MAX_VELOCITY));
  vy = -2;
}
```

The setup() function initializes the screen, hides the mouse pointer with noCursor(), and sets the font that we will use to output messages (create the font using Processing's Tools > Create Font menu). Then we call initGame() to initialize the bricks array and the ball's current position and velocity. To make things more interesting, the velocity in x direction is set to a random value. We set the velocity for the y direction to -2, which makes the ball fall at a reasonable speed.

Now that everything is initialized, we can implement the game's main loop. Processing's draw() method is a perfect place:[5]

---

5. http://processing.org/reference/ has excellent documentation for all Processing classes.

MotionSensor/Game/Game.pde

```
void draw() {
  background(0);
  stroke(255);
  strokeWeight(3);

  done = drawBricks();
  if (done) {
    paused = true;
    printWinMessage();
  }

  if (paused)
    printPauseMessage();
  else
    updateGame();

  drawBall();
  drawPaddle();
}
```

We clear the screen and paint it black using background(). Then we set the stroke color to white and the stroke weight to three pixels. After that we draw the remaining bricks. If no bricks are left, we pause the game and print a "You Win!" message.

If the game is paused, we print a corresponding message, and if it's not, we update the game's current state. Finally, we draw the ball and the paddle at their current positions using the following functions:

MotionSensor/Game/Game.pde

```
boolean drawBricks() {
  boolean allEmpty = true;
  for (int x = 0; x < COLUMNS; x++) {
    for (int y = 0; y < ROWS; y++) {
      if (bricks[x][y] > 0) {
        allEmpty = false;
        fill(0, 0, 100 + y * 8);
        rect(
          MARGIN + x * BRICK_WIDTH,
          MARGIN + y * BRICK_HEIGHT,
          BRICK_WIDTH,
          BRICK_HEIGHT
        );
      }
    }
  }
  return allEmpty;
}
```

```
void drawBall() {
  strokeWeight(1);
  fill(128, 0, 0);
  ellipse(px, py, BALL_DIAMETER, BALL_DIAMETER);
}

void drawPaddle() {
  int x = xpos - PADDLE_WIDTH / 2;
  int y = height - (PADDLE_HEIGHT + MARGIN);
  strokeWeight(1);
  fill(128);
  rect(x, y, PADDLE_WIDTH, PADDLE_HEIGHT);
}
```

As you can see, the ball is nothing but a circle, and the bricks and the paddle are simple rectangles. To make them look more appealing, we give them a nice border.

Printing the game's messages is easy, too:

MotionSensor/Game/Game.pde

```
void printWinMessage() {
  fill(255);
  textSize(36);
  textAlign(CENTER);
  text("YOU WIN!", width / 2, height * 2 / 3);
}

void printPauseMessage() {
  fill(128);
  textSize(16);
  textAlign(CENTER);
  text("Press Button to Continue", width / 2, height * 5 / 6);
}
```

The update() function is very important, because it updates the game's state—it checks for collisions, moves the ball, and so on:

MotionSensor/Game/Game.pde

```
void updateGame() {
  if (ballDropped()) {
    initBall();
    paused = true;
  } else {
    checkBrickCollision();
    checkWallCollision();
    checkPaddleCollision();
    px += vx;
    py += vy;
  }
}
```

When the player does not hit the ball with the paddle and it drops out of the playfield, the game stops, and the user is allowed to continue after pressing the button. In the final game, you'd decrease some kind of a life counter and print a "Game Over" message when the counter reaches zero.

If the ball is still in play, we check for various collisions. We check if the ball has hit one or more bricks, if it has hit a wall, or if it has hit the paddle. Then we calculate the ball's new position. The collision checks look complicated, but they are fairly simple and only compare the ball's coordinates with the coordinates of all the other objects on the screen:

MotionSensor/Game/Game.pde

```
boolean ballDropped() {
  return py + vy > height - BALL_RADIUS;
}

boolean inXRange(final int row, final int v) {
  return px + v > row * BRICK_WIDTH &&
         px + v < (row + 1) * BRICK_WIDTH + BALL_DIAMETER;
}

boolean inYRange(final int col, final int v) {
  return py + v > col * BRICK_HEIGHT &&
         py + v < (col + 1) * BRICK_HEIGHT + BALL_DIAMETER;
}

void checkBrickCollision() {
  for (int x = 0; x < COLUMNS; x++) {
    for (int y = 0; y < ROWS; y++) {
      if (bricks[x][y] > 0) {
        if (inXRange(x, vx) && inYRange(y, vy)) {
          bricks[x][y] = 0;
          if (inXRange(x, 0)) // Hit top or bottom of brick.
            vy = -vy;
          if (inYRange(y, 0)) // Hit left or right side of brick.
            vx = -vx;
        }
      }
    }
  }
}

void checkWallCollision() {
  if (px + vx < BALL_RADIUS || px + vx > width - BALL_RADIUS)
    vx = -vx;

  if (py + vy < BALL_RADIUS || py + vy > height - BALL_RADIUS)
    vy = -vy;
}
```

More Fun with Motion-Sensing Technologies

Since motion-sensing technologies became popular and cheap, people have used them to create some unbelievably cool and funny projects. A hilarious example is the Brushduino.* A father built it to encourage his young children to brush their teeth properly. Its main component—apart from an Arduino— is a three-axis accelerometer. The Brushduino indicates which section of the mouth to brush next using LEDs, and whenever the child has successfully finished a section, it plays some music from the Super Mario Brothers video game.

But you do not need an accelerometer to detect motion and to create cool new electronic toys. An ordinary tilt sensor is sufficient to build an interactive hacky-sack game, for example.[†] This hacky-sack blinks and beeps whenever you kick it, and after 30 successful kicks, it plays a song.

---

[*]. http://camelpunch.blogspot.com/2010/02/blog-post.html
[†]. http://blog.makezine.com/archive/2010/03/arduino-powered_hacky-sack_game.html

```
void checkPaddleCollision() {
  final int cx = xpos;
  if (py + vy >= height - (PADDLE_HEIGHT + MARGIN + 6) &&
      px >= cx - PADDLE_WIDTH / 2 &&
      px <= cx + PADDLE_WIDTH / 2)
  {
    vy = -vy;
    vx = int(
          map(
            px - cx,
            -(PADDLE_WIDTH / 2), PADDLE_WIDTH / 2,
            -MAX_VELOCITY,
            MAX_VELOCITY
          )
        );
  }
}
```

Note that the collision checks also change the velocity of the ball if necessary.

Now that the ball is moving, it'd be only fair to move the paddle, too. As said before, you control the paddle by tilting the game controller around the x-axis. Here's the code that gets the controller data via the serial port:

MotionSensor/Game/Game.pde

```
Line 1   void serialEvent(Serial port) {
           final String arduinoData = port.readStringUntil(LINE_FEED);

           if (arduinoData != null) {
     5       final int[] data = int(split(trim(arduinoData), ' '));
             if (data.length == 4) {
               buttonPressed = (data[3] == 1);
               if (buttonPressed) {
                 paused = !paused;
    10           if (done) {
                   done = false;
                   initGame();
                 }
               }

    15
               if (!paused)
                 xpos = int(map(data[0], X_AXIS_MIN, X_AXIS_MAX, 0, WIDTH));
             }
           }
    20   }
```

Processing calls the serialEvent() function whenever new data is available on the serial port. The controller sends its data line by line. Each line contains the current acceleration of the x-, y-, and z-axes and the current state of the button. It separates all attributes by blanks. So, in serialEvent(), we read the new line, split it at the blank characters, and convert the resulting strings into int values. This all happens in line 5.

We check whether we actually got all four attributes, and then we see whether the player has pushed the button on the game controller. If yes, we toggle the pause state: if the game currently is in pause mode, we continue the game; otherwise, we pause it. Also, we check whether the game has been finished. If yes, we start a new game.

Finally, we read the current X acceleration in line 17 and map it to the possible x positions of our paddle. That's really all we have to do to move the paddle using our own game controller. Also, it doesn't matter if you use the controller to control a game or a completely different type of software. You only have to read four integer values from the serial port when you need them.

In this section, you have learned much more about game programming than about Arduino programming or hardware. But you should

> ### Creating Games with the Arduino
>
> You can use the Arduino to build more than your own cool game controllers. You can also use it to build some cool games. With the right extension shields, you can even turn an Arduino into a powerful gaming console.* It's pricey, but suddenly your Arduino has a 320x200 pixel OLED touch screen, an analog stick, two buttons, and even an vibration motor for force feedback effects.
>
> While looking for a cheaper solution, someone built a Super Mario Bros clone with minimal hardware requirements.† It's a perfect example of the unbelievable creativity that the Arduino sets free.
>
> ---
>
> *. http://antipastohw.blogspot.com/2009/02/getting-started-with-gamepack-in-3.html
> †. http://blog.makezine.com/archive/2010/03/super_mario_brothers_with_an_arduino.html

have also learned that it's easy to integrate a well-designed electronics project into your regular software projects. We carefully analyzed the analog data returned by the accelerometer, and then we eliminated all unwanted jitter. This is a technique you'll use often in your electronics projects, and we will use it again in the next chapter.

6.7 More Projects

If you keep your eyes open, you'll quickly find many more applications for accelerometers than you might imagine. Here's a small collection of both commercial and free products:

- Nike's iPod Sport Kit supports you in your daily exercise, and it's based on an accelerometer, too. You can learn a lot from its inner workings.[6]

- It's a lot of fun to create a marble maze computer game and control it using the game controller we build in this chapter. How much more fun will it be to build a real marble maze?[7]

---

6. http://www.runnerplus.com/read/1-how_does_the_nike_ipod_sport_kit_accelerometer_work/
7. http://www.electronicsinfoline.com/New/Everything_Else/marble-maze-that-is-remote-controlled-using-an-accelerometer.html

- In this chapter, we have measured only direct acceleration; that is, we usually have the accelerometer in our hand and move it. But you can also build many interesting projects that measure indirect acceleration, such as when you are driving a car.[8]

6.8 What If It Doesn't Work?

All advice from Section 5.10, *What If It Doesn't Work?*, on page 116 also applies to the project in this section. Still, we have some special items such as the protoshield. Make sure that it sits correctly on top of the Arduino and that none of its connectors accidentally slipped past its socket. Sometimes the headers are out of shape, so it might happen.

Check if you have soldered the pin header correctly to the breakout board. Use a magnifying glass and study every single solder joint carefully. Did you use enough solder? Did you use too much and connect two joints?

6.9 Exercises

- Create your own computer mouse using the ADXL335 accelerometer. It should work in free air, and it should emit the current acceleration around the x- and y-axes. It should also have a left button and a right button. Write some Processing code (or perhaps code in a programming language of your choice?) to control a mouse pointer on the screen.

---

8. http://www.dimensionengineering.com/appnotes/Gmeter/Gmeter.htm

Chapter 7

Tinkering with the Wii Nunchuk

One of the most entertaining electronic activities is tinkering: taking an existing product and turning it into something different or using it for an unintended purpose. Sometimes you have to open the product and void its warranty; other times you can safely make it part of your own project.

In this chapter, you'll learn how to hijack a Nintendo Nunchuk controller. It's a perfect candidate for tinkering: it comes with a three-axis accelerometer, an analog joystick, and two buttons, and it is very cheap (less than $20 at the time of this writing). Even better: because of its good design and its easy-to-access connectors, you can integrate it into your own projects surprisingly easily.

We'll use an ordinary Nunchuk controller and transfer the data it emits to our computer using an Arduino. You'll learn how to wire it to the Arduino; how to write software that reads the controller's current state; and how to move, rotate, and scale a 3D cube on the screen using your Nunchuk. You don't even need a Nintendo Wii to do any of this—you only need a Nunchuk controller.

7.1 What You Need

- An Arduino board such as the Uno, Duemilanove, or Diecimila

- A USB cable to connect the Arduino to your computer

- A Nintendo Nunchuk controller

- Four wires

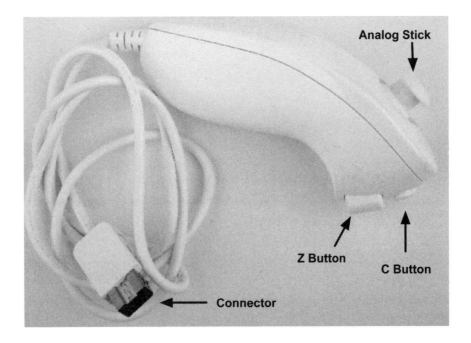

Figure 7.1: A NINTENDO NUNCHUK CONTROLLER

7.2 Wiring a Wii Nunchuk

Wiring a Nunchuk to an Arduino really is a piece of cake. You don't have to open the Nunchuk or modify it in any way. You only have to put four wires into its connector and then connect the wires to the Arduino. Here's the pinout of a Nunchuk plug:

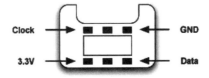

It has six connectors, but only four of them are active: GND, 3.3 V, Data, and Clock. Put a wire into each connector, and then connect the wires to the Arduino. Connect the data wire to analog pin 4 and the clock wire to analog pin 5. The GND wire has to be connected to the Arduino's ground pin and the 3.3 V wire belongs to the Arduino's 3.3 V pin.

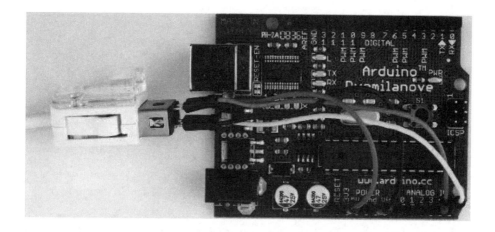

Figure 7.2: HOW TO CONNECT A NUNCHUK TO AN ARDUINO

That's really all you have to do to connect a Nunchuk controller to an Arduino. In the next section, you'll see that the two wires connected to analog pins 4 and 5 are all we need to interface with the controller.

7.3 Talking to a Nunchuk

No official documentation shows how a Nunchuk works internally or how you can use it in a non-Wii environment. But some smart hackers and makers on the Internet invested a lot of time to reverse-engineer what's happening inside the controller.[1]

All in all, it's really simple, because the Nunchuk uses the Two-Wire Interface (TWI), also known as I^2C (Inter-Integrated Circuit) protocol.[2] It enables devices to communicate via a master/slave data bus using only two wires. You transmit data on one wire (DATA), while the other synchronizes the communication (CLOCK).

The Arduino IDE comes with a library named Wire that implements the I^2C protocol. It expects the data line to be connected to analog pin 4 and the clock line to analog pin 5. We'll use it shortly to communicate with the Nunchuk, but before that, we'll have a look at the commands the controller understands.[3]

---

1. http://www.windmeadow.com/node/42
2. http://en.wikipedia.org/wiki/I2c
3. At http://todbot.com/blog/2010/09/25/softi2cmaster-add-i2c-to-any-arduino-pins/, you can find a library that allows you to use any pair of pins for I^2C communication.

Improve People's Life with Tinkering

Because of its popularity, peripheral equipment for modern game consoles often is unbelievably cheap. Also, it's no longer limited to classic controllers; you can buy things like snowboard simulators or cameras. So, it comes as no surprise that creative people have built many interesting projects using hardware that was originally built for playing games.

An impressive and useful tinkering project is the Eyewriter.* It uses the PlayStation Eye (a camera for Sony's PlayStation 3) to track the movement of human eyes.

A team of hackers built it to enable their paralyzed friend to draw graffiti using his eyes. Because of a disease, this friend, an artist, is almost completely physically paralyzed and can only move his eyes. With the Eyewriter, he is able to create amazing artwork again.

It's not an Arduino project but definitely worth a look.

*. http://www.eyewriter.org/

To be honest, the Nunchuk understands only a single command: "Give me all your data." Whenever it receives this command, it returns six bytes that have the following meaning (see the data structure in Figure 7.3, on the facing page):

- Byte 1 contains the analog stick's x-axis value, and in byte 2 you'll find the stick's y-axis value. Both are 8-bit numbers and range from about 29 to 225.

- Acceleration values for the x-, y-, and z-axes are three 10-bit numbers. Bytes 3, 4, and 5 contain their eight most significant bits. You can find the missing two bits for each of them in byte 6.

- Byte 6 has to be interpreted bit-wise. Bit 0 (the least significant bit) contains the status of the Z-button. It's 0 if the button was pressed; otherwise, it is 1. Bit 1 contains the C-button's status.

  The remaining six bits contain the missing least significant bits of the acceleration values. Bits 2 and 3 belong to the X axis, bits 4 and 5 belong to Y, and bits 6 and 7 belong to Z.

Now that we know how to interpret the data we get from the Nunchuk, we can start to build a Nunchuk class to control it.

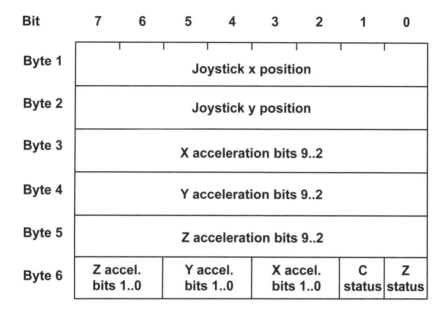

Figure 7.3: THE NUNCHUK ALWAYS RETURNS 6 BYTES OF DATA.

Scientific Applications Using Wii Equipment

Because of the Wii's accuracy and cheap price, many scientists use Wii equipment for other things than gaming. Some hydrologists use it for measuring evaporation on a body of water.* Usually, you'd need equipment costing more than $500 to do that.

Some doctors at the University of Melbourne had a closer look at the Wii Balance Board, because they were looking for a cheap device to help stroke victims recover.[†] They've published a scientific paper verifying that the board's data is clinically comparable to that of a lab-grade "force platform" for a tiny fraction of the costs.

*. http://www.wired.com/wiredscience/2009/12/wiimote-science/
†. http://www.newscientist.com/article/mg20527435.300-wii-board-helps-physios-strike-a-balance-after-strokes.html

7.4 Building a Nunchuk Class

The interface of our Nunchuk class (and the main part of its implementation) looks as follows:

MotionSensor/NunchukDemo/nunchuk.h

```
Line 1   #ifndef __NUNCHUK_H__
    -    #define __NUNCHUK_H__
    -
    -    #define NUNCHUK_BUFFER_SIZE 6
    5
    -    class Nunchuk {
    -    public:
    -      void initialize();
    -      bool update();
   10
    -      int joystick_x() const { return _buffer[0]; }
    -      int joystick_y() const { return _buffer[1]; }
    -
    -      int x_acceleration() const {
   15        return ((int)(_buffer[2]) << 2) | ((_buffer[5] >> 2) & 0x03);
    -      }
    -
    -      int y_acceleration() const {
    -        return ((int)(_buffer[3]) << 2) | ((_buffer[5] >> 4) & 0x03);
   20      }
    -
    -      int z_acceleration() const {
    -        return ((int)(_buffer[4]) << 2) | ((_buffer[5] >> 6) & 0x03);
    -      }
   25
    -      bool z_button() const { return !(_buffer[5] & 0x01); }
    -      bool c_button() const { return !(_buffer[5] & 0x02); }
    -
    -    private:
   30      void request_data();
    -      char decode_byte(const char);
    -
    -      unsigned char _buffer[NUNCHUK_BUFFER_SIZE];
    -    };
   35
    -    #endif
```

This small C++ class is all you need to use a Nunchuk controller with your Arduino. It starts with a double-include prevention mechanism: it checks whether a preprocessor macro named __NUNCHUK_H__ has been defined already using #ifndef. If it hasn't been defined, we define it and continue with the declaration of the Nunchuk class. Otherwise, the preprocessor skips the declaration, so you can safely include this header file more than once in your application.

In line 4, we create a constant for the size of the array we need to store the data the Nunchuk returns. We define this array in line 33, and in this case, we define the constant using the preprocessor instead of the **const** keyword, because array constants must be known at compile time in C++.

Then the actual declaration of the Nunchuk class begins. To initiate the communication channel between Arduino and Nunchuk, you have to invoke the initialize() method once. Then you call update() whenever you want the Nunchuk to send new data. You'll see the implementation of these two methods shortly.

We have public methods for getting all attributes the Nunchuk returns: the x and y positions of the analog stick, the button states, and the acceleration values of the x-, y-, and z-axes. All these methods operate on the raw data you can find in the buffer in line 33. Their implementation is mostly trivial and requires only a single line of code. Only the assembly of the 10-bit acceleration values needs some tricky bit operations (see Section B.2, *Bit Operations*, on page 237).

At the end of the class declaration you find two private helper methods we need to implement: initialize() and update():

MotionSensor/NunchukDemo/nunchuk.cpp

```
Line 1   #include <WProgram.h>
   -     #include <Wire.h>
   -     #include "nunchuk.h"

   5     #define NUNCHUK_DEVICE_ID 0x52
   -
   -     void Nunchuk::initialize() {
   -       Wire.begin();
   -       Wire.beginTransmission(NUNCHUK_DEVICE_ID);
  10       Wire.send(0x40);
   -       Wire.send(0x00);
   -       Wire.endTransmission();
   -       update();
   -     }
  15
   -     bool Nunchuk::update() {
   -       delay(1);
   -       Wire.requestFrom(NUNCHUK_DEVICE_ID, NUNCHUK_BUFFER_SIZE);
   -       int byte_counter = 0;
  20       while (Wire.available() && byte_counter < NUNCHUK_BUFFER_SIZE)
   -         _buffer[byte_counter++] = decode_byte(Wire.receive());
   -       request_data();
   -       return byte_counter == NUNCHUK_BUFFER_SIZE;
   -     }
```

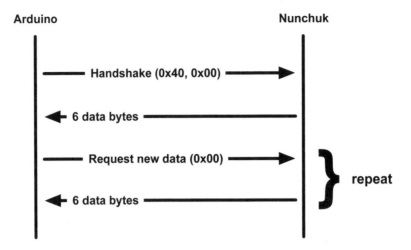

Figure 7.4: Message flow between Arduino and Nunchuk

```
25
     void Nunchuk::request_data() {
       Wire.beginTransmission(NUNCHUK_DEVICE_ID);
       Wire.send(0x00);
       Wire.endTransmission();
30   }

     char Nunchuk::decode_byte(const char b) {
       return (b ^ 0x17) + 0x17;
     }
```

After including all libraries we need, we define the NUNCHUK_DEVICE_ID
constant. I^2C is a master/slave protocol; in our case, the Arduino will
be the master, and the Nunchuk will be the slave. The Nunchuk regis-
ters itself at the data bus using a certain ID (0x52), so we can address
it whenever we need something.

In initialize(), we establish the connection between the Arduino and the
Nunchuk by sending a handshake. In line 8, we call Wire's begin()
method, so the Arduino joins the I^2C bus as a master (if you pass
begin() an ID, it joins the bus as a slave having this ID). Then we begin
a new transmission to the device identified by NUNCHUCK_DEVICE_ID: our
Nunchuk.

We send two bytes (0x40 and 0x00) to the Nunchuk, and then we end the transmission. This is the whole handshake procedure, and now we can ask the Nunchuk for its current status by calling update(). In Figure 7.4, on the facing page, we see the message flow between an Arduino and a Nunchuk.

update() first pauses for a millisecond to let things settle a bit. Then we request six bytes from the Nunchuk, calling Wire.requestFrom(). This does not actually return the bytes, but we have to read them in a loop and fill our buffer. Wire.available() returns the number of bytes that are available on the data bus, and Wire.receive() returns the current byte. We cannot use the bytes we get from the Nunchuk directly, because the controller obfuscates them a bit. "Decrypting" them is easy as you can see in decode_byte().

Finally, we call request_data() to tell the Nunchuk to prepare new data. It transmits a single zero byte to the Nunchuk, which means "prepare the next six bytes."

Before we actually use our Nunchuk class in the next section, take a look at the documentation of the Wire library. In the Arduino IDE's menu, choose Help > Reference, and click the Libraries link.

7.5 Using Our Nunchuk Class

Let's use the Nunchuk class to see what data the controller actually returns:

MotionSensor/NunchukDemo/NunchukDemo.pde

```
#include <Wire.h>
#include "nunchuk.h"

const unsigned int BAUD_RATE = 19200;

Nunchuk nunchuk;

void setup() {
  Serial.begin(BAUD_RATE);
  nunchuk.initialize();
}

void loop() {
  if (nunchuk.update()) {
    Serial.print(nunchuk.joystick_x());
    Serial.print(" ");
    Serial.print(nunchuk.joystick_y());
```

```
        Serial.print(" ");
        Serial.print(nunchuk.x_acceleration());
        Serial.print(" ");
        Serial.print(nunchuk.y_acceleration());
        Serial.print(" ");
        Serial.print(nunchuk.z_acceleration());
        Serial.print(" ");
        Serial.print(nunchuk.z_button());
        Serial.print(" ");
        Serial.println(nunchuk.c_button());
    }
}
```

No big surprises here: we define a global Nunchuk object and initialize it in the setup() function. In loop(), we call update() to request the controller's current status and output all attributes to the serial port.

Compile and upload the program, and then open the serial monitor and play around with the Nunchuk. Move the stick, move the controller, and press the buttons, and you should see something like this:

```
46 109 428 394 651 1 1
49 132 414 380 656 1 0
46 161 415 390 651 1 0
46 184 429 377 648 1 0
53 199 404 337 654 1 0
53 201 406 359 643 1 0
```

You have successfully connected a Nunchuk controller to your Arduino. It really isn't rocket science, and in the next section you'll learn how to control objects on the screen using the Nunchuk.

7.6 Rotating a Colorful Cube

The Nunchuk was primarily designed for controlling video games by turning physical movements in the real world into virtual movements on a computer screen. So, in this section, we'll do exactly that and manipulate a 3D cube on the screen with a Nunchuk (see a screenshot in Figure 7.5, on the next page).

Before we start to draw the cube and use the controller, we have to talk about an aspect we have ignored until now: jitter. Like the game controller we built in Chapter 6, *Building a Motion-Sensing Game Controller*, on page 117, the Nunchuk acceleration data has to be stabilized. We use the same technique as in Section 6.4, *Finding and Polishing Edge Values*, on page 122, but this time we'll implement it in our Processing code instead of on the Arduino:

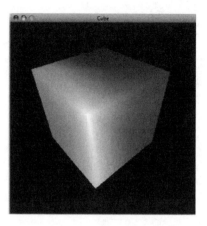

Figure 7.5: CONTROLLING A ROTATING CUBE WITH A NUNCHUK

MotionSensor/Cube/SensorDataBuffer.pde

```
Line 1   class SensorDataBuffer {
           private int _maxSamples;
           private int _bufferIndex;
           private int[] _xBuffer;
    5      private int[] _yBuffer;
           private int[] _zBuffer;

           public SensorDataBuffer(final int maxSamples) {
             _maxSamples = maxSamples;
   10        _bufferIndex = 0;
             _xBuffer = new int[_maxSamples];
             _yBuffer = new int[_maxSamples];
             _zBuffer = new int[_maxSamples];
           }
   15
           public void addData(final int x, final int y, final int z) {
             if (_bufferIndex >= _maxSamples)
               _bufferIndex = 0;

   20        _xBuffer[_bufferIndex] = x;
             _yBuffer[_bufferIndex] = y;
             _zBuffer[_bufferIndex] = z;
             _bufferIndex++;
           }
   25
           public int getX() {
             return getAverageValue(_xBuffer);
           }
```

```
30    public int getY() {
        return getAverageValue(_yBuffer);
      }

      public int getZ() {
35      return getAverageValue(_zBuffer);
      }

      private int getAverageValue(final int[] buffer) {
        int sum = 0;
40      for (int i = 0; i < _maxSamples; i++)
          sum += buffer[i];
        return (int)(sum / _maxSamples);
      }
    }
```

SensorDataBuffer encapsulates three buffers for the acceleration data of the x-, y-, and z-axes. It also stores a buffer index that contains the current position in the three buffers. The constructor beginning in line 8 expects the maximum number of samples (the buffer size) and initializes the buffers and the index.

The addData() method takes new values for all three space axes and appends them to their corresponding buffers. If the buffer runs full, the oldest buffer entries will be dropped. With getX(), getY(), and getZ(), you can request the current average acceleration value for each axis. All three methods delegate their work to the getAverageValue() method.

So, now let's start and work toward drawing a 3D cube. First we initialize all things related to the serial communication with the Arduino controlling the Nunchuk:

MotionSensor/Cube/Cube.pde

```
import processing.serial.*;

final int LINE_FEED = 10;
final int MAX_SAMPLES = 16;

Serial arduinoPort;
SensorDataBuffer sensorData = new SensorDataBuffer(MAX_SAMPLES);
```

As usual, we import the libraries for serial communication and initialize a global Serial object, and this time we also create a SensorDataBuffer object.

Now we need some constants for the screen dimensions, the Nunchuk data ranges, and for our 3D calculations:

MotionSensor/Cube/Cube.pde

```
final int WIDTH = 500;
final int HEIGHT = 500;
final int BAUD_RATE = 19200;
final int X_AXIS_MIN = 300;
final int X_AXIS_MAX = 700;
final int Y_AXIS_MIN = 300;
final int Y_AXIS_MAX = 700;
final int Z_AXIS_MIN = 300;
final int Z_AXIS_MAX = 700;
final int MIN_SCALE = 5;
final int MAX_SCALE = 128;
final float MX = 2.0 / (X_AXIS_MAX - X_AXIS_MIN);
final float MY = 2.0 / (Y_AXIS_MAX - Y_AXIS_MIN);
final float MZ = 2.0 / (Z_AXIS_MAX - Z_AXIS_MIN);
final float BX = 1.0 - MX * X_AXIS_MAX;
final float BY = 1.0 - MY * Y_AXIS_MAX;
final float BZ = 1.0 - MZ * Z_AXIS_MAX;
```

X_AXIS_MIN and X_AXIS_MAX define the minimum and maximum acceleration values returned by the Nunchuk for the x-axis. The same is true for Y_AXIS_MIN, and so on. We'll need the remaining constants (MX, BX, and so on) to turn acceleration values into angles later, so don't worry too much about them.

Next we need some variables to store the cube's current state: its position, the rotation angle for the different axes, and its current scaling:

MotionSensor/Cube/Cube.pde

```
int xpos = WIDTH / 2;
int ypos = HEIGHT / 2;
int scale = 90;

float xrotate = 0.0;
float yrotate = 0.0;
float zrotate = 0.0;
```

In the setup() method, we initialize the screen and the serial port:

MotionSensor/Cube/Cube.pde

```
Line 1  void setup() {
2         size(WIDTH, HEIGHT, P3D);
3         noStroke();
4         colorMode(RGB, 1);
5         background(0);
6         println(Serial.list());
7         arduinoPort = new Serial(this, Serial.list()[0], BAUD_RATE);
8         arduinoPort.bufferUntil(LINE_FEED);
9       }
```

The only thing worth mentioning is the call to colorMode() in line 4. It determines that we specify colors as RGB values in the range from 0 to 1. This helps us make the cube very colorful (the 3D drawing portion of this code was derived from one of Processing's standard examples).

You can draw the cube with Processing as follows:

MotionSensor/Cube/Cube.pde

```
void draw() {
  background(0);
  pushMatrix();

  translate(xpos, ypos, -30);
  rotateX(yrotate);
  rotateY(xrotate);
  rotateZ(zrotate);
  scale(scale);

  beginShape(QUADS);
  fill(0, 1, 1); vertex(-1,  1,  1);
  fill(1, 1, 1); vertex( 1,  1,  1);
  fill(1, 0, 1); vertex( 1, -1,  1);
  fill(0, 0, 1); vertex(-1, -1,  1);

  fill(1, 1, 1); vertex( 1,  1,  1);
  fill(1, 1, 0); vertex( 1,  1, -1);
  fill(1, 0, 0); vertex( 1, -1, -1);
  fill(1, 0, 1); vertex( 1, -1,  1);

  fill(1, 1, 0); vertex( 1,  1, -1);
  fill(0, 1, 0); vertex(-1,  1, -1);
  fill(0, 0, 0); vertex(-1, -1, -1);
  fill(1, 0, 0); vertex( 1, -1, -1);

  fill(0, 1, 0); vertex(-1,  1, -1);
  fill(0, 1, 1); vertex(-1,  1,  1);
  fill(0, 0, 1); vertex(-1, -1,  1);
  fill(0, 0, 0); vertex(-1, -1, -1);

  fill(0, 1, 0); vertex(-1,  1, -1);
  fill(1, 1, 0); vertex( 1,  1, -1);
  fill(1, 1, 1); vertex( 1,  1,  1);
  fill(0, 1, 1); vertex(-1,  1,  1);

  fill(0, 0, 0); vertex(-1, -1, -1);
  fill(1, 0, 0); vertex( 1, -1, -1);
  fill(1, 0, 1); vertex( 1, -1,  1);
  fill(0, 0, 1); vertex(-1, -1,  1);
  endShape();

  popMatrix();
}
```

draw() defines and fills the six surfaces of the cube using fill() and vertex(). We define the vertices using base coordinates because we're scaling the cube to a reasonable size in line 9 anyway. Moving and rotating the cube happens in lines 5 to 8.

Because Processing's draw() method resets all matrix manipulations performed by translate() and the rotate methods, we use pushMatrix() and popMatrix() to store and restore them.

Finally, we have to take the Nunchuk data and turn it into suitable arguments for our vector manipulation functions:

MotionSensor/Cube/Cube.pde

```
Line 1  void serialEvent(Serial port) {
          final String arduinoData = port.readStringUntil(LINE_FEED);

          if (arduinoData != null) {
    5       final int[] data = int(split(trim(arduinoData), ' '));
            if (data.length == 7) {
              xpos = int(map(data[0], 0x1e, 0xe1, 0, WIDTH));
              ypos = int(map(data[1], 0x1d, 0xdf, HEIGHT, 0));

   10         if (data[5] == 1) scale++;
              if (data[6] == 1) scale--;
              if (scale < MIN_SCALE) scale = MIN_SCALE;
              if (scale > MAX_SCALE) scale = MAX_SCALE;

   15         sensorData.addData(data[2], data[3], data[4]);

              final float gx = MX * sensorData.getX() + BX;
              final float gy = MY * sensorData.getY() + BY;
              final float gz = MZ * sensorData.getZ() + BZ;
   20
              xrotate = atan2(gx, sqrt(gy * gy + gz * gz));
              yrotate = atan2(gy, sqrt(gx * gx + gz * gz));
              zrotate = atan2(sqrt(gx * gx + gy * gy), gz);
            }
   25     }
        }
```

Reading, splitting, and converting the data we read from the serial port is business as usual. The interesting part starts in line 7 where we map the analog stick's x position to a new x coordinate for our cube. In the following line, we do the same for the y coordinate.

We handle the state of the Nunchuk buttons in lines 10 to 13. If you press the Z-button, the cube will grow. Press the C-button to shrink it.

The rest of the serialEvent() method turns the controller's acceleration values into angles. I won't explain the underlying math in detail—it's rather complicated and pretty much unrelated to our main topic.

Start the program and play around with the cube. Isn't it great how easy it is? We only needed four wires and a small piece of software, and now we can use the superb but cheap Nunchuk hardware for our own projects, both software and hardware. We could use it to control a robot; some people even use it to make music.[4]

The next time you buy a new piece of hardware, try to imagine how to use it in a different context. Often it's easier than you think. Oh, and whenever you create a class such as our Nunchuk class, consider turning your code into a library and making it available on the Internet (see Chapter 4, *Building a Morse Code Generator Library*, on page 71 to learn how to create your own libraries).

7.7 What If It Doesn't Work?

From a maker's perspective, this project is an easy one. Still, things can go wrong, especially with the wiring. Make sure you have connected the right pins on the Arduino and on the Nunchuk. Also check that the wires tightly fit into the Nunchuk's and the Arduino's sockets. When in doubt, use wire with a larger diameter.

7.8 Exercises

- Rewrite the game we implemented in Section 6.6, *Writing Your Own Game*, on page 129, so it supports the Nunchuk controller. It should support both the analog stick and the accelerometer. Perhaps you can switch between them using the Nunchuk buttons?

- Tinkering with Nintendo's WiiMotion is a bit more complicated.[5] But it's a nice and cheap way to sharpen your tinkering skills.

---

4. http://www.youtube.com/watch?v=J4GPS83Rm6M
5. http://randomhacksofboredom.blogspot.com/2009/07/motion-plus-and-nunchuck-together-on.html

Chapter 8

Networking with Arduino

With a stand-alone Arduino, you can create countless fun and useful projects. But as soon as you turn the Arduino into a networking device, you open up a whole new world of possibilities.

You now have access to all information on the Internet, so you could turn your Arduino into a nice geeky weather station simply by reading data from a weather service. You can also turn the Arduino into a web server that provides sensor data for other devices or computers on your network.

We will build an emailing burglar alarm in this chapter. It detects motion in your living room, and the Arduino will send you an email whenever it detects movement during your absence. Because this is a somewhat advanced project, we'll first work on some smaller projects to learn all techniques and skills needed.

We'll start with a "naked" Arduino that doesn't have any network capabilities. You can still attach it to the Internet, as long as you connect it to a PC.

For our second project, we'll improve the situation dramatically with an Ethernet shield. Now your Arduino becomes a full-blown network device that can directly access IP services such as a DAYTIME service. This will turn your Arduino into a very accurate clock.

Once we are able to access IP services, we'll then learn how to send emails directly from an Arduino with an Ethernet shield. For our burglar alarm, we then only need to know how to detect motion. We'll use a passive infrared sensor (PIR) for this purpose, so in this chapter, you'll

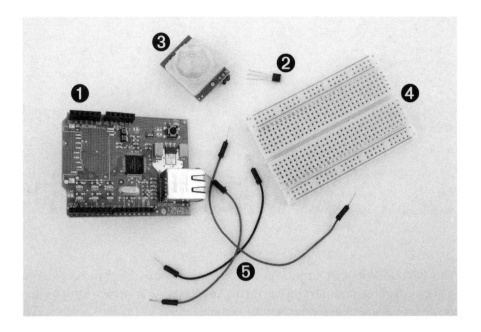

Figure 8.1: ALL THE PARTS YOU NEED IN THIS CHAPTER

learn not only various networking technologies but also how to use PIR sensors.

Finally, we'll combine all the things we learned and build the emailing burglar alarm. You'll feel much safer as soon as it's running.

8.1 What You Need

1. An Ethernet shield for the Arduino

2. An TMP36 temperature sensor

3. A PIR infrared motion sensor

4. A breadboard

5. Some wires

6. An Arduino board such as the Uno, Duemilanove, or Diecimila

7. A USB cable to connect the Arduino to your computer

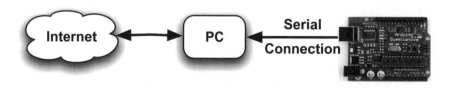

Figure 8.2: CONNECT YOUR ARDUINO TO THE INTERNET USING YOUR PC.

8.2 Using Your PC to Transfer Sensor Data to the Internet

Remember when you connected your PC to the Internet, oh, around fifteen years ago? It all started with a 38,400 baud modem, Netscape Navigator 3, and one of those AOL floppy disks or CD-ROMs you got in the mail. Today you probably have broadband access via cable, satellite, or DSL, and it's probably available everywhere in your house via WiFi. So, we'll start by using your existing connection to connect your Arduino to the Internet.

In Figure 8.2, you can see a typical setup for connecting an Arduino to the Internet. A program runs on your PC and communicates with the Arduino using the serial port. Whenever the application needs Internet access, the program on the PC deals with it. Using this architecture, you can tweet[1] interesting sensor data.

We'll build a system that tweets a message as soon as the temperature in your working room or office exceeds a certain threshold, that is, 32 degrees Celsius (90 degrees Fahrenheit). Build the temperature sensor example from Section 5.4, *Increasing Precision Using a Temperature Sensor*, on page 98 again (try to do it without looking at Figure 5.6, on page 99), and upload the following sketch to your Arduino:

Ethernet/TwitterTemperature/TwitterTemperature.pde

```
Line 1   #define CELSIUS

    -    const unsigned int TEMP_SENSOR_PIN = 0;
    -    const unsigned int BAUD_RATE = 9600;
    5    const float SUPPLY_VOLTAGE = 5.0;
```

---

1. http://twitter.com

```
       void setup() {
         Serial.begin(BAUD_RATE);
       }
10
       void loop() {
         const int sensor_voltage = analogRead(TEMP_SENSOR_PIN);
         const float voltage = sensor_voltage * SUPPLY_VOLTAGE / 1024;
         const float celsius = (voltage * 1000 - 500) / 10;
15  #ifdef CELSIUS
         Serial.print(celsius);
         Serial.println(" C");
     #else
         Serial.print(9.0 / 5.0 * celsius + 32.0);
20       Serial.println(" F");
     #endif
         delay(5000);
       }
```

This is nearly the same sketch we have used before. Keep in mind that you have to set SUPPLY_VOLTAGE to 3.3 in line 5, if you're using an Arduino that runs with 3.3V instead of 5V.

We support both Celsius and Fahrenheit values now, and you can control which unit should be used with a preprocessor constant. If you set the constant CELSIUS in the first line, the application outputs the temperature in degree Celsius. If you remove the first line or turn it into a comment line, Fahrenheit will be used.

To change the application's behavior, we use the **#ifdef** preprocessor directive. It checks whether a certain preprocessor constant has been set, and then it compiles code conditionally. In our case, it will compile the Celsius-to-Fahrenheit formula in line 19 only if the constant CELSIUS has not been set.

Upload the sketch, and it will output the current temperature to the serial port every five seconds. Its output looks as follows:

```
27.15 C
26.66 C
27.15 C
```

What we need now is a program running on your PC that reads this output and tweets a message as soon as the temperature is greater than 32 degrees Celsius (90 degrees Fahrenheit). We could use any programming language that is capable of reading from a serial port and that supports Twitter, but because we have used Processing in all other examples, we'll use it for this project as well.

Web Services for Publishing Sensor Data

With the advent of cheap open source hardware and sensors, web services for publishing sensor data have become popular over the past few years. Such services allow you to publish, read, and analyze sensor data. People from all over the world publish data from their weather stations, environmental sensors, and so on, and make it available for free on the Internet.

The most popular services are Pachube* and Sensorpedia.[†] In principle, they all work the same: you register an account, and you get back an API key. Then you can use this key to authenticate against the service and upload sensor data.

---

*. http://pachube.com
†. http://sensorpedia.com/

8.3 Registering an Application with Twitter

Before we start coding, we have to register our application at the Twitter website to get an OAuth access token.[2] OAuth is an authentication scheme that allows applications to use other applications' resources. In our case, we'll grant our very own application the right to update our Twitter feed without using our Twitter username and password.

For a long time, Twitter supported HTTP Basic Authentication.[3] Automatic services only needed a username and password to request or update Twitter feeds. But as of August 2010, Twitter has removed support for Basic Authentication and now uses OAuth.

To get the OAuth access token, register your new application in the developer section of the Twitter website.[4] After you've logged in, click the "Register an app" link, and fill out the form you see in Figure 8.3, on the next page. Make sure you set the application type to Client and the default access type to Read & Write. You can set the application name to an arbitrary string, and it will appear on your Twitter channel whenever you use the application to tweet messages. If you set it to RescueMeFromWork, for example, your tweets will be published via RescueMeFromWork.

---

2. http://en.wikipedia.org/wiki/Oauth
3. http://en.wikipedia.org/wiki/Basic_authentication
4. http://dev.twitter.com

Figure 8.3: REGISTER YOUR NEW TWITTER CLIENT APP FIRST.

After you've registered your new application successfully, go to the application's settings page to see your consumer key and consumer secret (see Figure 8.4, on the facing page). You need them together with your OAuth token and your OAuth token secret to allow your application to modify your Twitter status. To see the OAuth token and secret, follow the My Access Token link.

Copy the consumer key, the consumer secret, the access token, and the access token secret. You'll need them in the next section when we tweet messages using Processing.

8.4 Tweeting Messages with Processing

Processing doesn't have Twitter support, but in Processing programs, we have direct access to Java libraries, and you can find several good

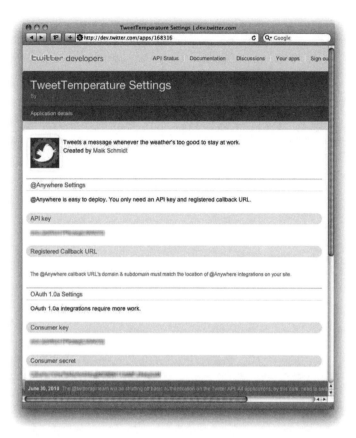

Figure 8.4: CONSUMER CREDENTIALS ARE ON THE SETTINGS PAGE.

Twitter libraries for Java. One of them is twitter4j.[5] We'll use it because it's very mature and has excellent OAuth support.

Download it from its website,[6] and unpack it to a temporary folder. Depending on the version you've downloaded, you'll find a file named twitter4j-core-x.y.z.jar or twitter4j-core-x.y.z-SNAPSHOT.jar in the folder. Open the Processing IDE, create a new sketch, and then drag and drop the .jar file to the IDE (the .jar file will automatically be copied to a local folder named code). That's all you have to do to give your application access to the twitter4j library.

---

5. http://twitter4j.org/
6. http://twitter4j.org/en/index.html#download

We proceed with some boilerplate code:

```
import processing.serial.*;

final float  MAX_WORKING_TEMP = 32.0;
final int    LINE_FEED = 10;
final int    BAUD_RATE = 9600;
final String CONSUMER_KEY = "<YOUR CONSUMER KEY>";
final String CONSUMER_SECRET = "<YOUR CONSUMER SECRET>";
final String ACCESS_TOKEN = "<YOUR ACCESS TOKEN>";
final String ACCESS_TOKEN_SECRET = "<YOUR ACCESS TOKEN SECRET>";

Serial arduinoPort;

void setup() {
  println(Serial.list());
  arduinoPort = new Serial(this, Serial.list()[0], BAUD_RATE);
  arduinoPort.bufferUntil(LINE_FEED);
}


void draw() {}
```

As usual, we import the serial libraries for communicating with the Arduino, and then we define some constants we'll need later. Most of them contain the credentials we need to access the Twitter service. With MAX_WORKING_TEMP, you can define at which temperature the application starts to tweet. This can be a degree Celsius or Fahrenheit value.

In the setup() method, we print out a list of all serial devices available, and we initialize our serialPort variable with the first one we find, hoping that it's the Arduino. You could loop through the list automatically and search for something that looks like an Arduino port name, but that'd be fragile, too. We don't need any graphical output for our application, so the draw() method remains empty.

Now let's implement the actual business logic of our "Take me to the beach" alarm:

```
void serialEvent(Serial port) {
  final String arduinoData = port.readStringUntil(LINE_FEED);

  if (arduinoData != null) {
    final String[] data = split(trim(arduinoData), ' ');
    if (data.length == 2 &&
        (data[1].equals("C") || data[1].equals("F")))
    {
      float temperature = float(data[0]);
```

```
      println(temperature);
      int sleepTime = 5 * 60 * 1000;
      if (temperature > MAX_WORKING_TEMP) {
        tweetAlarm();
        sleepTime = 120 * 60 * 1000;
      }
      try {
        Thread.sleep(sleepTime);
      }
      catch(InterruptedException ignoreMe) {}
    }
  }
}

void tweetAlarm() {
  TwitterFactory factory = new TwitterFactory();
  Twitter twitter = factory.getInstance();
  twitter.setOAuthConsumer(CONSUMER_KEY, CONSUMER_SECRET);
  AccessToken accessToken = new AccessToken(
    ACCESS_TOKEN,
    ACCESS_TOKEN_SECRET
  );
  twitter.setOAuthAccessToken(accessToken);
  try {
    Status status = twitter.updateStatus(
      "Someone, please, take me to the beach!"
    );
    println(
      "Successfully updated status to '" + status.getText() + "'."
    );
  }
  catch (TwitterException e) {
    e.printStackTrace();
  }
}
```

In Section 5.8, *Implementing Serial Communication in Processing*, on page 111, you learned how to implement serial communication in Processing. Whenever new data arrives on the serial port, the runtime environment calls the serialEvent() method. There we try to read a line of text, and then we check whether it contains a decimal number followed by a blank and a *C* or *F* character. This makes sure we've read an actual temperature data set and not some digital garbage.

If we got a syntactically correct temperature data set, we convert it into a float object and check to see if it's greater than MAX_WORKING_TEMP (no one should be forced to work at temperatures that high!). If yes, we call tweetAlarm() and tweet a message to encourage some followers to rescue us. Then we wait for two hours until our next check. Otherwise, we wait five minutes and check the temperature again.

Figure 8.5: I HOPE SOMEONE SEES YOUR CRY FOR HELP.

tweetAlarm() updates our Twitter channel and is simple. In good old Java tradition, we create a new Twitter instance using a TwitterFactory and set our consumer credentials by calling setOAuthConsumer(). Then we set the OAuth credentials calling setOAuthAccessToken(). Finally, we invoke updateStatus(). If everything went fine, we print a success message to the console. If anything goes wrong, updateStatus() will raise an exception, and we print its stack trace for debugging purposes.

That's all the code we need, so connect your Arduino to your PC and run it! In Figure 8.5, you can see what happens on Twitter when the temperature in my working room is greater than 32 degrees Celsius (for your first tests you might have to change 32.0 to a smaller value. If you don't have to change it, why aren't you at the beach?).

Using a full-blown PC as an Internet relay for your Arduino is convenient, but it's also overkill for most applications. In the next section, you'll learn how to turn an Arduino into a real networking device.

8.5 Communicating Over Networks Using an Ethernet Shield

In the previous section, you learned how to build network applications with an Arduino by using your PC's network connection. This approach works nicely, but it also has a few disadvantages. The biggest problem is

Tweeting Arduinos

One of the most popular hardware kits available is the *Botanicall*.* It checks whether your plants need water, and if they do, it sends a reminder message via http://twitter.com/. As soon as you water it, it dutifully sends a "Thank You" message. Although the official version of the Botanicall is a specialized piece of hardware, you can build it using an Arduino.†

Botanicalls certainly make your life a bit easier. Whether the *Twitwee Clock*‡ improves your life is a matter of taste. This modified cuckoo clock looks for Twitter updates using a wireless Internet connection. Whenever it finds a programmable search term, it displays the corresponding tweets on a display and also pops out a cuckoo making some noise. You'd better ask your family up front before you build this project and install it in your living room.

*. http://www.botanicalls.com/
†. http://www.botanicalls.com/archived_kits/twitter/
‡. http://www.haroonbaig.com/projects/TwitweeClock/

that you need a complete PC, while for many applications the Arduino's hardware capabilities would be sufficient. In this section, you'll learn how to solve this problem with an Ethernet shield.

You can't connect a naked Arduino to a network. Not only are its hardware capabilities too limited, it also doesn't have an Ethernet port. That means you can't plug an Ethernet cable into it, and to overcome this limitation, you have to use an Ethernet shield. Such shields come with an Ethernet chip and Ethernet connectors and turn your Arduino into a networking device immediately. You only have to plug it in.

You can choose from several products; they all are good and serve their purpose well.[7] For prototyping I prefer the "official" shield,[8] because it comes with sockets for all pins (it's on the left side in Figure 8.6, on the next page). Also at the time of this writing the Arduino team announced the Arduino Ethernet, an Arduino board that comes with an Ethernet port and does not need a separate shield.

---

7. See http://www.ladyada.net/make/eshield/, for example.
8. http://www.arduino.cc/en/Main/ArduinoEthernetShield

Figure 8.6: TWO ETHERNET SHIELDS FOR THE ARDUINO

Hardware is only one aspect of turning an Arduino into a network device. We also need some software for network communication. The Arduino IDE comes with a convenient Ethernet library that contains a few classes related to networking. We will use it now to access a DAYTIME service on the Internet.

A DAYTIME service[9] returns the current date and time as an ASCII string. DAYTIME servers listen on either TCP or UDP port 13. You can find many DAYTIME services on the Internet; one of them runs at *time.nist.gov*. Before we use the service programmatically with an Arduino, see how it works using the telnet command:

```
maik> telnet time.nist.gov 13
Trying 192.43.244.18...
Connected to time.nist.gov.
Escape character is '^]'.
55480 10-10-11 13:25:35 28 0 0 138.5 UTC(NIST) *
Connection closed by foreign host.
```

---

9. http://en.wikipedia.org/wiki/DAYTIME

As soon as the telnet command connects to the DAYTIME server, it sends back the current time and date.[10] Then the service closes the connection immediately.

Here's an implementation of exactly the same behavior for an Arduino with an Ethernet shield:

`Ethernet/TimeServer/TimeServer.pde`

```
Line 1   #include <SPI.h>
    -    #include <Ethernet.h>
    -
    -    const unsigned int DAYTIME_PORT = 13;
    5    const unsigned int BAUD_RATE = 9600;
    -
    -    byte mac[]        = { 0xDE, 0xAD, 0xBE, 0xEF, 0xFE, 0xED };
    -    byte my_ip[]      = { 192, 168, 2, 120 };
    -    byte time_server[] = { 192, 43, 244, 18 }; // time.nist.gov
    10
    -    Client client(time_server, DAYTIME_PORT);
    -
    -    void setup() {
    -      Ethernet.begin(mac, my_ip);
    15     Serial.begin(BAUD_RATE);
    -    }
    -
    -    void loop() {
    -      delay(1000);
    20     Serial.print("Connecting...");
    -
    -      if (!client.connect()) {
    -        Serial.println("connection failed.");
    -      } else {
    25       Serial.println("connected.");
    -        delay(1000);
    -
    -        while (client.available()) {
    -          char c = client.read();
    30         Serial.print(c);
    -        }
    -
    -        Serial.println("Disconnecting.");
    -        client.stop();
    35     }
    -    }
```

---

10. See http://www.nist.gov/physlab/div847/grp40/its.cfm for a detailed description of the date string's format.

First, we include the Ethernet library and define a constant for the DAYTIME service port (we also have to include the SPI library, because the Ethernet library depends on it). Then we define three byte arrays:

- mac contains the MAC address we are going to use for the Ethernet shield. A MAC address is a 48-bit number that uniquely identifies a network device.[11] Usually, the manufacturer sets this identifier, but for the Ethernet shield, we have to set it ourselves; we use an arbitrary number.

  Important note: the MAC address has to be unique on your network. If you connect more than one Arduino, make sure they all have different MAC addresses!

- Whenever you connect your PC to the Internet, it probably gets a new IP address via the Dynamic Host Configuration Protocol (DHCP).[12] For most Arduino applications, a DHCP implementation is comparatively costly, so you usually assign an IP address manually. In most cases, this will be a local address in the *192.168.x.y* range; we store this address in the my_ip array.

- To turn domain names such as *time.nist.gov* into an IP address, you need access to the Domain Name System (DNS). The Arduino's standard library doesn't support DNS, so we have to find out the IP address ourselves. We assign it to time_server. The telnet command already turned the DAYTIME service domain name into an IP address for us. Alternatively, you can use one of the following commands to determine a domain name's IP address:

```
maik> host time.nist.gov
time.nist.gov has address 192.43.244.18
maik> dig +short time.nist.gov
192.43.244.18
maik> resolveip time.nist.gov
IP address of time.nist.gov is 192.43.244.18
maik> ping -c 1 time.nist.gov
PING time.nist.gov (192.43.244.18): 56 data bytes
64 bytes from 192.43.244.18: icmp_seq=0 ttl=48 time=173.598 ms

--- time.nist.gov ping statistics ---
1 packets transmitted, 1 packets received, 0.0% packet loss
round-trip min/avg/max/stddev = 173.598/173.598/173.598/0.000 ms
```

---

11. http://en.wikipedia.org/wiki/Mac_address
12. http://en.wikipedia.org/wiki/Dynamic_Host_Configuration_Protocol

In line 11, we create a new Client object. This class is part of the Ethernet library and allows us to create network clients that connect to a certain IP address and port.

Now we have to initialize the Ethernet shield itself; we do this in line 14 in the setup() function. We have to invoke Ethernet.begin(), passing it our MAC and IP addresses. Then we initialize the serial port so that we can output some debug messages. At this point, we've initialized all the components we need, so we can finally connect to the DAYTIME server and read its output.

Please note that you can also pass the IP address of your network gateway and your subnet mask to Ethernet.begin(). This is necessary if you do not connect the Arduino directly to the Internet but use a router or a cable modem instead. In this case, you can pass the gateway address as follows:

```
// ...
byte mac[] = { 0xDE, 0xAD, 0xBE, 0xEF, 0xFE, 0xED };
byte my_ip[] = { 192, 168, 2, 120 };
byte time_server[] = { 192, 43, 244, 18 }; // time.nist.gov
// Insert IP address of your cable or DSL router below:
byte gateway[] = { 192, 168, 13, 254 };

Client client(time_server, DAYTIME_PORT);

void setup() {
  Ethernet.begin(mac, my_ip, gateway);
  Serial.begin(BAUD_RATE);
}
// ...
```

The loop() function of our sketch starts with a short delay, allowing all components to initialize properly. This is necessary because the Ethernet shield is an autonomous device that is capable of working in parallel to the Arduino. In line 22, we try to connect to the DAYTIME service. If the connection cannot be established, we print an error message. Otherwise, we wait for half a second to give the service some preparation time, and then we read and print its output character by character.

Note that the client's interface is similar to the interface of the Serial class. With available(), we can check whether some bytes are still available, and read() returns the next byte. At the end, we call stop() to disconnect from the service and then we start again.

Compile and upload the program to the Arduino. Then open the serial monitor, and you should see something like this:

More Fun with Networking Arduinos

Wearables and e-textiles are getting more and more popular, and they're still a good way to impress your colleagues and friends. Different types of interactive T-shirts are available in every well-assorted geek shop. Some of them show the current WiFi strength, while others come with a full-blown equalizer that analyzes ambient noise.

With an Arduino Lilypad,[*] a Bluetooth dongle, and an Android phone, you can build a T-shirt that displays the current number of unread emails in your inbox.[†]

Not only can you show the number of unread email messages on your T-shirt, you can also show your current mood using a pointer device on your desk—at least as long as you announce it in an IRC channel that you monitor with an Arduino.[‡]

Although not built with Arduinos, the Luminet project[§] is very impressive. It is a network of interconnected intelligent LED pixels, and the Luminet team used it to build a really cool interactive jacket.

---

[*]. http://arduino.cc/en/Main/ArduinoBoardLilyPad
[†]. http://blog.makezine.com/archive/2010/03/email-counting_t-shirt.html
[‡]. http://blog.makezine.com/archive/2010/01/arduino_powered_mood_meter.html
[§]. http://luminet.cc

```
Connecting...connected.

55480 10-10-11 13:32:23 28 0 0 579.9 UTC(NIST) *
Disconnecting.
Connecting...connected.

55480 10-10-11 13:32:26 28 0 0  34.5 UTC(NIST) *
Disconnecting.
```

We're done! Our Arduino is directly connected to the Internet, and it even does something useful: we've turned it into a very accurate clock.

All in all, networking with an Arduino doesn't differ much from networking with a PC, if you use the Ethernet shield. In the next section, you'll learn how to send emails with an Arduino.

> ## Useful Networking Libraries
>
> The Ethernet library that comes with the Arduino IDE is fairly limited and not very convenient. For example, it doesn't support DNS or DHCP. So for advanced projects, you should have a look at the Arduino Ethernet library.*
>
> If you want to turn your Arduino into a web server, you should take a look at the Webduino library.† It has some great features, and it is quite mature.
>
> But be warned: all these libraries consume quite a lot of memory, so there's not much left for your application code. Also, they are rather fragile, because they often rely upon the innards of the official Ethernet library that change from time to time. So, it might well be that they do not work with the latest Arduino IDE.
>
> ---
>
> *. http://gkaindl.com/software/arduino-ethernet
> †. http://code.google.com/p/webduino/

8.6 Emailing from the Command Line

Now that we know how to access network services, we'll continue to build a more advanced project: an automatic burglar alarm. In case someone is moving in our living room, we want to get an email, so we have to learn how to send emails from an Arduino.

Although email is an important service, only a few people know how it actually works behind the scenes. To send emails from an Arduino, we could choose the easy path and use a PC as an email relay as we did in Section 8.4, *Tweeting Messages with Processing*, on page 160 to tweet messages. As real hackers, we'll follow a more sophisticated path and implement a subset of the Simple Mail Transfer Protocol (SMTP).[13]

SMTP is a typical Internet protocol. It uses only text, and it is mainly line-based; that is, you exchange information line by line. A typical email consists of only a few attributes: a sender, a receiver, a subject, and a message body. To transmit an email, you have to send a request to an SMTP server. The request has to adhere to the SMTP specification.

---

13. http://en.wikipedia.org/wiki/Smtp

Before we send an email using an Arduino and an Ethernet shield, you should learn how to send an email from a command line using the telnet command. To do so, you have to find out the address of an SMTP server you can use first. The following instructions assume you're using a Google Mail account (http://gmail.com). If you use a different email provider, you have to adjust the domain names accordingly. In any case, don't abuse their service! When in doubt, read their usage terms!

Open a terminal, and enter the following:

```
maik> nslookup
> set type=mx
> gmail.com
Server:    192.168.2.1
Address:   192.168.2.1#53
Non-authoritative answer:
gmail.com mail exchanger = 5 gmail-smtp-in.l.google.com.
gmail.com mail exchanger = 10 alt1.gmail-smtp-in.l.google.com.
gmail.com mail exchanger = 20 alt2.gmail-smtp-in.
> exit
```

This command returns a list of all the Google Mail exchange servers (MX) available on your network. Take the first server name, and open a connection to the SMTP standard port 25 (replace the server name gmail-smtp-in.l.google.com and all email addresses accordingly):

```
⇐  maik> telnet gmail-smtp-in.l.google.com 25
⇒  Trying 74.125.77.27...
   Connected to gmail-smtp-in.l.google.com.
   Escape character is '^]'.
   220 mx.google.com ESMTP q43si10820020eeh.100
⇐  HELO
⇒  250 mx.google.com at your service
⇐  MAIL FROM: <arduino@example.com>
⇒  250 2.1.0 OK q43si10820020eeh.100
⇐  RCPT TO: <info@example.com>
⇒  250 2.1.5 OK q43si10820020eeh.100
⇐  DATA
⇒  354  Go ahead q43si10820020eeh.100
⇐  from: arduino@example.com
⇐  to: info@example.com
⇐  subject: This is a test
⇐
⇐  Really, this is a test!
⇐  .
⇒  250 2.0.0 OK 1286819789 q43si10820020eeh.100
⇐  QUIT
⇒  221 2.0.0 closing connection q43si10820020eeh.100
   Connection closed by foreign host.
```

Although it is way more complex, this session is similar to our DAYTIME example. We only send more complex commands (by the way, you do not have to write the commands in uppercase). First we send the HELO command (the spelling is correct) to establish a session with the SMTP server. Then we tell the server that we'd like to send an email using MAIL FROM:. The email address we provide with this command will be used by the server in case our email bounces back. Note that the server sends back a response line for every request. These responses always start with a three-digit status code.

The RCPT TO: command sets the recipient's email address. If you'd like to send an email to more than one recipient, you have to repeat the command for each of them.

With the DATA command, we tell the server that we now start to transmit the email's attributes. Email attributes are mainly a list of key/value pairs where key and value are delimited by a colon. So in the first three lines, we set the attributes "from," "to," and "subject," and they all have the meaning you'd expect when sending an email.

You separate the email's body from the attributes using a blank line. To mark the end of the email body, send a line containing a single period. Send the QUIT command to end the session with the SMTP server.

You should find a new email in your inbox. If not, try another MX server first. Still things can go wrong, and although simple in theory, SMTP can be a complex beast in practice. Often SMTP servers return helpful error messages that might help you to quickly solve your problem.

Don't proceed until you have successfully sent an email from the command line, because it is the basis for the next section where you'll learn how to send emails with an Arduino.

8.7 Emailing Directly from an Arduino

To send an email from the Arduino, we will basically implement the telnet session from the previous section line by line. Instead of simply hardwiring the email's attributes into the networking code, we will create a more advanced design.

We start with an Email class:

Ethernet/Email/email.h

```
#ifndef __EMAIL__H_
#define __EMAIL__H_

class Email {
  String _from, _to, _subject, _body;

  public:

  Email(
    const String& from,
    const String& to,
    const String& subject,
    const String& body
  ) : _from(from), _to(to), _subject(subject), _body(body) {}

  const String& getFrom()    const { return _from; }
  const String& getTo()      const { return _to; }
  const String& getSubject() const { return _subject; }
  const String& getBody()    const { return _body; }
};

#endif
```

This class encapsulates an email's four most important attributes—the email addresses of the sender and the recipient, a subject, and a message body. We store all attributes as String objects.

Wait a minute...a String class? Yes! Since version 19, the Arduino IDE comes with a full-blown string class.[14] It does not have as many features as the C++ or Java string classes, but it's still way better than messing around with **char** pointers. You'll see how to use it in a few paragraphs.

The rest of our Email class is pretty straightforward. In the constructor, we initialize all instance variables, and we have methods for getting every single attribute. We now need an SmtpService class for sending Email objects:

Ethernet/Email/smtp_service.h

```
Line 1  #ifndef __SMTP_SERVICE__H_
   -    #define __SMTP_SERVICE__H_

   -
   -    #include "email.h"
```

---

14. http://arduino.cc/en/Reference/StringObject

```
 5    class SmtpService {
 -      byte*           _smtp_server;
 -      unsigned int _port;
 -
10      void read_response(Client& client) {
 -        delay(4000);
 -        while (client.available()) {
 -          const char c = client.read();
 -          Serial.print(c);
15        }
 -      }
 -
 -      void send_line(Client& client, String line) {
 -        const unsigned int MAX_LINE = 256;
20        char buffer[MAX_LINE];
 -        line.toCharArray(buffer, MAX_LINE);
 -        Serial.println(buffer);
 -        client.println(buffer);
 -        read_response(client);
25      }
 -
 -    public:
 -
 -    SmtpService(
30      byte*               smtp_server,
 -      const unsigned int port) : _smtp_server(smtp_server),
 -                                 _port(port) {}
 -
 -      void send_email(const Email& email) {
35        Client client(_smtp_server, _port);
 -        Serial.print("Connecting...");
 -
 -        if (!client.connect()) {
 -          Serial.println("connection failed.");
40        } else {
 -          Serial.println("connected.");
 -          read_response(client);
 -          send_line(client, String("helo"));
 -          send_line(
45            client,
 -            String("mail from: <") + email.getFrom() + String(">")
 -          );
 -          send_line(
 -            client,
50            String("rcpt to: <") + email.getTo() + String(">")
 -          );
 -          send_line(client, String("data"));
 -          send_line(client, String("from: ") + email.getFrom());
 -          send_line(client, String("to: ") + email.getTo());
55          send_line(client, String("subject: ") + email.getSubject());
```

```
-        send_line(client, String(""));
-        send_line(client, email.getBody());
-        send_line(client, String("."));
-        send_line(client, String("quit"));
60       client.println("Disconnecting.");
-        client.stop();
-      }
-    }
-  };
65
-  #endif
```

Admittedly, this is a lot of code, but it's very simple. First, the SmtpService class encapsulates the SMTP server's IP address and its port.

To communicate with an SMTP server, we have to read its responses, and we do that using the private read_response() method starting on line 10. It waits for four seconds (SMTP servers usually are very busy, because they have to send a lot of spam), and then it reads all the data sent back by the server and outputs it to the serial port for debugging purposes.

Before we can process responses, we have to send requests. send_line() beginning in line 18 sends a single command to an SMTP server. You have to pass the connection to the server as a Client instance, and the line you'd like to send has to be a String object.

To send the data stored in a String object, we need to access the character data it refers to. At the moment of this writing, the Arduino reference documentation tells you to simply use toCharArray() or getBytes() to retrieve this information. Unfortunately, the documentation is wrong. That is, these two methods do not return a pointer. Instead, they expect you to provide a sufficiently large **char** array and its size. That's why we copy line's content to buffer before we output it to the serial and Ethernet port. After we've sent the data, we read the server's response and print it to the serial port.

In the public interface, you do not find any surprises. The constructor expects the SMTP server's IP address and its port. The send_email() method is the largest piece of code in our class, but it's also one of the simplest. It mimics exactly our telnet session, and the only thing worth mentioning is the string handling: we use the Arduino's new String class, and to use its concatenation operator (+), we turn every string into a String object.

Let's use our classes now to actually send an email:

Ethernet/Email/Email.pde

```
Line 1   #include <SPI.h>
    -    #include <Ethernet.h>
    -    #include "smtp_service.h"

    5    const unsigned int SMTP_PORT = 25;
    -    const unsigned int BAUD_RATE = 9600;

    -    byte mac[]   = { 0xDE, 0xAD, 0xBE, 0xEF, 0xFE, 0xED };
    -    byte my_ip[] = { 192, 168, 2, 120 };
   10
    -     // Insert IP of your SMTP server below!
    -    byte smtp_server[] = { 0, 0, 0, 0 };

    -    SmtpService smtp_service(smtp_server, SMTP_PORT);
   15
    -    void setup() {
    -      Ethernet.begin(mac, my_ip);
    -      Serial.begin(BAUD_RATE);
    -      delay(1000);
   20      Email email(
    -        "arduino@example.com",
    -        "info@example.net",
    -        "Yet another subject",
    -        "Yet another body"
   25      );
    -      smtp_service.send_email(email);
    -    }

    -    void loop() {}
```

No surprises here. We define constants, the MAC address, and so on, then create an SmtpService instance. In the setup() function, we initialize the serial port and the Ethernet shield, then wait for a second to let things settle down a bit. On line 20, we create a new Email object and call its send_email() method.

Now we know how to send emails with an Arduino, but to build our burglar alarm, we still have to learn how to detect motion.

8.8 Detecting Motion Using a Passive Infrared Sensor

Detecting motion is a useful technique, and you probably already know devices that turn on the light in your garden or at your door whenever someone is near enough. Most of them use *passive infrared sensors* (PIR)[15] for motion detection.

---

15. http://en.wikipedia.org/wiki/Passive_infrared_sensor

Figure 8.7: TOP AND BOTTOM OF A PASSIVE INFRARED SENSOR

Nearly every object emits infrared light, and a PIR sensor (see one in Figure 8.7) measures exactly this portion of light. Detecting motion is comparatively easy if you are already able to receive the infrared radiation emitted by objects in the sensor's field of view. If the sensor receives the infrared light emitted by a wall, for example, and suddenly a human being or an animal moves in front of the wall, the infrared light signal will change.

Off-the-shelf sensors hide these details, so you can use a single digital pin to check whether someone is moving in the sensor's field of view. The Parallax PIR sensor[16] is a good example of such a device, and we'll use it as the basis of our burglar alarm.

The PIR sensor has three pins: power, ground, and signal. Connect power to the Arduino's 5V supply, ground to one of the Arduino's GND pins, and signal to digital pin 2 (see a circuit diagram in Figure 8.8, on the facing page). The sensor also has a jumper that you can use for changing its behavior. For our project, it has to be in position H; that is, the jumper has to cover the pin next to the H (Lady Ada has an excellent tutorial on PIR sensors).[17]

Then enter the following code in the Arduino IDE:

---

16. http://www.parallax.com/Store/Sensors/ObjectDetection/tabid/176/ProductID/83/List/0/Default.aspx
17. http://www.ladyada.net/learn/sensors/pir.html

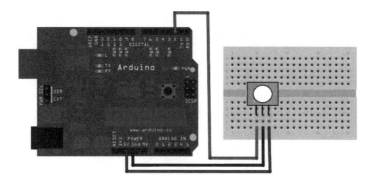

Figure 8.8: A MINIMALISTIC PIR SENSOR CIRCUIT

Ethernet/MotionDetector/MotionDetector.pde

```
const unsigned int PIR_INPUT_PIN = 2;
const unsigned int BAUD_RATE = 9600;

class PassiveInfraredSensor {
  int _input_pin;

  public:

  PassiveInfraredSensor(const int input_pin) {
    _input_pin = input_pin;
    pinMode(_input_pin, INPUT);
  }

  const bool motion_detected() const {
    return digitalRead(_input_pin) == HIGH;
  }
};

PassiveInfraredSensor pir(PIR_INPUT_PIN);

void setup() {
  Serial.begin(BAUD_RATE);
}

void loop() {
  if (pir.motion_detected()) {
    Serial.println("Motion detected");
  } else {
    Serial.println("No motion detected");
  }
  delay(200);
}
```

Figure 8.9: Typical output of a PIR sensor

With the constant PIR_INPUT_PIN, you can define the digital pin you've connected your PIR sensor to. In line 4, we begin the definition of a class named PassiveInfraredSensor that encapsulates all things related to PIR sensors.

We define a member variable named _input_pin that stores the number of the digital pin we've connected our sensor to. Then we define a constructor that expects the pin number as an argument and assigns it to our member variable.

The only method we need to define is motion_detected(). It returns true if it has currently detected a motion and false otherwise. So, it has to check only whether the current state of the sensor's digital pin is HIGH or LOW.

Compile the sketch, upload it to your Arduino, and you should see an output similar to Figure 8.9 when you start to wave with your hand in front of the sensor.

Now we've built the two main components of our burglar alarm, and the only thing left to do is to bring them both together. We'll do that in the next section.

Figure 8.10: AN EMAILING BURGLAR ALARM

8.9 Bringing It All Together

With our PassiveInfraredSensor and SmtpService classes, it's a piece of cake to build an emailing burglar alarm. Connect the PIR sensor to the Ethernet shield, as shown in Figure 8.10, and upload the following code to your Arduino:

Ethernet/BurglarAlarm/burglar_alarm.h

```
Line 1   #ifndef __BURGLAR_ALARM_H__
    -    #define __BURGLAR_ALARM_H__

    -    #include "pir_sensor.h"
    5    #include "smtp_service.h"

    -    class BurglarAlarm {
    -      PassiveInfraredSensor _pir_sensor;
    -      SmtpService           _smtp_service;
   10
    -      void send_alarm() {
    -        Email email(
    -          "arduino@example.com",
    -          "info@example.net",
   15          "Intruder Alert!",
    -          "Someone's moving in your living room!"
    -        );
    -        _smtp_service.send_email(email);
    -      }
   20
```

```
     public:

     BurglarAlarm(
       const PassiveInfraredSensor& pir_sensor,
25     const SmtpService&           smtp_service) :
         _pir_sensor(pir_sensor),
         _smtp_service(smtp_service)
     {
     }
30
     void check() {
       Serial.println("Checking");
       if (_pir_sensor.motion_detected()) {
         Serial.println("Intruder detected!");
35       send_alarm();
       }
     }
   };

40 #endif
```

This defines a class named BurglarAlarm that aggregates all the code we've written so far. It encapsulates a SmtpService instance and a PassiveInfraredSensor object. Its most complex method is send_alarm() that sends a predefined email.

The rest of the BurglarAlarm class is pretty straightforward. Beginning in line 23, we define the constructor that initializes all private members. The check() method checks whether the PIR sensor has detected a movement. If it did, we send an email.

Let's use the BurglarAlarm class:

Ethernet/BurglarAlarm/BurglarAlarm.pde

```
#include <SPI.h>
#include <Ethernet.h>
#include "burglar_alarm.h"

const unsigned int PIR_INPUT_PIN = 2;
const unsigned int SMTP_PORT = 25;
const unsigned int BAUD_RATE = 9600;

byte mac[]        = { 0xDE, 0xAD, 0xBE, 0xEF, 0xFE, 0xED };
byte my_ip[]      = { 192, 168, 2, 120 };

// Insert IP of your SMTP server below!
byte smtp_server[] = { 0, 0, 0, 0 };

PassiveInfraredSensor pir_sensor(PIR_INPUT_PIN);
SmtpService           smtp_service(smtp_server, SMTP_PORT);
```

Figure 8.11: THE BURGLAR ALARM'S OUTPUT

```
BurglarAlarm            burglar_alarm(pir_sensor, smtp_service);

void setup() {
  Ethernet.begin(mac, my_ip);
  Serial.begin(BAUD_RATE);
  delay(20 * 1000);
}

void loop() {
  burglar_alarm.check();
  delay(3000);
}
```

First we define all the libraries we need, and we define constants for the PIR sensor pin and our MAC address. Then we define SmtpService and PassiveInfraredSensor objects and use them to define a BurglarAlarm instance.

In the setup() method, we define the serial port and the Ethernet shield. I've also added a delay of twenty seconds, which gives you enough time to leave the room before the alarm begins to work.

The loop() function is simple, too. It delegates all the work to the Burglar-Alarm's check() method. In Figure 8.11, on the previous page, you can see what happens when the burglar alarm detects an intruder.

Did you notice how easy object-oriented programming on an embedded device can be? We've cleanly hidden the complexity of both email and the PIR sensor in two small classes. To build the burglar alarm, we then only had to write some glue code.

One word regarding privacy: do not abuse the project in this chapter to observe other people without their knowledge. Not only is it unethical, but in many countries it even is illegal!

In this chapter, you learned different ways of connecting the Arduino to the Internet. Some of them need an additional PC, while others need an Ethernet shield, but they all open the door to a whole new range of embedded computing applications.

Networking is one of those techniques that may have a direct impact on the outside world. In the next chapter, you'll learn about another technique that has similar effects; you'll learn how to control devices remotely.

8.10 What If It Doesn't Work?

Networks are complex and complicated beasts, and many things can go wrong when trying the examples in this chapter. The most common problems are the following:

- You have chosen the wrong serial port in the Processing application. By default, the application uses the first serial port it can find. It might be that you have connected your Arduino to another port. In this case, you have to change the index 0 in the statement arduinoPort = new Serial(this, Serial.list()[0], BAUD_RATE); accordingly.

- You forgot to plug the Ethernet cable into the Ethernet shield.

- Your network router has a MAC whitelist that allows only certain MAC addresses to access the network. Make sure that the MAC address you use in your sketches is whitelisted. Check your router's documentation.

- You have used the same MAC address twice on your network.

Alternative Networking Technologies

Ethernet is one of the most popular and most powerful networking technologies. Using an Ethernet shield, you can easily connect your Arduino to the Internet both as a client and as a server.

Depending on your project's needs, it's sometimes better to use a wireless connection. With a WiFi shield* you can easily turn your Arduino into a wireless networking device.

But often you don't need the full power of Ethernet, especially if you only need short-range communication in a personal area network. You can choose from a variety of options, but Bluetooth and ZigBee† are probably the most popular. Excellent solutions for both of them are available for the Arduino.

Finally, you can even participate in cellular networks with your Arduino. Plug in a GSM shield‡ and your SIM card, and you are ready to go.

---

*. WiShield (http://www.asynclabs.com/) and WiFly (http://www.sparkfun.com/commerce/product_info.php?products_id=9954) are good products.
†. http://en.wikipedia.org/wiki/Zigbee
‡. http://www.hwkitchen.com/products/gsm-playground/

- You've used an IP address that is not allowed in your network or that is used already by another device. Double-check your IP address.

- You've used the wrong credentials for accessing a service such as Twitter. Make sure you use the right OAuth tokens.

- Twitter does not allow duplicate tweets. So, whenever your application fails to tweet a message, make sure you haven't tweeted it recently.

- Networks have become very reliable over the last decades, but sometimes they are still a bit fragile. So, it might well be that connections fail or that you run into timeouts. Increase the delays in your sketches accordingly.

8.11 Exercises

• Search the Web for other Ethernet shield projects, and build at least one of them. For example, you can find chat clients for the Arduino.[18]

• Build a project similar to the burglar alarm, but use another type of sensor. There's tons of inspiration out there on the Web.[19]

• Add the current time stamp to the burglar alarm's email. Get the timestamp from a DAYTIME service.

---

18. http://rapplogic.blogspot.com/2009/11/chatduino-aim-client-for-arduinowiznet.html
19. http://www.tigoe.net/pcomp/code/category/arduinowiring/873

Chapter 9

Creating Your Own Universal Remote Control

Remote controls add a lot of convenience to our lives, but they aren't without annoyances. Sometimes remotes don't have a certain function that you'd like to have, such as a sleep timer. Plus, remote controls seem to reproduce at the same rate as rabbits. They quickly occupy your whole coffee table, and you have to feed them with expensive batteries that you don't have at home when you need them during a Sunday evening football game. Universal remote controls reduce the pain a bit, but even the most expensive products aren't perfect.

Although we use remote controls every day, few of us understand how they work. In this chapter, you'll find out how remote controls work from the inside out, and then you'll build your own universal remote control that's better than a store-bought one because you can fully customize it to your needs. You can easily add all your favorite functions, and you can also add functions other remotes don't offer. If a commercial product doesn't support a certain vendor, you're usually stuck. With your own remote, you can easily add new protocols yourself. It's even possible not only to support infrared but to add more transmission technologies such as Bluetooth or WiFi.

You'll get started by learning the basics of infrared light signals, and you'll quickly build your first project using an infrared sensor to grab control codes from any remote you have on hand. Once you grab the control codes, you can emit them using an infrared LED, and you'll start to build your own universal remote control.

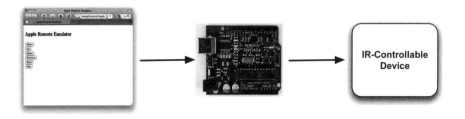

Figure 9.1: ARCHITECTURE OF THE INFRARED PROXY

Then we'll even take the idea of a remote control a step further. Once we have a universal remote, we'll control the Arduino itself using the serial port or an Ethernet connection. This way, you can control the Arduino using a web browser, so you can control your TV set or DVD recorder using the Internet (see Figure 9.1).

9.1 What You Need

1. An Ethernet shield for the Arduino.

2. A breadboard.

3. An infrared receiver, preferably the PNA4602.

4. A 100Ω resistor.

5. An infrared LED.

6. Some wires.

7. One or more infrared remote controls. They can be from your TV set, DVD player, or your Mac. To follow the chapter's examples, it'd be best to have a Mac and an Apple Remote, but it's not necessary. If you're not using an Apple Remote, be sure to adjust the protocol name, bit length, and control codes in the examples accordingly. If you're using a remote control belonging to a Sony TV set, for example, set the protocol name to SONY (you'll learn more about this in Section 9.3, *Grabbing Remote Control Codes*, on page 190).

8. An Arduino board such as the Uno, Duemilanove, or Diecimila.

9. A USB cable to connect the Arduino to your computer.

Figure 9.2: ALL THE PARTS YOU NEED IN THIS CHAPTER

9.2 Understanding Infrared Remote Controls

To control a device such as a TV set wirelessly, you need a sender and a receiver. The receiver usually is built into the device to be controlled, and the sender is part of a separate remote control. Although you can choose from a variety of technologies such as Bluetooth or WiFi, most modern remote controls still use infrared light for communication.

Using infrared light for transmitting signals has several advantages. It is invisible to human beings, so it doesn't bother you. Also, you can generate it cheaply with infrared LEDs that can be integrated easily into electronic circuits. So, for many purposes such as controlling devices in a typical household, it's an excellent choice.

But it also has some drawbacks. It doesn't work through walls or doors, and the distance between the remote control and the operated device is fairly limited. Even more importantly, the infrared signal is subject to interference with other light sources.

To reduce possible distortions caused by other light sources to a minimum, the infrared signal has to be modulated. That means you turn the LED on and off at a certain frequency, usually somewhere between 36KHz and 40KHz.

That's one of the problems that makes it a bit complicated to build a robust infrared remote control. The biggest problem is that vendors have invented countless incompatible protocols. They all use different frequencies, and they all interpret data differently. Some interpret "light on" as a 1 bit, while others treat it as 0, and they all define their own commands that have different lengths. So, to work successfully with different remote control protocols, we need to know how to obtain all these properties for a specific remote control.

To get this information, we'll take a pragmatic approach. In the next two sections, you'll learn how to read infrared signals from a commercial-grade remote control, and you'll also learn how to reproduce them.

9.3 Grabbing Remote Control Codes

Because remote controls from different vendors rarely use the same protocol or even the same commands, before we start sending remote control codes ourselves, we should know what we have to send to achieve a certain result. We have to get as much information as possible about the remote control we'd like to emulate.

We have two alternatives for obtaining remote control codes for a specific device: we could use a remote control database on the Internet such as the Linux Infrared Remote Control project,[1] or we could use an infrared receiver to read them directly from our device's remote. We will choose the latter approach, because we can learn a lot from it.

Infrared receivers (see Figure 9.3, on the facing page) are fairly complex on the inside, but they are easy to use. They automatically observe the infrared light spectrum at a certain frequency (usually between 36KHz and 40KHz), and they report their observations using a single pin. So, when you're using such a receiver, you don't have to deal with all the complicated transmission details. You can focus on reading and interpreting the incoming signals.

---

1. http://www.lirc.org/

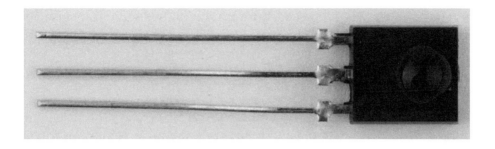

Figure 9.3: A PNA4602 INFRARED SENSOR

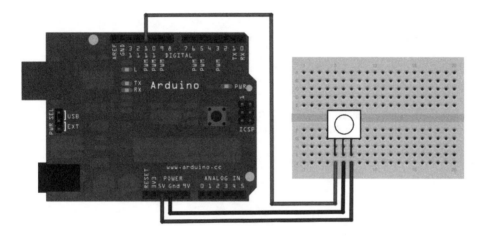

Figure 9.4: CONNECTING AN IR RECEIVER TO THE ARDUINO IS EASY.

In Figure 9.4, you can see how to connect a PNA4602 receiver to an Arduino. It's cheap, it's easy to use, and it works at a frequency of 38KHz, so it detects signals from a broad range of devices. Connect its ground connector to one of the Arduino's GND pins, the power supply to the Arduino's 5V pin, and the signal pin to digital pin 11.

You might be tempted to write a sketch that reads and outputs all incoming data on pin 11, and I won't stop you. Call digitalRead() in the loop() method and output the results to the serial port. Point your TV set's remote to the receiver and see what happens.

You'll probably have a hard time understanding the data you see. The problem is that decoding the incoming data isn't easy. Even if the receiver has already processed the data, it still has to be transformed and interpreted according to some complicated rules. Also, Arduino's digitalRead() method isn't always accurate enough to deal with all types of incoming signals. You have to directly access the micro-controller to get the best results.

Fortunately, we don't have to do this ourselves, because the IRremote library[2] hides the nasty details. It supports the most popular infrared protocols, and can both receive and send data. After you've down-loaded and extracted the ZIP file,[3] copy the directory IRremote to either ~/Documents/Arduino/libraries (on a Mac) or My Documents\Arduino\libraries (on a Windows box). Then restart your IDE.

With the following sketch, you can then decode incoming infrared signals, if the IRremote library supports their encoding:

RemoteControl/InfraredDumper/InfraredDumper.pde

```
Line 1   #include <IRremote.h>

         const unsigned int IR_RECEIVER_PIN = 11;
         const unsigned int BAUD_RATE = 9600;
    5
         IRrecv ir_receiver(IR_RECEIVER_PIN);
         decode_results results;

         void setup() {
   10      Serial.begin(BAUD_RATE);
           ir_receiver.enableIRIn();
         }

         void dump(const decode_results* results) {
   15      const int protocol = results->decode_type;
           Serial.print("Protocol: ");
           if (protocol == UNKNOWN) {
             Serial.println("not recognized.");
           } else {
   20        if (protocol == NEC) {
               Serial.println("NEC");
             } else if (protocol == SONY) {
               Serial.println("SONY");
             } else if (protocol == RC5) {
   25          Serial.println("RC5");
             } else if (protocol == RC6) {
               Serial.println("RC6");
             }
```

---

2. http://www.arcfn.com/2009/08/multi-protocol-infrared-remote-library.html
3. http://arcfn.com/files/IRremote.zip

```
          Serial.print("Value: ");
30        Serial.print(results->value, HEX);
          Serial.print(" (");
          Serial.print(results->bits, DEC);
          Serial.println(" bits)");
      }
35  }

    void loop() {
      if (ir_receiver.decode(&results)) {
        dump(&results);
40      ir_receiver.resume();
      }
    }
```

First we define an IRrecv object named ir_receiver that reads from pin 11. We also define a decode_result object that we'll use to store the attributes of incoming infrared signals. In setup(), we initialize the serial port, and we initialize the infrared receiver by calling enableIRIn().

Then we define a method named dump() that nicely formats and outputs the content of a decode_result object to the serial port. decode_result is one of the core data types of the IRremote library. It encapsulates data such as the protocol type, the length of a command code, and the command code itself. In line 15, we read the protocol type that has been used to encode the incoming signal. Whenever we receive a new signal, we output all these attributes to the serial port.

The loop() method is simple. We call decode() to check whether we've received a new signal. If yes, we call dump() to output it to the serial port, and then we call resume() to wait for the next signal.

Compile and upload the sketch to your Arduino, then start the serial monitor, and point a remote control at the receiver. Push some of the remote's buttons, and see what happens. In Figure 9.5, on the following page, you can see, for example, what happens when you point an Apple Remote to the receiver and press menu, up, down, previous, next, and play (if you see the code 0xffffffff from time to time, you've pressed one of the Apple Remote's keys for too long, because it is the "repeat code" that indicates that the last command should be repeated).

After you have grabbed a remote's control codes, you can use them to build your own remote. You'll learn how to do that in the next section.

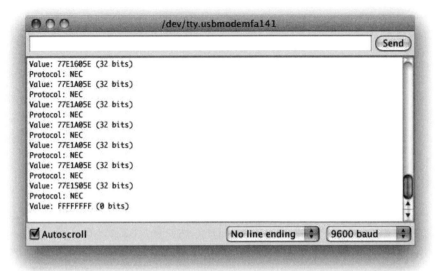

Figure 9.5: CAPTURING THE IR CODES OF AN APPLE REMOTE

9.4 Building Your Own Apple Remote

Now that you know the protocol and the codes of the commands the Apple Remote sends to a Mac, you can build your own Apple Remote. You only need an infrared LED that doesn't differ much from the LEDs we've used before. The only difference is that it emits "invisible" light. In Figure 9.6, on the next page, you can see how to connect it to pin 3 of an Arduino (the library we're using in this section expects the infrared LED to be connected to pin 3). Note that you can't use an LED without a resistor (see Section A.1, *Current, Voltage, and Resistance*, on page 225 to learn more about it).

We could try to generate the infrared signals ourselves, but that'd be tedious and error-prone. It's better to use the existing implementation in the IRremote library. We'll use it to create our own AppleRemote class that encapsulates all the gory protocol details. The class looks like this:

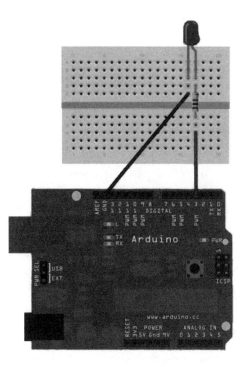

Figure 9.6: CONNECTING AN IR LED TO THE ARDUINO

RemoteControl/AppleRemote/AppleRemote.pde

```
#include <IRremote.h>

class AppleRemote {

  enum {
    CMD_LEN = 32,
    UP      = 0x77E15061,
    DOWN    = 0x77E13061,
    PLAY    = 0x77E1A05E,
    PREV    = 0x77E1905E,
    NEXT    = 0x77E1605E,
    MENU    = 0x77E1C05E
  };

  IRsend mac;

  void send_command(const long command) {
    mac.sendNEC(command, CMD_LEN);
  }
```

```
public:

  void menu()  { send_command(MENU); }
  void play()  { send_command(PLAY); }
  void prev()  { send_command(PREV); }
  void next()  { send_command(NEXT); }
  void up()    { send_command(UP);   }
  void down()  { send_command(DOWN); }
};
```

The code starts with an enumeration that contains all the constants we need: the length of each control code and the control codes themselves. Then we define an IRsend object named mac that we'll use to send commands using the send_command() method. send_command() uses IRsend's sendNEC() method because the Apple Remote uses the NEC protocol.

After we've established the basis, we can implement all commands with a single function call, so implementing menu(), play(), and so on, is a piece of cake.

Using the AppleRemote class is easy, too. In the following sketch, we use it to control a Mac from the Arduino's serial monitor:

RemoteControl/AppleRemote/AppleRemote.pde

```
AppleRemote apple_remote;
const unsigned int BAUD_RATE = 9600;

void setup() {
  Serial.begin(BAUD_RATE);
}

void loop() {
  if (Serial.available()) {
    const char command = Serial.read();
    switch(command) {
      case 'm':
        apple_remote.menu();
        break;
      case 'u':
        apple_remote.up();
        break;
      case 'd':
        apple_remote.down();
        break;
      case 'l':
        apple_remote.prev();
        break;
      case 'r':
```

```
      apple_remote.next();
      break;
    case 'p':
      apple_remote.play();
      break;
    default:
      break;
    }
  }
}
```

We define a global AppleRemote object named apple_remote, and in the setup() function we initialize the serial port. In loop(), we wait for new data on the serial port, and whenever a new byte arrives, we check whether it's one of the characters *m, u, d, l, r,* or *p.* Depending on the character we received, we send the control code for menu, up, down, previous, next, or play accordingly.

Compile and upload the sketch, and you can control a Mac using any serial monitor, which is quite cool already. The interface is still a bit awkward for less geeky people, so in the next section, you'll learn how to create a more user-friendly interface.

9.5 Controlling Devices Remotely with Your Browser

We've already created a lot of projects that you can control using a serial monitor. For programmers, that's a nice and convenient interface, but as soon as you want to present your projects to your non-technical friends or to your spouse, you'd better have something more user-friendly and colorful.

The Seriality[4] plug-in makes that possible. It adds support for serial port communication to your web browser's JavaScript engine.

At the moment, the plug-in is available only for Firefox, Safari, and Chrome on Mac OS X, but a Windows port is under development. Seriality is available as a disk image, so you can download it[5] and install it as usual.

After you've installed Seriality, you can turn your web browser into an Apple Remote simulator using the following mixture of HTML and JavaScript code:

---

4. http://www.zambetti.com/projects/seriality/
5. http://code.google.com/p/seriality/downloads/list

RemoteControl/AppleRemoteUI/ui.html

```
Line 1   <html>
    -      <title>Apple Remote Emulator</title>
    -      <head>
    -        <script type="text/javascript">
    5          var serial;
    -
    -          function setup() {
    -            serial = (document.getElementById("seriality")).Seriality();
    -            alert(serial.ports.join("\n"));
    10           serial.begin(serial.ports[0], 9600);
    -          }
    -        </script>
    -      </head>
    -
    15     <body onload="setup();">
    -        <object type="application/Seriality"
    -                id="seriality"
    -                width="0"
    -                height="0">
    20       </object>
    -        <h2>Apple Remote Emulator</h2>
    -        <form>
    -          <button type="button" onclick="serial.write('m');">
    -            Menu
    25         </button>
    -          <br/>
    -          <button type="button" onclick="serial.write('u');">
    -            Up
    -          </button>
    30         <br/>
    -          <button type="button" onclick="serial.write('d');">
    -            Down
    -          </button>
    -          <br/>
    35         <button type="button" onclick="serial.write('l');">
    -            Previous
    -          </button>
    -          <br/>
    -          <button type="button" onclick="serial.write('n');">
    40           Next
    -          </button>
    -          <br/>
    -          <button type="button" onclick="serial.write('p');">
    -            Play
    45         </button>
    -          <br/>
    -        </form>
    -      </body>
    -    </html>
```

This is a very simple HTML page, and we'll focus on the JavaScript parts. In lines 4 to 12, we define two things: a global variable named serial and a function named setup(). setup() initializes serial and assigns a Seriality object to it. We embed a Seriality object into the web page using the *<object>* tag. Its ID is "seriality," so we can access it using getElementById().

As soon as we have a reference to the object, we call JavaScript's alert() function and output all serial ports we have found. You have to look up the index of the serial port your Arduino is connected to and use it in the following call to the begin() method. For simplicity, we always pass it the first serial device we can find and a baud rate of 9,600. Using the first serial device is only a guess, and you might have to adjust it. You already know that pattern from our Processing examples.

We invoke setup() in the **onload** event handler of the *<body>* element. Then we can access the Seriality object in the **onclick** handlers of our six *<button>* elements.

Upload the sketch from Section 9.4, *Building Your Own Apple Remote*, on page 194 to your Arduino, and point your browser to the HTML page. After you have clicked the OK button of the alert box showing all serial ports, you should see a web page like Figure 9.7, on the following page. Click any button to perform the corresponding action. That's an interface even your Grandma could use, isn't it?

Please note that you cannot access the Arduino hardware directly using Seriality. You can only access the serial port, so all the things you'd like to happen on your Arduino have to be accessible via serial communication. But that's a common pattern anyway, so Seriality is really a useful tool that can greatly improve your project's user interface.

You still need to connect the Arduino to your computer's serial port to control it with a web browser. In the next section, you'll learn how to overcome this and control an Arduino without a serial connection.

9.6 Building an Infrared Proxy

All our previous remote control approaches have one major drawback: they all depend on a serial connection to a PC. In this section, you'll learn how to replace this connection with an Ethernet connection, so you no longer need a PC but only Internet access. You will directly plug

Figure 9.7: THE APPLE REMOTE EMULATOR IN ACTION

your Ethernet cable into an Ethernet shield connected to the Arduino (see Figure 9.8, on the next page), so it is available on your network.

This doesn't necessarily mean that you have to use your PC's web browser to access the Arduino. You could also use the browser on your PlayStation Portable, on your iPhone, or on your Nintendo DS. Yes, you can now control your TV set using your game consoles or your smartphone. Oh, and you could replace the Ethernet shield with a WiFi shield so you don't have to connect your Arduino physically to your network router.

Before we dive into the code, we should do a little planning ahead and make clear what we'd like to achieve. We'll build an infrared proxy—a device that receives commands via Ethernet and turns them into infrared signals (see Figure 9.1, on page 188). To make it easy to integrate the device into a network, we'll make it accessible via HTTP. This way, we can control it using a regular web browser.

We'll only implement a very small portion of the HTTP standard on the Arduino—we'll only support a certain URL scheme. The URLs we will support look as follows:

`http://«arduino-ip»/«protocol-name»/«command-length»/«command-code»`

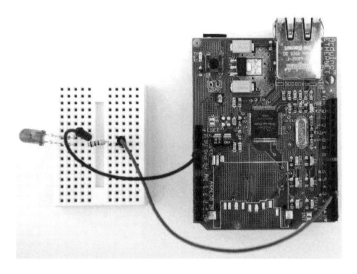

Figure 9.8: An ETHERNET-CONTROLLABLE REMOTE CONTROL

We'll replace «*arduino-ip*» with the IP address of the Arduino's Ethernet shield. The element «*protocol-name*» can be one of the supported protocols ("NEC," "SONY," "RC5," or "RC6"). «*command-length*» specifies the length of the command code in bits, and «*command-code*» contains the command code itself as a decimal number.

Let's assume we'd like to send the code for the menu key on an Apple Remote, and our Arduino has the IP address 192.168.2.42. Then we'd have to point our web browser to the following URL:

http://192.168.2.42/NEC/32/2011283550

In this case, the protocol name is NEC, the length of the command code is 32 bits, and the command code is 2011283550 (the decimal representation of the hexadecimal number 0x77E1C05E).

We've already used the Arduino as a web client in Chapter 8, *Networking with Arduino*, on page 155, but now we need to turn it into a web server. The server waits for new HTTP requests like the one shown previously, parses the URL, and emits the corresponding infrared signal.

We'll hide all these details in a class named InfraredProxy, and to keep things as easy and as concise as possible, we'll make use of both the Ethernet and the IRremote library. The InfraredProxy class is still one of the book's most sophisticated examples of Arduino code. Here it is:

RemoteControl/InfraredProxy/InfraredProxy.pde

```
Line 1  #include <SPI.h>
    -   #include <Ethernet.h>
    -   #include <IRremote.h>
    -
    5   class InfraredProxy {
    -     IRsend _infrared_sender;
    -
    -     void read_line(Client& client, char* buffer, const int buffer_length) {
    -       int buffer_pos = 0;
   10       while (client.available() && (buffer_pos < buffer_length - 1)) {
    -         const char c = client.read();
    -         if (c == '\n')
    -           break;
    -         if (c != '\r')
   15           buffer[buffer_pos++] = c;
    -       }
    -       buffer[buffer_pos] = '\0';
    -     }
    -
   20     bool send_ir_data(const char* protocol, const int bits, const long value) {
    -       bool result = true;
    -       if (!strcasecmp(protocol, "NEC"))
    -         _infrared_sender.sendNEC(value, bits);
    -       else if (!strcasecmp(protocol, "SONY"))
   25         _infrared_sender.sendSony(value, bits);
    -       else if (!strcasecmp(protocol, "RC5"))
    -         _infrared_sender.sendRC5(value, bits);
    -       else if (!strcasecmp(protocol, "RC6"))
    -         _infrared_sender.sendRC6(value, bits);
   30       else
    -         result = false;
    -       return result;
    -     }
    -
   35     bool handle_command(char* line) {
    -       strsep(&line, " ");
    -       char* path = strsep(&line, " ");
    -
    -       char* args[3];
   40       for (char** ap = args; (*ap = strsep(&path, "/")) != NULL;)
    -         if (**ap != '\0')
    -           if (++ap >= &args[3])
    -             break;
    -       const int  bits = atoi(args[1]);
   45       const long value = atol(args[2]);
    -       return send_ir_data(args[0], bits, value);
    -     }
    -
    -   public:
```

```
50      void receive_from_server(Server server) {
          const int MAX_LINE = 256;
          char line[MAX_LINE];
          Client client = server.available();
55        if (client) {
            while (client.connected()) {
              if (client.available()) {
                read_line(client, line, MAX_LINE);
                Serial.println(line);
60              if (line[0] == 'G' && line[1] == 'E' && line[2] == 'T')
                  handle_command(line);
                if (!strcmp(line, "")) {
                  client.println("HTTP/1.1 200 OK\n");
                  break;
65              }
              }
            }
            delay(1);
            client.stop();
70        }
        }
      };
```

After including all libraries needed, we declare the InfraredProxy class. We define a member variable named _infrared_sender that stores an IRsend object we need to emit infrared control codes.

In line 8, we define a read_line() method that reads one line of data sent by a client. A line ends either with a newline character (\n) or with a carriage return character followed by a newline character (\r\n). read_line() expects the Ethernet Client object to read data from, a character buffer to store the data in (buffer), and the maximum length of the character buffer (buffer_length). The method ignores all newline and carriage return characters, and it sets the line's last character to \0, so the buffer to be filled will always be a null-terminated string.

The next method (send_ir_data()) starts in line 20 and emits an infrared command specified by a protocol type (protocol), the length of the code measured in bits (bits), and the code value to be sent (value). Depending on the name of the protocol, the method delegates all the real work to our IRsend instance.

handle_command() implements one of the most difficult aspects of our InfraredProxy: it parses the URL addressed by the HTTP request. To understand what this method does, we have to understand how HTTP requests work. If you wander up to your web browser's address bar and enter a URL like http://192.168.2.42/NEC/32/2011283550, your browser will send an HTTP request that looks like this:

```
GET /NEC/32/2011283550 HTTP/1.1
host: 192.168.2.42
```

The first line is a GET request, and handle_command() expects a string containing such a request. It extracts all information encoded in the path (/NEC/32/2011283550) and uses it to emit an infrared signal. Parsing the information is a bit tricky, but using C's strsep() function, it's not too difficult. strsep() separates strings delimited by certain characters. It expects a string containing several separated strings and a string containing all delimiters. strsep() replaces the first occurrence of any character in the delimiter string with a \0 character. It returns a pointer to the original string. Before that, it replaces the pointer to the string we wanted to split with a pointer pointing to the first string.

We use strsep() in two different contexts. In the first case, we extract the path from the GET command: we strip off the string "GET" and the string "HTTP/1.1." Both are separated from the path by a blank character. All this happens in lines 36 and 37. If you were to pass the URL http://192.168.2.42/NEC/32/2011283550 to handle_command(), for example, path would contain /NEC/32/2011283550.

At this stage, we have a string consisting of three strings separated by a slash character (/). It's time to use strsep() again, and if you understand what happens in lines 40 to 43, then you can call yourself familiar with both C and the strsep() function. In the end, the array args contains all three path elements. We can pass the protocol name directly to send_ir_data(), but we have to turn the bit length and the value of the code into **int** and **long** values before. For the conversion, we use the atoi() and atol() functions.

Now we have defined all helper methods we need, and we only have to implement the public interface of the InfraredProxy class. It contains only one method named receive_from_server(). This method finally implements the core logic of our InfraredProxy class. It expects an instance of the Server class that is defined in the Ethernet library. It waits for a client to connect using Server's available() method in line 54. Whenever the server is connected to a client, it checks whether the client has new data using Client's available() method in line 57.

receive_from_server() reads the data sent by the client line by line calling read_line(). It prints each line to the serial port for debugging purposes, and for every line it checks whether it begins with "GET." If yes, it calls handle_command(); otherwise, it checks whether the line is empty, because all HTTP messages are terminated by an empty line. In this case, receive_from_server() sends back an "OK" response, waits for a millisecond to give the client some time to process the response, and then disconnects from the client calling stop().

Admittedly that was a lot of code, but the effort was well worth it. Using the InfraredProxy is really simple now:

RemoteControl/InfraredProxy/InfraredProxy.pde

```
const unsigned int PROXY_PORT = 80;
const unsigned int BAUD_RATE = 9600;

byte mac[] = { 0xDE, 0xAD, 0xBE, 0xEF, 0xFE, 0xED };
byte ip[] = { 192, 168, 2, 42 };

Server server(PROXY_PORT);
InfraredProxy ir_proxy;

void setup() {
  Serial.begin(BAUD_RATE);
  Ethernet.begin(mac, ip);
  server.begin();
}

void loop() {
  ir_proxy.receive_from_server(server);
}
```

As usual, we define the MAC and IP addresses we'd like to use. Then we define a Server object, passing it the port it should listen to, 80 (the standard HTTP port). Also, we initialize a new InfraredProxy object.

In the setup() method, we initialize the serial port for debug purposes. We also initialize the Ethernet shield, and we call Server's begin() method to start our server's listener. In loop(), we only call the InfraredProxy's receive_from_server() method, passing it our Server instance.

Let's finally test the code! Attach the Ethernet shield to your Arduino, and attach the infrared LED circuit to the shield. Configure the MAC and IP addresses, compile it, and upload it to your Arduino. Point your web browser to http://192.168.2.42/NEC/32/2011283550 (adjust the URL to your local settings!), and see what happens to your Mac or whatever device you want to control (in Figure 9.9, on the following page, you can see a typical output of the infrared proxy on the serial monitor).

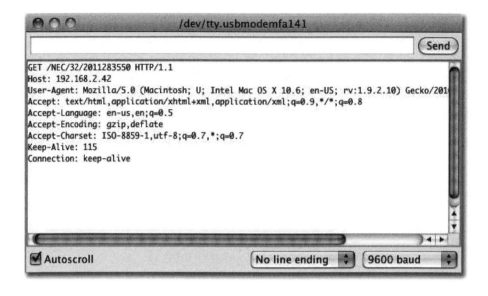

Figure 9.9: ACCESSING THE INFRARED PROXY WITH FIREFOX

Although we've used only a minimum amount of hardware (a cheap and simple infrared LED), this chapter's projects are very useful and fairly sophisticated, at least from a software development point of view. We can now not only control any device that understands infrared signals, but we can do it using a computer's serial port or even a web browser.

Also, you no longer need to connect the Arduino to your computer's USB port. The Infrared proxy, for example, only needs the USB port to get some power. Plug an AC adapter into your Arduino, and you can get rid of your USB cable.

For the first time, we've controlled real-world devices using an Arduino. We'll continue to do so in the next chapter, where you'll learn how to control motors.

9.7 What If It Doesn't Work?

In this chapter, we mainly used LEDs and an Ethernet shield, so all the advice from Chapter 3, *Building Binary Dice*, on page 45 and Chapter 8, *Networking with Arduino*, on page 155 also apply to this chapter.

In addition, you have to be careful about more things. For example, the distance between an infrared LED and its receiver is important.

> ### Control Everything
>
> All the projects in this chapter are based on devices you can control already using an infrared remote control. But you can also add an infrared receiver to existing devices or build completely new gadgets that come with an infrared receiver.
>
> In principle, you could control your refrigerator or your microwave oven with a remote control. But have you ever thought about a remote-controlled lawn mower?* I bet not.
>
> ---
> *. http://www.instructables.com/id/Arduino-RC-Lawnmower/

To be on the safe side, you should position the LED near the receiver. It should also be placed right in front of the receiver, and you should make sure that there's not too much ambient light that might disturb the infrared signal.

For debugging purposes, it's useful to replace invisible infrared LED with a regular LED from time to time. This way, you can see whether your circuit works in principle.

If you're trying to control a Mac, you should unpair any other remote controls in the security area of the Mac's system preferences menu.

Finally, you might be using a device that uses a protocol that is not supported by the IRremote library. In this case, you have to add it. This can be tricky, but IRremote is open source, so at least it's possible.

9.8 Exercises

- Build an emulator for a remote control you find in your household. Make its commands available via serial port and via Ethernet.

- Instead of controlling the Arduino via a serial monitor or web browser, control it using a Nintendo Nunchuk. For example, you could move the analog stick up and down to control your TV set's volume, and you could move it left or right to change the channels.

- Design a real universal remote control based on an Arduino. Look for a touch screen, a button pad, an SD card shield, and a Bluetooth module. I bet you didn't think you could build a device like this—but you know everything you need to do it now.

Chapter 10

Controlling Motors with Arduino

So far, we've created projects that have had an impact on the real world. We've made LEDs shine, and we've controlled devices using infrared light. In this chapter, we'll create an even more intense experience: we'll control motors that will actually move things. We won't go so far as to build a full-blown autonomous robot, but we'll create a small device that does something useful and funny.

First, though, you'll learn a bit about the basics of different motor types and their pros and cons. Today you can choose from a variety of motor types for your projects, and this chapter starts with a brief description of their differences.

We'll concentrate on servo motors, because you can use them for a wide range of projects and they're cheap and easy to use. You'll learn to use the Arduino servo library and to control a servo using the serial port.

Based on these first steps, we'll then build a more sophisticated project. It's a blaming device that uses nearly the same hardware as the first project in the chapter but more elaborate software. You'll probably find many applications for it in your office!

10.1 What You Need

1. A servo motor such as the Hitec HS-322HD
2. Some wires
3. A TMP36 temperature sensor (it's optional, and you need it only for the exercises)
4. An Arduino board such as the Uno, Duemilanove, or Diecimila
5. A USB cable to connect the Arduino to your computer

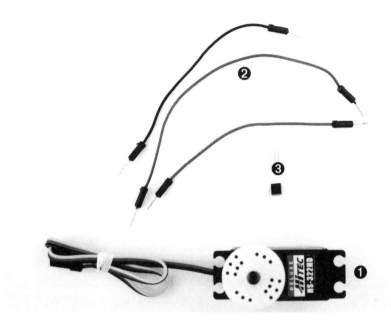

Figure 10.1: ALL THE PARTS YOU NEED IN THIS CHAPTER

10.2 Introducing Motors

Depending on your project's needs, you can choose from a variety of motors today. For hobby electronics, you'll usually use DC motors, servo motors, or stepper motors (in Figure 10.2, on the next page, you see a few different types of motors; no DC motor is shown). They mainly differ in speed, precision of control, power consumption, reliability, and price.

DC motors are fast and efficient, so you can use them in drill machines, electric bicycles, or remote-control cars. You can control DC motors easily, because they have only two connectors. Connect one to a power supply and the other to ground, and the motor starts to spin. Swap the connections, and the motor will spin the other way around. Add more voltage, and the motor spins faster; decrease voltage, and it spins slower.

DC motors aren't a good choice if you need precise control. In such cases, it's better to use a stepper motor, which allows for precise control in a range of 360 degrees. Although you might not have noticed

Figure 10.2: MOTOR TYPES FROM LEFT TO RIGHT: STANDARD SERVO, CONTINUOUS ROTATION SERVO, STEPPER

it, you're surrounded by stepper motors. You hear them when your printer, scanner, or disk drive is at work. Controlling stepper motors isn't rocket science, but it is a bit more complicated than controlling DC motors and servos.

Servo motors are the most popular among hobbyists, because they are a good compromise between DC motors and steppers. They're affordable, reliable, and easy to control. You can move standard servos only in a range of 180 degrees, but that's sufficient for many applications. With continuous rotation servos, you can increase the range to 360 degrees, but you lose the ease of control.

In the next section, you'll learn how easy it is to control standard servo motors with an Arduino.

10.3 First Steps with a Servo Motor

The Arduino IDE comes with a library for controlling servo motors that we'll use for our first experiments. In Figure 10.3, on the following page,

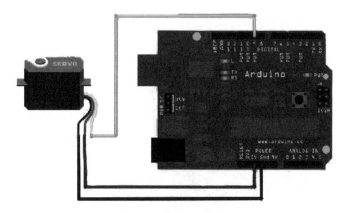

Figure 10.3: BASIC CIRCUIT FOR A 5V SERVO MOTOR

---

you can see a basic circuit for connecting an Arduino to a servo motor. Connect the ground wire to one of the Arduino's GND pins, connect power to the Arduino's 5V pin, and connect the control line to pin 9.

Please note that this works only for a 5V servo! Many cheap servos use 9V, and in this case, you need an external power supply, and you can no longer connect the servo to the Arduino's 5V pin. If you have a 9V servo, attach an external power supply such as an AC-to-DC adapter or a DC power supply to your Arduino's power jack. Then connect the servo to the Vin pin.[1] You should also check the specification of your Arduino board. For example, you should not use an Arduino BT[2] to control motors, because it can only cope with a maximum of 5.5V.

Figure 10.4, on the next page shows how to connect your servo motor to your Arduino using wires. You can also use pin headers, but wires give you more flexibility.

Controlling servo motors is convenient, because you can set the motor's shaft to an angle between 0 and 180. With the following sketch, you can send a degree value via the serial port and move the servo motor accordingly:

---

1.   http://www.arduino.cc/playground/Learning/WhatAdapter

2.   http://arduino.cc/en/Main/ArduinoBoardBluetooth

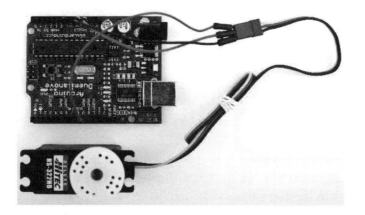

Figure 10.4: PLUG THREE WIRES INTO THE SERVO'S CONNECTOR TO ATTACH IT TO THE ARDUINO.

Motors/SerialServo/SerialServo.pde

```
Line 1   #include <Servo.h>

         const unsigned int MOTOR_PIN = 9;
         const unsigned int MOTOR_DELAY = 15;
    5    const unsigned int SERIAL_DELAY = 5;
         const unsigned int BAUD_RATE = 9600;

         Servo servo;

   10    void setup() {
           Serial.begin(BAUD_RATE);
           servo.attach(MOTOR_PIN);
           delay(MOTOR_DELAY);
           servo.write(1);
   15      delay(MOTOR_DELAY);
         }

         void loop() {
           const int MAX_ANGLE = 3;
   20
           char degrees[MAX_ANGLE + 1];

           if (Serial.available()) {
             int i = 0;
   25        while (Serial.available() && i < MAX_ANGLE) {
               const char c = Serial.read();
               if (c != -1 && c != '\n')
                 degrees[i++] = c;
```

```
   -              delay(SERIAL_DELAY);
  30            }
   -            degrees[i] = 0;
   -            Serial.print(degrees);
   -            Serial.println(" degrees.");
   -            servo.write(atoi(degrees));
  35            delay(MOTOR_DELAY);
   -          }
   -        }
```

We include the Servo library, and in line 8, we define a new Servo object. In the setup() function, we initialize the serial port, and we attach() the Servo object to the pin we have defined in MOTOR_PIN. After that, we wait for 15 milliseconds so the servo motor has enough time to process our command. Then we call write() to move back the servo to 1 degree. We could also move it back to 0 degrees, but some of the servos I have worked with make some annoying noise in this position.

The main purpose of the loop() function is to read new degree values from the serial port. These values are in a range from 0 to 180, and we read them as ASCII values. So, we need a string that can contain up to four characters (remember, strings are null-terminated in C). That's why we declare the degrees string with a length of four in line 21.

Then we wait for new data to arrive at the serial port and read it character by character until no more data is available or until we have read enough. We terminate the string with a zero byte and print the value we've read to the serial port. Finally, we convert the string into an integer value using atoi() and pass it to the write() method of the Servo object in line 34. Then we wait again for the servo to do its job.

Compile and upload the sketch, and then open the serial monitor. After the servo motor has initialized, send some degree values such as 45, 180, or 10. See how the motor moves to the angle you have specified. To see the effect a bit better, turn a wire or a piece of paper into an arrow, and attach it to the motor's gear.

It's easy to control a servo via the serial port, and the circuit we've built can be the basis for many useful and fun projects. In the next section, we'll use it to build an automatic blaming device.

10.4 Building a Blaminatr

Finger-pointing isn't nice, but it can be perversely satisfying. In this section, we'll build a device that I call *Blaminatr*. Instead of blaming

---

Arduino Arts

You can use the Arduino not just for gadgets or fun projects but also in artistic ways. Especially in the new-media art area you will find many amazing projects built with the Arduino. One of them is Anthros,* a responsive environment that observes a small area using a webcam. The area contains some "tentacles," and whenever a person crosses the area, the tentacles move into the person's direction. Servos move the tentacles, and an Arduino controls the servos.

For all people interested in new-media art, Alicia Gibb's thesis "New Media Art, Design, and the Arduino Microcontroller: A Malleable Tool"[†] is a must-read.

---

*. http://www.richgilbank.ca/anthros
†. http://aliciagibb.com/thesis/

---

someone directly, you can tell the Blaminatr to do so. In Figure 10.5, on the following page, you can see the device in action. Tell it to blame me, and it moves an arrow, so it points to "Maik."

Blaminatrs are perfect office toys that you can use in many situations. For software developers, it can be a good idea to attach one to your continuous integration (CI) system. Continuous integration systems such as CruiseControl.rb[3] or Luntbuild[4] help you continuously check whether your software is in good shape.

Whenever a developer checks in changes, the CI automatically compiles the software and runs all tests. Then it publishes the results via email or as an RSS feed. You can easily write a small piece of software that subscribes to such a feed. Whenever someone breaks the build, you'll find a notification in the feed, and you can use the Blaminatr to point to the name of the developer who has committed the latest changes.[5]

In the previous section, you learned all about servo motors you need to build the Blaminatr. Now we only need some creativity to build the device's display, and we need more elaborate software. We start with

---

3. http://cruisecontrolrb.thoughtworks.com/
4. http://luntbuild.javaforge.com/
5. At http://urbanhonking.com/ideasfordozens/2010/05/19/the_github_stoplight/, you can see an alternative project. It uses a traffic light to indicate your project's current status.

Figure 10.5: THE BLAMINATR: BLAMING HAS NEVER BEEN EASIER.

a class named Team that represents the members of our team; that is, the potential "blamees":

Motors/Blaminatr/Blaminatr.pde

```
Line 1  const unsigned int MAX_MEMBERS = 10;

        class Team {
          char** _members;
     5    int     _num_members;
          int     _positions[MAX_MEMBERS];

          public:

    10    Team(char** members) {
            _members = members;

            _num_members = 0;
            char** member = _members;
    15      while (*member++)
              _num_members++;
```

```
       const int share = 180 / _num_members;
       int pos = share / 2;
20     for (int i = 0; i < _num_members; i++) {
         _positions[i] = pos;
         pos += share;
       }
     }

25
     int get_position(const char* name) const {
       int position = 0;
       for (int i = 0; i < _num_members; i++) {
         if (!strcmp(_members[i], name)) {
30         position = _positions[i];
           break;
         }
       }
       return position;
35   }
};
```

The code defines several member variables: _members contains a list of up to ten team member names, _num_members contains the actual number of people on the team, and we store the position (angle) of the team member's name on the Blaminatr display in _positions.

The constructor expects an array of strings that contains the team members' names and that is terminated by a NULL pointer. We store a reference to the list, and then we calculate the number of team members. We iterate over the array until we find a NULL pointer. All this happens in lines 13 to 16.

Then we calculate the position of each team member's name on the Blaminatr's display. Every team member gets their fair share on the 180-degree display, and the Blaminatr will point to the share's center, so we divide the share by 2. We store the positions in the _positions array that corresponds to the _members array. That means the first entry of _positions contains the position of the first team member, and so on.

With the get_position() method, we get back the position belonging to a certain name. We walk through the _members array and check whether we have found the right member using the strcmp() function. As soon as we've found it, we return the corresponding entry of the _positions array. If we couldn't find a team member with the name we are looking for, we return 0.

Implementing a Blaminatr class is easy now:

Motors/Blaminatr/Blaminatr.pde

```
#include <Servo.h>

const unsigned int MOTOR_PIN = 9;
const unsigned int MOTOR_DELAY = 15;

class Blaminatr {
  Team  _team;
  Servo _servo;

  public:

  Blaminatr(const Team& team) : _team(team) {}

  void attach(const int sensor_pin) {
    _servo.attach(sensor_pin);
    delay(MOTOR_DELAY);
  }

  void blame(const char* name) {
    _servo.write(_team.get_position(name));
    delay(MOTOR_DELAY);
  }
};
```

A Blaminatr object aggregates a Team object and a Servo object. The constructor initializes the Team instance while we can initialize the Servo instance by calling the attach() method.

The most interesting method is blame(). It expects the name of the team member to blame, calculates his position, and moves the servo accordingly. Let's put it all together now:

Motors/Blaminatr/Blaminatr.pde

```
Line 1  const unsigned int MAX_NAME = 30;
    -   const unsigned int BAUD_RATE = 9600;
    -   const unsigned int SERIAL_DELAY = 5;
    -
    5   char* members[] = { "nobody", "Bob", "Alice", "Maik", NULL };
    -   Team team(members);
    -   Blaminatr blaminatr(team);
    -
    -   void setup() {
   10     Serial.begin(BAUD_RATE);
    -     blaminatr.attach(MOTOR_PIN);
    -     blaminatr.blame("nobody");
    -   }
    -
   15   void loop() {
    -     char name[MAX_NAME + 1];
```

```
     if (Serial.available()) {
       int i = 0;
       while (Serial.available() && i < MAX_NAME) {
20       const char c = Serial.read();
         if (c != -1 && c != '\n')
           name[i++] = c;
         delay(SERIAL_DELAY);
       }
25     name[i] = 0;
       Serial.print(name);
       Serial.println(" is to blame.");
       blaminatr.blame(name);
     }
30 }
```

We define a list of member names that is terminated by a NULL pointer. The list's first entry is "nobody," so we don't have to deal with the rare edge case when nobody is to blame. Then we use members to initialize a new Team object and pass this object to the Blaminatr's constructor.

In the setup() function, we initialize the serial port and attach the Blaminatr's servo motor to the pin we defined in MOTOR_PIN. Also, we initialize the Blaminatr by blaming "nobody."

The loop() function is nearly the same as in Section 10.3, *First Steps with a Servo Motor*, on page 211. The only difference is that we do not control a servo directly but call blame() in line 28.

That's it! You can now start to draw your own display and create your own arrow. Attach them directly to the motor or—even better—put everything into a nice box. Compile and upload the software and start to blame.

Of course, you can use motors for more serious projects. For example, you can use them to build robots running on wheels or similar devices. But you cannot attach too many motors to a "naked" Arduino, because it is not meant for driving bigger loads. So if you have a project in mind that needs a significant number of motors, you should consider buying a motor shield[6] or use a special shield such as the Roboduino.[7]

10.5 What If It Doesn't Work?

Working with motors is surprisingly easy, but still a lot of things can go wrong. The biggest problem is that motors consume a lot of power,

---

6. You can find them at http://adafruit.com or http://makershed.com.
7. http://store.curiousinventor.com/roboduino.html

More Motors Projects

Motors are fascinating. Search the 'net and you'll find numerous projects combining the Arduino with them. A fun project is the Arduino Hypnodisk.* It uses a servo motor to rotate a hypno disc—a rotating disk with a spiral printed on it that has an hypnotic effect. An infrared rangefinder changes the motor's speed, so the closer you get to the disc, the faster it spins.

A useful and exciting project is the USB hourglass.† It uses an Arduino and a servo motor to turn a sand timer, and it observes the falling sand using an optical sensor. Whenever all the sand has fallen through, the device turns the timer automatically.

That's all nice, but the device's main purpose is to generate true random numbers. Falling sand is a perfect basis for generating true randomness (see the sidebar on page 55), and the USB hourglass uses the signals from its optical sensor to generate random numbers, sending them to the serial port.

---

*. http://www.flickr.com/photos/kevino/4583084700/in/pool-make
†. http://home.comcast.net/~hourglass/

---

so you cannot simply attach every motor to an Arduino. Also, you cannot easily drive more than one motor, especially not with the small amount of power you get from a USB port. If your motor does not run as expected, check its specification, and attach an AC or DC adapter to your Arduino if necessary.

You also shouldn't attach too much weight to your motor. Moving an arrow made of paper is no problem, but you might run into problems if you attach bigger and heavier things. Also, be careful not to put any obstacles into the motor's way. The motor's shaft always needs to move freely.

Some motors have to be adjusted from time to time, and usually you have to do that with a very small screw driver. Refer to the motor's specification for detailed instructions.

10.6 Exercises

- Add an Ethernet shield to the Blaminatr so you can blame people via Internet and not only via the serial port. Pointing your

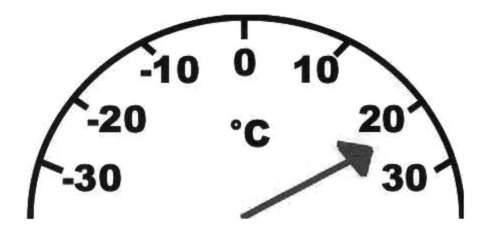

Figure 10.6: A MOTORIZED THERMOMETER

web browser to an address such as http://192.168.1.42/blame/Maik should blame me, for example.

- Create a thermometer based on a TMP36 temperature sensor and a servo motor. Its display could look like Figure 10.6; that is, you have to move an arrow that points to the current temperature.

- Use an IR receiver to control the Blaminatr. For example, you could use the channel key of your TV set's remote control to proceed the Blaminatr from one name to the other.

Part III

Appendixes

Basics of Electronics

We didn't need a lot of theory or background to create our first Arduino projects. But it's a good idea to learn a bit about electricity and about soldering if you want to build bigger and more sophisticated projects.

In this appendix, you'll learn the basics of electricity, and you'll learn about Ohm's law, which is probably the most important law in electronics. Also, you'll learn more about resistors, and you'll see that soldering isn't as difficult as it might seem.

A.1 Current, Voltage, and Resistance

To build your first projects with the Arduino, you didn't need to know much about electricity. But at some point, you'll need to understand what current, voltage, and resistance is all about. For example, you already know that you always have to put a resistor in front of an LED, but you might not know exactly why, and you might not know how to calculate the resistor's size for a given LED. Let's remedy that.

An electrical circuit resembles a water circuit in many respects. In Figure A.1, on the following page, you can see a water circuit on the left and an electrical circuit on the right. Isn't it fascinating how similar they are and that you can even find a connection between them when you use a water-driven dynamo that acts as a power supply? Let's take a closer look at their most important attributes.

While water flows in a water circuit, electrons flow in an electrical circuit. Voltage is electricity's equivalent of water pressure and is measured in volts (V). Voltage is the initial cause for a current, and the higher the voltage, the faster the current flows.

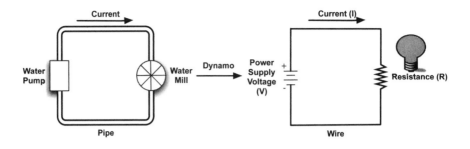

Figure A.1: WATER CIRCUITS AND ELECTRICAL CIRCUITS ARE SIMILAR.

In electronics, current is the amount of electricity flowing through an electric line. It is the equivalent of the actual flow of water in a water circuit. While we measure the water flow in liters per minute, we measure current in ampere. One ampere means that approximately 6.24×10^{18} electrons are flowing per second.

Every component in a circuit—be it water or electricity—resists some amount of current. In a water circuit, it's the pipes the water is flowing through or perhaps a water mill. In an electrical circuit, it is the wire or a light bulb. Resistance is an important physical phenomenon that is closely related to current and voltage. We measure it in Ohms, and its official symbol is Ω.

The German physicist Georg Ohm found out that current depends on voltage and resistance. He postulated the following form we call *Ohm's law* today:[1]

- I (current) = V (voltage) / R (resistance)

This is equivalent to the following:

- R (resistance) = V (voltage) / I (current)

- V (voltage) = R (resistance) $\times$ I (current)

So, for two given values, you can calculate the third one. Ohm's law is the only formula you'll absolutely have to learn when learning electron-

---

1. We use I as the current's letter for historical reasons. In the past, it stood for inductance.

ics. When working with LEDs, for example, it helps you calculate the size of the resistor you need.

If you look at a LED's data sheet, you'll usually find two values: a forward voltage and a current rating. The forward voltage usually is somewhere between 1.8V and 3.6V, and the maximum current often is 20 mA (milliamperes). Let's say we have an LED with a maximum of 2.5 volts and a safe current of 20 mA. We also assume that we have a power supply delivering 5 volts (as the Arduino does, for example). What's the right size of the resistor we need to put in front of the LED?

We have to make sure that the resistor takes 5 – 2.5 = 2.5 volts from the circuit, so only 2.5 volts are left for the LED. This value is called *voltage drop*. Also, we want a maximum of 20 mA to flow through the LED. This implies that a maximum of 20 mA (0.02 A) should flow through our resistor also.

Now that we know that 2.5 V and 0.02 A should pass the LED, we can use Ohm's law to calculate the resistance R:

$R = V / I$

In our case, we have the following:

$R = 2.5V / 0.02A = 125\Omega$

This means we need a 125Ω resistor for our LED. If you do not have a 125Ω resistor, use a bigger one such as 150Ω or 220Ω. It will still protect the LED and only slightly decrease its brightness. That's because we'd decrease the current even more:

$I = 2.5V / 150\Omega = 17mA$

$I = 2.5V / 220\Omega = 11mA$

Resistors

You'll hardly ever find an electronics project that doesn't need resistors. So, you'll need them often and should get familiar with them a bit more. Usually you'll use carbon or metal resistors. Metal resistors are more precise and don't create so much noise, but carbon resistors are a bit cheaper. In simple circuits, it usually doesn't matter which type you use.

The most important attribute of a resistor is its resistance value that is measured in Ohm. Only a few vendors actually print this value on the resistor, because resistors are small parts, and it's hard to read text

	Color	Code	Zeros
⬛	Black	0	-
⬛	Brown	1	0
⬛	Red	2	00
⬛	Orange	3	000
⬜	Yellow	4	0000
⬜	Green	5	00000
⬛	Blue	6	000000
⬛	Violet	7	0000000
⬛	Gray	8	00000000
	White	9	000000000

Figure A.2: Resistor values are encoded using colors.

that is so small it fits on them. So, they use a trick and encode the value using colored stripes.

Usually you find four or five stripes on a resistor (at least on through-hole parts; SMD resistors don't have them). One of them is separated from the others by a gap (see Figure A.3, on the next page). The separate stripe is on the right side of the resistor, and it tells you about the resistor's accuracy. Gold stands for an accuracy of ±5 percent, silver for ±10 percent, and no stripe means ±20 percent. Using the remaining stripes, you can calculate the resistor value.

You read the stripes from left to right, and every color stands for a digit (see Figure A.2). The rightmost stripe—that is the third or fourth one—stands for an amount of zeros to be added to the preceding digits. In Figure A.3, on the next page, you can see three examples:

- On the first resistor we find four stripes: brown (1), green (5), brown (1 zero), silver (±10%). That means we have a resistor value of 150Ω.

- The second resistor has four stripes again: yellow (4), violet (7), orange (3 zeros), gold (± 5%). So, this resistor has a value of 47000Ω = 47k Ω.

- The third resistor has five stripes: brown (1), red (2), red (2), green (5 zeros), silver (±10%), so the value is 12,200,000Ω = 12.2MΩ.

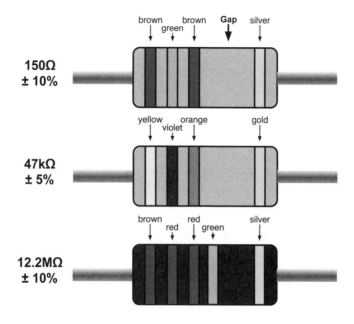

Figure A.3: COLORED STRIPES TELL YOU ABOUT RESISTOR VALUES.

In the beginning, the color coding seems to be complicated, but you'll get used to it quickly. Also, you can find countless tools for determining resistor values on the Internet.[2]

For the book's projects, this is all the theory of electricity you need to know. To learn more about electronics, have a look at *Make: Electronics* [Pla10] or at http://lcamtuf.coredump.cx/electronics/.

A.2 Learning How to Solder

You can build nearly all of the book's projects by plugging parts into a breadboard or directly into the Arduino board. But sooner or later you'll have to learn how to solder if you want to become an expert in electronics. That's mainly because you'll learn the most by building projects, and even the simplest kits require some sort of soldering.

A lot of people think that soldering is difficult or requires expensive equipment, so they never try to do it. The truth is that it's cheap and

---

2. http://harkopen.com/tutorials/using-wolfram-alpha-electric-circuits

pretty easy. It requires some practice, but after only a few solder joints you'll see that it's not rocket science.

In this book, we have one project that requires you to solder a pin header to an ADXL335 breakout board. We need it for building the motion-sensing game controller in Chapter 6, *Building a Motion-Sensing Game Controller*, on page 117. In this section, you'll learn how to do it, and you'll need the following equipment (shown in Figure A.4):

- A 25–30 watt soldering iron with a tip (preferably 1/16") and a soldering stand.

- Standard 60/40 solder (rosin-core) spool for electronics work. It should have a 0.031" diameter.

- A sponge.

Before you start to solder, prepare your work area. Make sure that you can easily access all your tools and that you have something to protect your work area from drops of solder. Wearing safety glasses is always a good idea! Even seemingly simple and harmless activities such as cutting wires, for example, can be very dangerous!

Bring all parts into the right position: attach the pin header to the breakout board, and make sure you cannot accidentally move it while soldering.

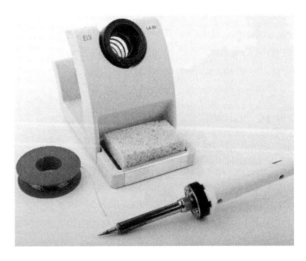

Figure A.4: YOU NEED THESE TOOLS FOR SOLDERING.

Figure A.5: YOU HAVE TO ATTACH THE PIN HEADER TO THE BREAKOUT BOARD.

People get very creative when it comes to locking parts into a certain position. But you have to be careful—don't use flammable materials to bring parts together. You should not use parts that distribute heat very well either, especially if they are in touch with other parts. Duct tape might work in some cases, but be careful with it, too.

Try to find a piece of wood or something similar that has the right height: the height of the pin headers. Then you can put the breakout board on top of it and attach the pin headers. If you're planning to solder more often and build some electronics projects, you should always look for these little tools that make your life easier.

In Figure A.5, you can see how I have prepared all parts with a *helping hand*, a useful tool for locking parts into a position. They usually come with a magnifying glass, and they are cheap. If you plan to solder often, you should get one (see Figure A.6, on the next page).

After you've prepared everything, it's time to heat up the soldering iron. The main purpose of soldering is to join metallic surfaces. In our case,

Figure A.6: A "HELPING HAND" REALLY DESERVES ITS NAME.

we'd like to join the surface of the pin header with the metal in the breakout board. To achieve this, we'll heat up the metallic parts and then connect them using molten solder.

This process depends on a certain temperature, and the wrong temperature is one of the most common soldering problems. If the temperature is too low, your solder joints might become fragile, and you also might have to touch the parts for too long, so you can damage them. An extremely high temperature can damage your parts right away. Experts can debate for hours and days about "the right temperature," but 600 to 650 F (315 to 350 C) is a good compromise.

Wet the sponge (it shouldn't be too wet), and clean the tip by wiping it over the sponge a few times. Then *tin* the tip by putting a small amount of solder back onto the tip. This helps protect the tip, and it also improves the heat transfer to components:

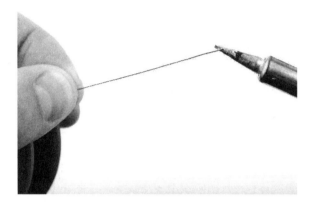

Soldering is mainly about heat distribution, and now it's time to heat the joint. Make sure the tip of the soldering iron touches the part (pin header) and the pad of the breakout board at the same time:

Keep it there for about a second, and then feed a small amount of solder between the tip and the pin:

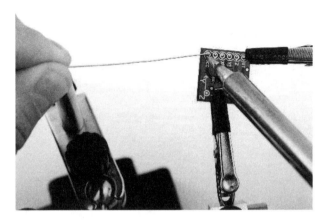

As soon as the solder starts to flow, you're safer, because the solder distributes heat automatically. Feed some more solder (not too much!) until you have a nice, shiny solder joint. The whole process shouldn't take more than two to three seconds. When you're done, remove the iron tip quickly, and give the joint a few seconds to cool down.

Repeat this for all six pin headers, and the result should look like this:,

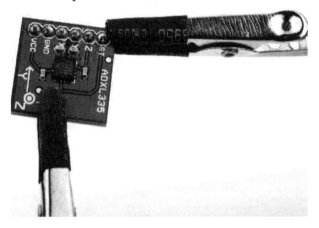

Test it by building the motion-sensing game controller, and play a video game to relax a bit.

Congratulations! You have just finished your first soldering job!

This tutorial is only a starting point for your new shiny soldering career. At least you know by now that soldering isn't too difficult. You can now try to build some beginner's kits. All electronics stores offer them, and they usually come with soldering instructions, too. You can also find excellent tutorials and even videos on the Internet to build your skills.[3]

---

3. http://store.curiousinventor.com/guides/How_to_Solder

Advanced Arduino Programming

In reality, the Arduino programming language is nothing but C++, but it has some restrictions, and it uses a special tool suite. In this appendix, you'll learn what the restrictions are. Also, you'll find a short section showing how bit operators work, because you need them often when working with sensors and other devices.

B.1 The Arduino Programming Language

The first sketches you'll write for an Arduino might seem to be written in a special "Arduino Language," but they aren't. To program the Arduino, you usually use plain old C/C++ and have to cross-compile your source code into machine code suitable for the Arduino's microcontroller.

These microcontrollers are all part of the AVR family produced by a company named Atmel. To make software development for AVR micro-controllers as easy as possible, Atmel has developed a whole tool chain based on the GNU compiler tools. All tools work like the originals, but they have been optimized for generating code for the AVR microcon-trollers.

For nearly all GNU development tools such as gcc, ld, or as, there's an AVR variant: avr-gcc, avr-ld, and so on. You can find them in the hardware/tools/bin directory of the Arduino IDE.

The IDE is mainly a graphical wrapper that helps you avoid using the command-line tools directly. Whenever you compile or upload a pro-gram using the IDE, it delegates all work to the AVR tools. As a seri-ous software developer, you should turn on a more verbose output, so you can see all command-line tool invocations. Edit preferences.txt as described in Section 2.3, *Changing Preferences*, on page 29, and set both build.verbose and upload.verbose to true. Then load our blinking LED sketch and compile it. The output in the message panel should look similar to Figure 2.3, on page 31.

The command invocations look a bit weird at first, because of the names of the many temporary files that are created. You should still be able to identify all compile and link steps that are necessary to build even a simple sketch like our blinking LED example. That's the most important thing that the Arduino team did: they hid all these nasty details well behind the IDE, so even people with no software development experience are able to program the Arduino. For programmers, it's a good idea to work in verbose mode, because the best way to learn about all the AVR tools is to see them in action.

Upload the program to the Arduino now to see avrdude in action. This tool is responsible for loading code into the Arduino and can be used for programming many other devices, too. Interestingly, the AVR tools make it even possible to use the Arduino IDE for non-Arduino projects such as the Meggy Jr.[1]

"But wait!" you say, "I'm a C++ programmer, and I'm missing a main() function!" And you're right: that's another difference between Arduino programming and regular old C++ code. When programming for the Arduino, you don't define main() yourself, because it is already defined in the libraries provided by the Arduino developers. As you might have guessed, it calls setup() first and then runs the loop() function in a loop.

There are further restrictions when programming C++ on AVR microcontrollers:[2]

- You cannot use the Standard Template Library (STL), because it's way too big for the small AVR microcontrollers.

- Exception handling is not supported. That's why you see the -fno-exceptions switch often when the avr-gcc compiler is invoked.

- Dynamic memory management using new() and delete() is currently not supported.

In addition to all that, you should keep an eye on performance. For example, C++ automatically creates a lot of functions (copy construc-

---

1. http://www.evilmadscientist.com/article.php/meggyjr
2. http://www.nongnu.org/avr-libc/user-manual/FAQ.html#faq_cplusplus

tors, assignment operators, and so on) in the background that are rarely needed on the Arduino. Even with these restrictions, the Arduino supports a powerful subset of the C++ programming language. So, there's no excuse for sloppy coding!

B.2 Bit Operations

In embedded computing, you often have to manipulate bits. For example, you sometimes have to read single bits to get some sensor data. In other cases, you have to set bits to turn a device into a certain status or make it perform some action.

For bit manipulation, you need only a few operations. The simplest is the *not* operation that inverses a bit. It turns a 0 into a 1, and vice versa. Most programming languages implement the *not* operation with a *!*-operator:

```
int x = 42; // In binary this is 101010
int y = !x; // y == 010101
```

In addition, you'll find three binary operations named *AND*, *OR*, and *XOR* (eXclusive OR). Most programming languages call the corresponding operators &, |, and ^, and their definitions are as follows:

a	b	a AND b a & b	a OR b a | b	a XOR b a ^ b
0	0	0	0	0
1	0	0	1	1
0	1	0	1	1
1	1	1	1	0

With these operators, it's possible to *mask* bits in a number. For example, you can extract certain bits. If you're interested only in the lower two bits of a number, you can do it as follows:

```
int x = 42;        // In binary this is 101010
int y = x & 0x03; // y == 2 == B10
```

You can also set or clear one or more bits in a number using the *OR* operation. The following code sets the fifth bit in x no matter if this bit is 0 or 1.

```
int x = 42;        // In binary this is 101010
int y = x | 0x10; // y == 58 == B111010
```

The bit shift operators << and >> let you move bits to a certain position before you work with them. The first one moves bits to the left, and the second moves them to the right:

```
int x = 42;       // In binary this is 101010
int y = x << 1;   // y == 84 == B1010100
int z = x >> 2;   // z == 10 == B1010
```

Shifting operations might seem intuitive, but you have to be careful when shifting signed values.[3] Although they look similar, binary operators are not the same as boolean operators. Boolean operators such as && and || do not operate on the bit level. They implement the rules of boolean algebra.[4]

---

3. http://en.wikipedia.org/wiki/Arithmetic_shift
4. http://en.wikipedia.org/wiki/Boolean_algebra_%28logic%29

Advanced Serial Programming

In nearly all the book's projects, we've used the Arduino's serial port. Sometimes we only emitted debug messages to monitor the current state of our sketches, but often we needed it to actually output information or to send commands. And the fact is, we've used the Serial class without explaining how serial communication actually works. We catch that up in this appendix.

To communicate with an Arduino, we used the Processing programming language, and we used JavaScript. But many developers prefer other languages, and in this appendix, you'll also learn how to use C/C++, Java, Ruby, Python, and Perl to talk to an Arduino.

C.1 Learning More About Serial Communication

In Chapter 2, *Inside the Arduino*, on page 27, you saw that you only need three wires for serial communication: a common ground, a line for transmitting data (TX), and one for receiving data (RX) (see the diagram on page 32).

Data is transmitted as electrical pulses, so both communication partners need a reference for the voltage level, and that's what the common ground is for. The transmission line is used to send data to the recipient and has to be connected to the recipient's receiving line. This enables full-duplex communication where both partners can send and receive data simultaneously (wouldn't it be great if people could also communicate full-duplex?).

We now know how to connect two devices, but we still have to transmit some data. Therefore, both communication partners have to agree on

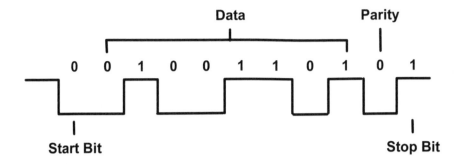

Figure C.1: SERIAL COMMUNICATION ON THE BIT LEVEL

a protocol, and in Figure C.1, you can see what a typical serial communication looks like. The different states of a bit are represented by different voltage levels. Usually, a 0 bit is represented by 0 volts, while 5 volts stands for a 1 bit (some protocols use -12V and 12V, respectively).

The following parameters control a serial communication:

- A *start bit* indicates the beginning of a data word and is used to synchronize transmitter and receiver. It is always 0.

- A *stop bit* tells us when the last data bit has been sent and separates two consecutive data words. Depending on the particular protocol agreement, there can be more than one stop bit, but that happens rarely.

- Information is transferred as binary *data bits*; that is, if you'd like to transmit the letter *M* for example, you have to turn it into a number first. Several character set encodings are available, but when working with the Arduino, the ASCII encoding fits best. In ASCII, an uppercase *M* is encoded as the decimal number 77, which is 01001101 in binary. This is the bit sequence that eventually gets transmitted.

- The *parity bit* indicates whether the number of 1s in the data has been odd or even. This is a simple error checking algorithm that is rarely used and that stems from a time when network connections have been less reliable than they are today.

Parity control can be "none" (no parity bit is sent), "odd" (the parity bit is set if the amount of 1s in the data bits is odd; otherwise, it is 0), or "even" (the parity bit is set if the amount of 1s in the data bits is even; otherwise, it is 0). We chose odd parity for our data, and because there are 4 bits set to 1 in 01001101, the parity bit is 0.

- The *baud rate* defines the transmission speed and is measured in transmission steps per second. When working with the Arduino, typical baud rates are 9600, 14400, 19200, or even 115200. Note that the baud rate does not define how much data is actually transferred per second, because you have to take the control bits into account. If your connection settings are 1 start bit, 1 stop bit, no parity, and 8 bits per byte, then you have to transfer 1 + 1 + 8 = 10 bits to transfer a single byte. With a baud rate set to 9600, you can then theoretically send 9600 / 10 = 960 bytes per second—at least if every bit gets transferred in exactly one transmission step.

C.2 Serial Communication Using Various Programming Languages

In this book, we've already used different programming languages to access an Arduino connected to your computer's serial port. In Chapter 6, *Building a Motion-Sensing Game Controller*, on page 117, we used Processing, and in Chapter 9, *Creating Your Own Universal Remote Control*, on page 187, we used JavaScript.

When working with the Arduino, you often have to program serial ports. So in this section, you'll learn how to do that in various programming languages. For demonstration purposes, we'll use the same Arduino sketch for all of them:

SerialProgramming/AnalogReader/AnalogReader.pde
```
const unsigned int BAUD_RATE = 9600;
const unsigned int SERIAL_DELAY = 5;
const unsigned int NUM_PINS = 6;

void setup() {
  Serial.begin(BAUD_RATE);
}

void loop() {
  const int MAX_PIN_NAME = 3;
```

```
    char pin_name[MAX_PIN_NAME + 1];

  if (Serial.available()) {
    int i = 0;
    while (Serial.available() && i < MAX_PIN_NAME) {
      const char c = Serial.read();
      if (c != -1 && c != '\n')
        pin_name[i++] = c;
      delay(SERIAL_DELAY);
    }
    pin_name[i] = 0;
    if (strlen(pin_name) > 1 &&
        (pin_name[0] == 'a' || pin_name[0] == 'A'))
    {
      const int pin = atoi(&pin_name[1]);
      if (pin < NUM_PINS) {
        Serial.print(pin_name);
        Serial.print(": ");
        Serial.println(analogRead(pin));
      } else {
        Serial.print("Unknown pin: ");
        Serial.println(pin);
      }
    } else {
      Serial.print("Unknown pin name: ");
      Serial.println(pin_name);
    }
  }
}
```

This program waits for the name of an analog pin (a0, a1, ... a5) and returns its current value. So, all our clients have to send data to the Arduino (the name of the pin), and they have to receive the result (in Figure C.2, on the next page, you can see it working with the IDE's serial monitor).

All clients will look similar: they expect the name of the serial port to connect to as a command-line argument. They will constantly send the string "a0" to the Arduino to get back the current value of analog pin 0. Then they print the result to the console. They all use a constant baud rate of 9600, and they all wait for two seconds after opening the serial port, because many Arduinos reboot upon opening a serial connection. To learn more about serial communication in general, take a look at Section C.1, *Learning More About Serial Communication*, on page 239.

For some of the clients, you need to install additional libraries. In some cases, you have to do that as an admin user on your machine. I won't mention that explicitly in the following sections. Also, you should make

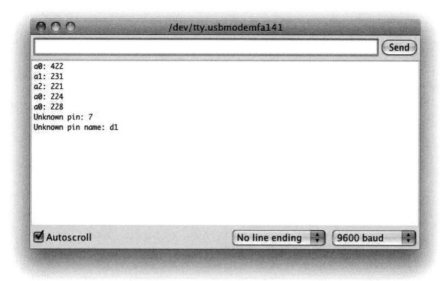

Figure C.2: OUR TEST SKETCH RETURNS THE CURRENT VALUES OF ANA-
LOG PINS.

sure you do not have any serial monitor windows open when running
one of the examples in the following sections.

C/C++

Although you program the Arduino in C++, you don't need to write
clients talking to the Arduino in C++ or C. Still, you can, and it's easy,
if you use Tod E. Kurt's excellent arduino_serial.c[1] as a basis.

The original program implements a complete command-line tool offer-
ing a lot of useful options. For our purpose, that's not necessary, so I've
extracted its four major functions into a C header file:

SerialProgramming/c/arduino-serial.h

```
#ifndef __ARDUINO_SERIAL__
#define __ARDUINO_SERIAL__

#include <fcntl.h>
#include <sys/ioctl.h>
```

---

1. http://todbot.com/blog/2006/12/06/arduino-serial-c-code-to-talk-to-arduino/

```
#include <termios.h>
#include <stdint.h>
#include <string.h>

int serialport_init(const char* serialport, int baud);
int serialport_writebyte(int fd, uint8_t b);
int serialport_write(int fd, const char* str);
int serialport_read_until(int fd, char* buf, char until);

#endif
```

Their meaning is as follows:

- serialport_init() opens a serial port connection. It expects the name of the serial port to be opened and the baud rate to be used. It returns a file descriptor if everything went fine, and it returns -1 otherwise.

- With serialport_writebyte(), you can send a single byte to an Arduino connected to your computer's serial port. Simply pass it the file descriptor returned by serialport_init() and the byte to be written. It returns -1 if an error occurred. Otherwise, it returns 0.

- serialport_write() writes an entire string to the serial port. It expects a file descriptor and the string to be written. It returns -1 if an error occurred. Otherwise, it returns 0.

- Use serialport_read_until() to read data from a serial port. Pass it a file descriptor and a buffer to be filled with the data read. The method also expects a delimiter character. serial_port_read_until() reads data until it finds that character and it always returns 0.

Just for the sake of completeness, we'll have a look at the implementation of our four functions:

SerialProgramming/c/arduino-serial.c

```
#include "arduino-serial.h"

int serialport_writebyte(int fd, uint8_t b) {
  int n = write(fd, &b, 1);
  return (n != 1) ? -1 : 0;
}

int serialport_write(int fd, const char* str) {
  int len = strlen(str);
  int n = write(fd, str, len);
  return (n != len) ? -1 : 0;
}
```

```c
int serialport_read_until(int fd, char* buf, char until) {
  char b[1];
  int i = 0;
  do {
    int n = read(fd, b, 1);
    if (n == -1)
      return -1;
      if (n == 0) {
        usleep(10 * 1000);
        continue;
      }
      buf[i++] = b[0];
  } while (b[0] != until);

  buf[i] = 0;
  return 0;
}

int serialport_init(const char* serialport, int baud) {
  int fd = open(serialport, O_RDWR | O_NOCTTY | O_NDELAY);
  if (fd == -1) {
    perror("init_serialport: Unable to open port");
    return -1;
  }

  struct termios toptions;
  if (tcgetattr(fd, &toptions) < 0) {
    perror("init_serialport: Couldn't get term attributes");
    return -1;
  }

  speed_t brate = baud;
  switch(baud) {
    case 4800:   brate = B4800;   break;
    case 9600:   brate = B9600;   break;
    case 19200:  brate = B19200;  break;
    case 38400:  brate = B38400;  break;
    case 57600:  brate = B57600;  break;
    case 115200: brate = B115200; break;
  }
  cfsetispeed(&toptions, brate);

  toptions.c_cflag &= ~PARENB;
  toptions.c_cflag &= ~CSTOPB;
  toptions.c_cflag &= ~CSIZE;
  toptions.c_cflag |= CS8;
  toptions.c_cflag &= ~CRTSCTS;
  toptions.c_cflag |= CREAD | CLOCAL;
  toptions.c_iflag &= ~(IXON | IXOFF | IXANY);
  toptions.c_lflag &= ~(ICANON | ECHO | ECHOE | ISIG);
  toptions.c_oflag &= ~OPOST;
```

```
    toptions.c_cc[VMIN]  = 0;
    toptions.c_cc[VTIME] = 20;

    if (tcsetattr(fd, TCSANOW, &toptions) < 0) {
      perror("init_serialport: Couldn't set term attributes");
      return -1;
    }

    return fd;
}
```

If you're familiar with Unix file handling, everything will make perfect sense to you. If not, well, then you still have the code to access an Arduino connected to your computer's serial port. Here's how to use the code for communicating with our analog reader sketch (note that the following code will run on your PC and not on your Arduino):

SerialProgramming/c/analog_reader.c

```
Line 1  #include <stdio.h>
     -  #include <unistd.h>
     -  #include "arduino-serial.h"
     -
     5  #define MAX_LINE 256
     -
     -  int main(int argc, char* argv[]) {
     -    if (argc == 1) {
     -      printf("You have to pass the name of a serial port.\n");
    10      return -1;
     -    }
     -
     -    int baudrate = B9600;
     -    int arduino = serialport_init(argv[1], baudrate);
    15    if (arduino == -1) {
     -      printf("Could not open serial port %s.\n", argv[1]);
     -      return -1;
     -    }
     -    sleep(2);
    20
     -    char line[MAX_LINE];
     -    while (1) {
     -      int rc = serialport_write(arduino, "a0\n");
     -      if (rc == -1) {
    25        printf("Could not write to serial port.\n");
     -      } else {
     -        serialport_read_until(arduino, line, '\n');
     -        printf("%s", line);
     -      }
    30    }
     -    return 0;
     -  }
```

First we import all the libraries we need, and we define a constant for the maximum length of the lines we are going to read from the Arduino. Then we define a main() function.

After we've made sure that the name of a serial port was passed on the command line, we initialize a serial port in line 14. Then we sleep for two seconds to give the Arduino some time to get ready. After that, we start a loop where we constantly send the string "a0" to the Arduino in line 23. We check the result of serialport_write(), and if it was successful, we read the result sent by the Arduino in line 27. Let's compile our little program:

```
maik> gcc arduino-serial.c analog_reader.c -o analog_reader
```

Determine what serial port your Arduino is connected to (mine is connected to /dev/tty.usbmodemfa141), and run the program like this:

```
maik> ./analog_reader /dev/tty.usbmodemfa141
a0: 495
a0: 376
a0: 368
^C
```

Everything works as expected, and accessing a serial port using C isn't that difficult. To embed this code into a C++ program, you should wrap it in a class named SerialPort or something similar.

Java

The Java platform standardizes a lot, and it also defines how to access a serial port in the Java Communications API.[2] But the API is only a specification that still has to be implemented. A good implementation is the RXTX project.[3]

Download the most current release, and follow the installation instructions for your platform. Make sure that RXTXcomm.jar is on your class path. Then enter the following code in your favorite IDE or text editor:

SerialProgramming/java/AnalogReaderTest.java

```
import java.io.InputStream;
import java.io.OutputStream;
import gnu.io.CommPortIdentifier;
import gnu.io.SerialPort;

class AnalogReader {
```

---

2. http://java.sun.com/products/javacomm/
3. http://rxtx.qbang.org/

```java
    private InputStream  _input;
    private OutputStream _output;

    public AnalogReader(
      final String portName,
      final int    baudRate) throws Exception
    {
      final int timeout = 1000;
      final String appName = "analog reader client";
      CommPortIdentifier portId =
        CommPortIdentifier.getPortIdentifier(portName);
      SerialPort port = (SerialPort)portId.open(
        appName,
        timeout
      );
      _input = port.getInputStream();
      _output = port.getOutputStream();
      port.setSerialPortParams(
        baudRate,
        SerialPort.DATABITS_8,
        SerialPort.STOPBITS_1,
        SerialPort.PARITY_NONE
      );
    }

  public void run() throws Exception {
    byte[] buffer = new byte[255];
    Thread.sleep(2000);
    while (true) {
      _output.write("a0\n".getBytes());
      Thread.sleep(100);
      if (_input.available() > 0) {
        _input.read(buffer);
        System.out.print(new String(buffer));
      }
    }
  }
}

public class AnalogReaderTest {
  public static void main(String[] args) throws Exception {
    if (args.length != 1) {
      System.out.println(
        "You have to pass the name of a serial port."
      );
      System.exit(1);
    }
    AnalogReader analogReader = new AnalogReader(args[0], 9600);
    analogReader.run();
  }
}
```

This file defines two classes named AnalogReader and AnalogReaderTest. AnalogReader actually encapsulates access to the Arduino. It stores an InputStream object in _input to receive data, and it stores an OutputStream object in _output to send data to the Arduino.

The constructor initializes the serial port connection and assigns its input and output streams to our member variables. To obtain a serial port connection, we have to get a CommPortIdentifier object first. From this object, we can then create a SerialPort object. This object gives us access to the underlying streams, and it also allows us to set the port's parameters, such as the baud rate.

We implement the protocol for our Arduino sketch in the run() method. There we wait for two seconds, and then we start a loop. In the loop, we send the string "a0" to the serial port using OutputStream's write() method. Before we send the string, we turn it into a byte array calling getBytes(). To give the Arduino some time to create a result, we wait for another 100 milliseconds. Afterward, we check if a result is available and read it by invoking InputStream's read() method.

AnalogReaderTest is only a small driver class that implements a main() method, creates an AnalogReader object, and calls run() on it. Here's how to compile and use the program:

```
maik> javac AnalogReaderTest.java
maik> java AnalogReaderTest /dev/tty.usbmodemfa141
Experimental:  JNI_OnLoad called.
Stable Library
=========================================
Native lib Version = RXTX-2.1-7
Java lib Version   = RXTX-2.1-7
a0: 496
a0: 433
a0: 328
a0: 328
^C
```

After some debug output from the libraries we are using, the AnalogReaderTest does exactly what it's intended to do: it permanently prints the values of the analog pin 0. Accessing a serial port in Java is a piece of cake if you use the right libraries.

Ruby

Even dynamic languages such as Ruby give you instant access to your computer's serial port and to an Arduino if you connect it to it. But before that, you need to install the serialport gem:

```
maik> gem install serialport
```

Using it, you can connect to the Arduino in just 30 lines of code.

SerialProgramming/ruby/analog_reader.rb

```
Line 1  require 'rubygems'
     -  require 'serialport'
     -
     -  if ARGV.size != 1
     5    puts "You have to pass the name of a serial port."
     -    exit 1
     -  end
     -
     -  port_name = ARGV[0]
    10  baud_rate = 9600
     -  data_bits = 8
     -  stop_bits = 1
     -  parity    = SerialPort::NONE
     -
    15  arduino = SerialPort.new(
     -    port_name,
     -    baud_rate,
     -    data_bits,
     -    stop_bits,
    20    parity
     -  )
     -
     -  sleep 2
     -  while true
    25    arduino.write "a0"
     -    line = arduino.gets.chomp
     -    puts line
     -  end
```

We create a new SerialPort object in line 15, passing it all the usual parameters. After we sleep for two seconds, we start a loop and call write() on the SerialPort object. To get the result back from the Arduino, we call gets() and then we print the result to the console. Here you can see the program in action:

```
maik> ruby analog_reader.rb /dev/tty.usbserial-A60061a3
a0: 496
a0: 456
a0: 382
^Canalog_reader.rb:21:in `gets': Interrupt
    from analog_reader.rb:21
```

Using Ruby for accessing an Arduino is a good choice, because you can fully concentrate on your application. All the ugly real-world details you have to deal with in other programming languages are well hidden.

Python

Python is another dynamic programming language that you can use to quickly create Arduino clients. For programming a serial port, download and install the pyserial library first.[4] There is a special installer for Windows, but usually it's sufficient to install it like this:

maik> **python setup.py install**

After you've installed pyserial, you can use it to create a client for our analog reader sketch:

SerialProgramming/python/analog_reader.py

```
Line 1  import sys
     -  import time
     -  import serial
     -
     5  if len(sys.argv) != 2:
     -    print "You have to pass the name of a serial port."
     -    sys.exit(1)
     -
     -  serial_port = sys.argv[1]
    10  arduino = serial.Serial(
     -    serial_port,
     -    9600,
     -    serial.EIGHTBITS,
     -    serial.PARITY_NONE,
    15    serial.STOPBITS_ONE)
     -  time.sleep(2)
     -
     -  while 1:
     -    arduino.write('a0')
    20    line = arduino.readline().rstrip()
     -    print line
```

We make sure that we have the name of a serial port on the command line. Then we create a new Serial object in line 10, passing it all the parameters we'd like to use for serial communication.

After sleeping for two seconds, we start an infinite loop. In the loop, we send the string "a0" to the serial port calling write(). We read the result returned by the Arduino using the readline() method and output the result to the console. Here's what a typical session looks like:

```
maik> python analog_reader.py /dev/tty.usbserial-A60061a3
a0: 497
a0: 458
a0: 383
^C
```

---

4. http://sourceforge.net/projects/pyserial/files/

Isn't that code beautiful? With about 20 lines of Python code, you get full control over your Arduino sketch. So, Python is another excellent choice for writing Arduino clients.

Perl

Perl is still one of the most widely used dynamic programming languages, and it has good support for serial communication. Some distributions come with libraries for programming the serial port, but usually you have to install a module first.

Windows users should have a look at Win32::SerialPort.[5] For the rest, Device::SerialPort is a good choice. You can install it as follows:

```
maik> perl -MCPAN -e 'install Device::SerialPort'
```

Then use it like this:

SerialProgramming/perl/analog_reader.pl

```
use strict;
use warnings;
use Device::SerialPort;

if ($#ARGV != 0) {
  die "You have to pass the name of a serial port.";
}

my $serial_port = $ARGV[0];
my $arduino = Device::SerialPort->new($serial_port);
$arduino->baudrate(9600);
$arduino->databits(8);
$arduino->parity("none");
$arduino->stopbits(1);
$arduino->read_const_time(1);
$arduino->read_char_time(1);

sleep(2);
while (1) {
  $arduino->write("a0\n");
  my ($count, $line) = $arduino->read(255);
  print $line;
}
```

We check whether the name of a serial port was passed on the command line. Then we create a new Device::SerialPort instance in line 10. We configure all serial port parameters, and in line 15, we set a timeout

---

5. http://search.cpan.org/dist/Win32-SerialPort/

value for read() calls. If we did not set it, read() would return immediately, giving the Arduino no time to respond. read_char_time() sets a
timeout for the waiting period between two characters.

Then we sleep for two seconds and start an infinite loop. Here we send
the string "a0" to the serial port and read Arduino's response using the
read() method. read() expects a maximum number of bytes to be read,
and it returns the actual number of bytes read and the data it received.
Finally, we output the result to the console. A typical program run looks
as follows:

```
maik> perl analog_reader.pl /dev/tty.usbserial-A60061a3
a0: 496
a0: 366
a0: 320
^C
```

That's it! It takes only about twenty lines of Perl code to create a client
for the analog reader Arduino sketch. So, Perl is a good choice for programming Arduino clients, too.

Appendix D

Bibliography

[But09]   Paul Butcher. *Debug It!: Find, Repair, and Prevent Bugs in Your Code.* The Pragmatic Programmers, LLC, Raleigh, NC, and Dallas, TX, 2009.

[Gre07]   Ira Greenberg. *Processing: Creative Coding and Computational Art.* Apress, Berkeley, CA, USA, 2007.

[KR98]   Brian W. Kernighan and Dennis Ritchie. *The C Programming Language.* Prentice Hall PTR, Englewood Cliffs, NJ, second edition, 1998.

[Mey97]   Scott Meyers. *Effective C++: 50 Specific Ways to Improve Your Programs and Designs.* Addison Wesley Longman, Reading, MA, second edition, 1997.

[Pin06]   Chris Pine. *Learn to Program.* The Pragmatic Programmers, LLC, Raleigh, NC, and Dallas, TX, 2006.

[Pla10]   Charles Platt. *Make: Electronics.* O'Reilly Media, Inc., Sebastopol, CA, 2010.

[Str00]   Bjarne Stroustrup. *The C++ Programming Language.* Addison Wesley Longman, Reading, MA, 2000.

Index

Symbols

A

B

B

Debugging & Better SQL

Debug It!

Debug It! will equip you with the tools, techniques, and approaches to help you tackle any bug with confidence. These secrets of professional debugging illuminate every stage of the bug life cycle, from constructing software that makes debugging easy; through bug detection, reproduction, and diagnosis; to rolling out your eventual fix. Learn better debugging whether you're writing Java or assembly language, targeting servers or embedded micro-controllers, or using agile or traditional approaches.

Debug It! Find, Repair, and Prevent Bugs in Your Code
Paul Butcher
(232 pages) ISBN: 978-1-9343562-8-9. $34.95
http://pragprog.com/titles/pbdp

SQL Antipatterns

If you're programming applications that store data, then chances are you're using SQL, either directly or through a mapping layer. But most of the SQL that gets used is inefficient, hard to maintain, and sometimes just plain wrong. This book shows you all the common mistakes, and then leads you through the best fixes. What's more, it shows you what's *behind* these fixes, so you'll learn a lot about relational databases along the way.

SQL Antipatterns: Avoiding the Pitfalls of Database Programming
Bill Karwin
(300 pages) ISBN: 978-19343565-5-5. $34.95
http://pragprog.com/titles/bksqla

More On Languages

Seven Languages in Seven Weeks

In this book you'll get a hands-on tour of Clojure, Haskell, Io, Prolog, Scala, Erlang, and Ruby. Whether or not your favorite language is on that list, you'll broaden your perspective of programming by examining these languages side-by-side. You'll learn something new from each, and best of all, you'll learn how to learn a language quickly.

Seven Languages in Seven Weeks: A Pragmatic Guide to Learning Programming Languages
Bruce A. Tate
(300 pages) ISBN: 978-1934356-59-3. $34.95
http://pragprog.com/titles/btlang

Language Implementation Patterns

Learn to build configuration file readers, data readers, model-driven code generators, source-to-source translators, source analyzers, and interpreters. You don't need a background in computer science—ANTLR creator Terence Parr demystifies language implementation by breaking it down into the most common design patterns. Pattern by pattern, you'll learn the key skills you need to implement your own computer languages.

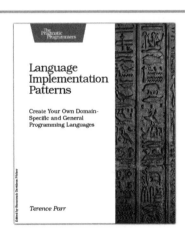

Language Implementation Patterns: Create Your Own Domain-Specific and General Programming Languages
Terence Parr
(350 pages) ISBN: 978-1934356-45-6. $34.95
http://pragprog.com/titles/tpdsl

Apple iOS & Mac

Beginning Mac Programming

Aimed at beginning developers without prior programming experience. Takes you through concrete, working examples, giving you the core concepts and principles of development in context so you will be ready to build the applications you've been imagining. It introduces you to Objective-C and the Cocoa framework in clear, easy-to-understand lessons, and demonstrates how you can use them together to write for the Mac, as well as the iPhone and iPod.

Beginning Mac Programming: Develop with Objective-C and Cocoa
Tim Isted
(300 pages) ISBN: 978-1934356-51-7. $34.95
http://pragprog.com/titles/tibmac

iPad Programming

It's not an iPhone and it's not a laptop: the iPad is a groundbreaking new device. You need to create true iPad apps to take advantage of all that is possible with the iPad. If you're an experienced iPhone developer, *iPad Programming* will show you how to write these outstanding new apps while completely fitting your users' expectation for this device.

iPad Programming: A Quick-Start Guide for iPhone Developers
Daniel H Steinberg and Eric T Freeman
(250 pages) ISBN: 978-19343565-7-9. $34.95
http://pragprog.com/titles/sfipad

Ruby & Rails

Programming Ruby 1.9 (The Pickaxe for 1.9)

The Pickaxe book, named for the tool on the cover, is the definitive reference to this highly-regarded language.

• Up-to-date and expanded for Ruby version 1.9
• Complete documentation of all the built-in classes, modules, and methods   • Complete descriptions of all standard libraries   • Learn more about Ruby's web tools, unit testing, and programming philosophy

Programming Ruby 1.9: The Pragmatic Programmers' Guide
Dave Thomas with Chad Fowler and Andy Hunt
(992 pages) ISBN: 978-1-9343560-8-1. $49.95
http://pragprog.com/titles/ruby3

Agile Web Development with Rails

Rails just keeps on changing. Rails 3 and Ruby 1.9 bring hundreds of improvements, including new APIs and substantial performance enhancements. The fourth edition of this award-winning classic has been reorganized and refocused so it's more useful than ever before for developers new to Ruby and Rails. This book isn't just a rework, it's a complete refactoring.

Agile Web Development with Rails: Fourth Edition
Sam Ruby, Dave Thomas, and David Heinemeier Hansson, et al.
(500 pages) ISBN: 978-1-93435-654-8. $43.95
http://pragprog.com/titles/rails4

Be Agile

Agile in a Flash

The best agile book isn't a book: Agile in a Flash is a unique deck of index cards that fit neatly in your pocket. You can tape them to the wall. Spread them out on your project table. Get stains on them over lunch. These cards are meant to be used, not just read.

Agile in a Flash: Speed-Learning Agile Software Development
Jeff Langr and Tim Ottinger
(110 pages) ISBN: 978-1-93435-671-5. $15.00
http://pragprog.com/titles/olag

The Agile Samurai

Faced with a software project of epic proportions? Tired of over-committing and under-delivering? Enter the dojo of the agile samurai, where agile expert Jonathan Rasmusson shows you how to kick-start, execute, and deliver your agile projects. You'll see how agile software delivery really works and how to help your team get agile fast, while having fun along the way.

The Agile Samurai: How Agile Masters Deliver Great Software
Jonathan Rasmusson
(275 pages) ISBN: 9781934356586. $34.95
http://pragprog.com/titles/jtrap

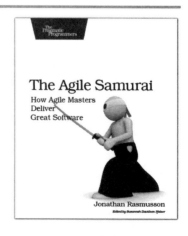

Be More Effective

Pragmatic Thinking and Learning

Software development happens in your head. Not in an editor, IDE, or design tool. In this book by Pragmatic Programmer Andy Hunt, you'll learn how our brains are wired, and how to take advantage of your brain's architecture. You'll master new tricks and tips to learn more, faster, and retain more of what you learn.

• Use the Dreyfus Model of Skill Acquisition to become more expert   • Leverage the architecture of the brain to strengthen different thinking modes
• Avoid common "known bugs" in your mind
• Learn more deliberately and more effectively
• Manage knowledge more efficiently

Pragmatic Thinking and Learning:
Refactor your Wetware
Andy Hunt
(288 pages) ISBN: 978-1-9343560-5-0. $34.95
http://pragprog.com/titles/ahptl

Pomodoro Technique Illustrated

Do you ever look at the clock and wonder where the day went? You spent all this time at work and didn't come close to getting everything done. Tomorrow, try something new. In *Pomodoro Technique Illustrated*, Staffan Nöteberg shows you how to organize your work to accomplish more in less time. There's no need for expensive software or fancy planners. You can get started with nothing more than a piece of paper, a pencil, and a kitchen timer.

Pomodoro Technique Illustrated: The Easy Way to Do More in Less Time
Staffan Nöteberg
(144 pages) ISBN: 9781934356500. $24.95
http://pragprog.com/titles/snfocus

The Pragmatic Bookshelf

The Pragmatic Bookshelf features books written by developers for developers. The titles continue the well-known Pragmatic Programmer style and continue to garner awards and rave reviews. As development gets more and more difficult, the Pragmatic Programmers will be there with more titles and products to help you stay on top of your game.

Visit Us Online

Home Page for Arduino: A Quick-Start Guide
http://pragprog.com/titles/msard
Source code from this book, errata, and other resources. Come give us feedback, too!

Register for Updates
http://pragprog.com/updates
Be notified when updates and new books become available.

Join the Community
http://pragprog.com/community
Read our weblogs, join our online discussions, participate in our mailing list, interact with our wiki, and benefit from the experience of other Pragmatic Programmers.

New and Noteworthy
http://pragprog.com/news
Check out the latest pragmatic developments, new titles and other offerings.

Save on the eBook

Save on the eBook versions of this title. Owning the paper version of this book entitles you to purchase the electronic versions at a terrific discount.

PDFs are great for carrying around on your laptop—they are hyperlinked, have color, and are fully searchable. Most titles are also available for the iPhone and iPod touch, Amazon Kindle, and other popular e-book readers.

Buy now at pragprog.com/coupon.

Contact Us

Online Orders:	www.pragprog.com/catalog
Customer Service:	support@pragprog.com
Non-English Versions:	translations@pragprog.com
Pragmatic Teaching:	academic@pragprog.com
Author Proposals:	proposals@pragprog.com
Contact us:	1-800-699-PROG (+1 919 847 3884)